Black Male Fiction
and the
Legacy of Caliban

Black Male Fiction

and the

Legacy of Caliban

James W. Coleman

THE UNIVERSITY PRESS OF KENTUCKY

Scholarly publisher for the Commonwealth,
serving Bellarmine University, Berea College, Centre
College of Kentucky, Eastern Kentucky University,
The Filson Historical Society, Georgetown College,
Kentucky Historical Society, Kentucky State University,
Morehead State University, Murray State University,
Northern Kentucky University, Transylvania University,
University of Kentucky, University of Louisville,
and Western Kentucky University.
All rights reserved.

Editorial and Sales Offices: The University Press of Kentucky
663 South Limestone Street, Lexington, Kentucky 40508-4008

05 04 03 02 01   5 4 3 2 1

Library of Congress Cataloging-in-Publication Data

Coleman, James W. (James Wilmouth), 1946–
Black male fiction and the legacy of Caliban / James W. Coleman.
        p.   cm.
Includes bibliographical references.
ISBN 0-8131-2204-X (cloth : alk. paper)
1. American fiction—African American authors—History and criticism.
2. American fiction—Male authors—History and criticism. 3. American
fiction—20th century—History and criticism. 4. Shakespeare, William, 1564–
1616—Influence. 5. Postmodernism (Literature)—United States.
6. African American men in literature. 7. Caliban (Fictitious character).
8. Blacks in literature. 9. Men in literature. I. Title.
PS374.N4 C64 2001
813'.5099286'0899073—dc21   00–012686

This book is printed on acid-free recycled paper meeting
the requirements of the American National Standard
for Permanence in Paper for Printed Library Materials.

Manufactured in the United States of America.

For my sons Jay and Lee
whose love has supported me.
And for Aunt Ade.

Contents

Introduction
Defining Calibanic Discourse
in the Black Male Novel and Black Male Culture
1

1
The Conscious and Unconscious Dimensions
of Calibanic Discourse Thematized
in *Philadelphia Fire*
18

2
The Thematized Black Voice
in John Edgar Wideman's
The Cattle Killing and *Reuben*
37

3
Clarence Major's Quest to Define
and Liberate the Self and the Black Male Writer
59

4
Charles Johnson's Response
to "Caliban's Dilemma"
81

5
Calibanic Discourse in Postmodern
and Non-Postmodern Black Male Texts
100

6
Ralph Ellison and the Literary Background
of Contemporary Black Male Postmodern Writers
129

Conclusion
The "Special Edge" Tension
Between the Conscious and Unconscious
in the Contemporary Black Male Postmodern Novel
148

Notes
156

Works Cited
180

Index
184

Introduction

Defining Calibanic Discourse in the Black Male Novel and Black Male Culture

Why do contemporary African American male writers write the kind of novels they write, and why do these works lack the appeal of novels by African American women? There is, of course, no one simple answer to this question. But some critics and readers say that over approximately the last three decades, black male fiction has become increasingly more bizarre, negative, and difficult. Male writers set up plot situations in which their fictional characters have the opportunity to confront oppression, but then they "don't do anything with" these situations. Texts written by black males seem to become laden by oppression instead of successfully confronting it like those written by black women. The highly postmodern works by black male writers are probably the most controversial in terms of negative perception, but what I have said applies to many more male texts. I want to change the way that we think about black male texts.

The attempt to tell a story of liberation as a response to what I call "Calibanic discourse"—and the restriction of this response—is the central feature uniting a broad range of contemporary black male texts that in other ways are very different. My overall conclusion is that Calibanic discourse influences a tradition of modernist and postmodernist African American male novels. With that in mind, I focus on Ralph Ellison's *Invisible Man* (1952), a novel with both modernist and postmodernist characteristics, as the chief literary influence. Calibanic discourse restricts voice in *Invisible Man,* and the novel is a literary influence that conflates with Calibanic discourse to restrict voice in contemporary black male novels.

I do not claim that this is the central feature in all contemporary black male texts. However, if some different well-known writers (Ishmael Reed and Ernest Gaines, for example) were also focuses of the study, the specifics of the analysis would change to fit the writers, but the overall critical stance would not have to change. Karla Holloway has said in *Moorings and Metaphors* that "[e]vil is an omnipresent, earth-bound presence in black male texts" (9). In part at least, Holloway is talking about what for her is the universal failure of voice in black male texts as compared to its realization in black women's texts. My assessment of black male texts is positive, and Holloway's is negative. However, within the context of my analysis specifying Calibanic discourse's challenge and compromise of voice, I agree with her that gender makes a difference across a broad range of black male texts that are considered "serious" texts.

Shakespeare's *The Tempest* is a symbolic and iconic text in this study. In the play, Prospero takes Caliban's island and makes Caliban a slave for him and his daughter Miranda. Miranda in turn tries to teach Caliban language, the language of Prospero. According to Miranda, Caliban was a "savage" who did not "Know [his] own meaning, but wouldst gabble like / A thing most brutish, I endowed [his] purposes / With words that made them known . . . " (I.ii.427–30). The language that Miranda gives Caliban forces his definition in her terms and in Prospero's: Caliban / cannibal—the savage brute whose "purpose" is enslavement. Caliban tries to use the language for his own benefit, but he cannot: "You taught me language, and my profit on't / Is I know how to curse. The red plague rid you / For learning me your language!" (I.ii.437–39). Caliban cannot use the patriarch Prospero's language for his own "profit," because using it this way would counter Prospero's goals, and Prospero has too much control over him and over the language for this to happen.

John Edgar Wideman talks about the effects on black people of the practice of a "foreign" language:

Tension and resistance characterize the practices African-descended peoples have employed to keep their distance from imposed tongues, imposed disciplines. Generation after generation has been compelled to negotiate—for better or worse, and with self-determination and self-realization at stake—the quicksand of a foreign language that continues by its structure, vocabulary, its deployment in social interaction, its retention of racist assumptions, expressions and attitudes, its contamination by theories of racial hierarchy to recreate the scenario of master and slave.
Uneasiness and a kind of disbelief of this incriminating language we've been forced to adopt never go away. . . . (Wideman, "In Praise of Silence" 548)[1]

Thus, the patriarchy controls the symbols of signification. In the context of the Caliban trope, Caliban can "curse" and (re)inscribe his inferiority by sounding vulgar and brutish, unable to use language in a civilized fashion and unable to learn, or he can remain in "passive compliance in the restrictive terms meted out" in Prospero's language (Baker 141). Caliban's attempted revolutionary act of having sex with Miranda—"Would't had been done! / . . . I had peopled else / This isle with Calibans" (I.ii.419–21)—also (re)inscribes his savagery and bestiality, because any act against Prospero by Caliban (particularly sex with his daughter) is savage and bestial in the language of Prospero.[2] Miranda concludes that Caliban is an "Abhorrèd slave, / . . . Who . . . deserved more than a prison" (I.ii.422–36). He is antithetical to Prospero's civilization and threatens to corrupt it with his bestiality and to destroy it with his sexual contamination. He deserves prison and, implicitly, even death. Although he tries, Caliban cannot escape his predicament; scholars have made him synonymous with the oppression and generally negative perception of black men and other nonwhite males.[3]

Calibanic discourse is the perceived history and story of the black male in Western culture that has its genesis and tradition in language and nonlinguistic signs. It denotes slavery, proscribed freedom, proscribed sexuality, inferior character, and inferior voice. In summary, the black male is the slave or servant who is the antithesis of the reason, civilized development, entitlement, freedom, and power of white men, and he never learns the civilized use of language.[4] His voice is unreliable; his words fail to signify his humanity. He also preys on civilization and represents bestial, contaminating sexuality. Clearly, Western culture must confine the black male to roles and places befitting his inferiority, and/or it must punish him, and even brutalize and kill him, for his criminality and reprobate character.[5]

In the context of the Caliban trope, Calibanic discourse began with the words Prospero imposed on Caliban that gave his "purposes" "meaning." Its "meaning" is an integral part of the English language and of Western signs and symbols. It is always there, even when those who use the language and respond to signs and symbols are unconscious of it. It is part of the language, but it resides in physical signs, too. Perhaps its most vivid manifestation is the association of the physical bodies of black men—even by other black men—with criminality, danger, and inferiority; fundamentally, "black men" is synonymous with these terms and with a larger story. Discrete physical signs tell the larger story of Calibanic discourse, and the larger story incorporates the discrete signs.

In black male fictions, Calibanic discourse and a responsive story of liberation are largely inseparable. The main thematic contours of the responsive story of liberation (most of which are inscribed through a variety of formal features) are the black male's quest to speak in an empowering voice, to achieve freedom from slavery and racism, to define the self, to fashion a humane character and a secure, empowered status in a racist world, and to attain freedom from proscribed sexuality. Besides representing the intention to portray black men seriously and substantively, the story of liberation is an unconscious response to Calibanic discourse. Many times the direct evidence of Calibanic discourse is the (re)inscription of some of its essential elements during a text's process of telling the responsive story of liberation, also recognizable through one or more of its thematic features. Often toward the end, the texts turn subtly but substantively from the story of liberation back toward restating one or more of the themes of the Calibanic legacy, which obviously opposes the portrayal of positive black male character, culture, and life. (Re)inscription takes place largely through character portrayal and also through a general type of narrative, variously expressed, that symbolizes the restriction of voice in its structure and explicitly or symbolically undercuts voice in its thematic development. Ambiguity and paradox—both in the narration of the black male character's and the text's liberation quests as well as in the text's structure—are the main formal aspects of the story of liberation that enable the (re)inscription of Calibanic discourse. The main point is that Calibanic discourse has an unconscious power that even many black male writers cannot clearly subvert or rewrite, and in spite of their intentions to redefine black men, their stories challenge (that is, contest) and compromise (that is, restrict) their own ends by reaffirming Calibanic definitions.[6]

My primary focus is the manifestation of Calibanic discourse in the contemporary postmodern novels of Wideman, Clarence Major, and Charles Johnson—three very important black male writers whose novels highlight and manifest the effect of Calibanic discourse to a greater extent than nonpostmodern black male texts. I use Wideman's *Philadelphia Fire* (1990), a postmodern meta-narrative, as a foundational text. The novel presents Shakespeare's *The Tempest* as a theme and links its portrayal of Caliban to the oppression of black men and the inability of the novel's writer figures to tell a liberating story. A negative, unconscious discourse of Caliban dictates the writers' stories, although it is a conscious theme in parts of the text.[7] The discourse's reality is, according to the novel, "buried," "unmentionable," and "signified" in the language (141). It is essentially an unconscious discourse inherent in the language, and the writers, one of them being Wideman, a character in the book, cannot change it. In Major's and Johnson's texts this discourse is also largely an unconscious influence.

Linda Hutcheon links concepts of the historical and the political in her critique of postmodernism.[8] Broadly and generally speaking, she says that we always construct the past through our ideology and discourse in the present. The past is therefore always open-ended, because given different ideologies and consequent discourses, we interpret it and (re)interpret it, construct it and (re)construct it. Consequently, a postmodern fiction is not the truth, but it is someone's version of truth. All fictions are equal, and that means both equally true from the creator's perspective and equally problematized by personal, class, race, and gender bias. The concept of the postmodern is liberating because in placing all stories on an equal basis, it allows everyone to construct and (re)construct identity and subjectivity. (See Hutcheon's *A Poetics of Postmodernism* [1988] and *The Politics of Postmodernism* [1989]).

All of this is "white," however, and fails to go as far as constituting the necessary grounds for black terms of liberation. (White) postmodernism can potentially be liberating for black writers, because its indeterminacy de-centers and destabilizes "grand," hegemonic racist narratives and opens up possibilities for producing new fictions of black truth that are equal to white fictions. Black writers do indeed very much want to seize the liberating potential of (white) postmodernism; however, its liberating potential is still not the same as it is for white writers. The racism embedded in Western linguistic and non-linguistic discourse poses a uniquely strong resistance to positive black signification. Black writers do not start from a position of equality, and to realize postmodern potential, they must generate the voice to construct black liberating fictions *against* the hegemony of Western discourse.

Because black male writers have difficulty doing this, the potential of (white) postmodernism highlights the restriction of liberating voice and highlights the anti-liberating power of Western discourse.[9] (White) postmodernism is theoretically liberating, but the great anti-liberating power of Western discourse essentializes black men. Contemporary black male postmodern novels clearly reflect the oppressive power of Western Calibanic discourse in the underlying unconscious story because of their contrasting, thematized potential for liberating voice in the conscious narrative. (As my later analysis will show, Johnson's case is somewhat more complex among the male postmodern writers that I study.)

While revealing that language is the source of black male oppression, *Philadelphia Fire* also thematizes the postmodernist possibilities of changing the Calibanic story by controlling language. The text's black male writers have a very urgent personal, political, and social need to speak in a black voice that refutes white racism and changes its very real effects. The writers would like to create the black fictions that de-center Calibanic discourse and that counter white versions of history. Human beings construct the history and reality of black male oppression in the present through language, and theoretically black male writers in the present can deconstruct and change this; in effect, that would be realizing liberating postmodernist potential. But to the contrary, their language and narrative are inadequate against the hegemony of Calibanic discourse; (white) postmodernism's liberating potential makes Calibanic discourse's limitation of voice stand out clearly.

Calibanic discourse initiates a process in American culture that parallels the one in texts. Black male signifying is a familiar cultural formation. Because signifying is a counter-response to Calibanic discourse in American culture, this study uses the term "counter-signifying" instead of signifying.

According to Michel Foucault, the "significations of a culture" make and exclude possibility for the individual subject (380); however, the black male subject's signification as a response to counter Calibanic discourse is more complicated. Among black men, counter-signifying discourse produces dynamics that make possible power and prestige for the black male subject in symbolic phallic terms and in the sexual terms of the penis. At the same time, the white male subject signifies black men in terms of Calibanic discourse, emphasizing Calibanic phallicism, and obversely signifies the possibility of his own white male phallocentric power. Calibanic discourse, especially Calibanic phallicism, overlays black male discourse and compromises possibility for the black male subject.

Words are the privileged signs, not the only ones, in black male counter-signifying. Counter-signifying includes non-linguistic ritual acts and forms, and it manifests itself in everything that black males do and say—most markedly and definitively when black men interact with each other. Two prominent scholars, Stephen Henderson and Henry Louis Gates Jr., use Rap Brown's poem as an example of what black men call "signifying," what I am calling "counter-signifying" in the context of this study.

Signifying is more humane. Instead of coming down on somebody's mother, you come down on them. But, before you can signify you got to be able to rap. A session would start maybe by a brother saying, "Man, before you mess with me you'd rather run rabbits, eat shit, and bark at the moon." Then, if he was talking to me, I'd tell him:

Man, you must don't know who I am.
I'm sweet peeter jeeter the womb beater
The baby maker the cradle shaker
The deerslayer the buckbinder the women finder
Known from the Gold Coast to the rocky shores of Maine
Rap is my name and love is my game.
I'm the bed tucker the cock plucker the mother fucker

The milk shaker the record breaker the population maker
The gun slinger the baby bringer
The hum-dinger the pussy ringer
The man with the terrible middle finger.
The hard hitter the bullshitter the polynussy getter
The beast from the East the Judge the sludge
The women's pet the men's fret and the punks' pin-up boy.
They call me Rap the dicker the ass kicker
The cherry picker the city slicker the titty licker
And I ain't giving nothing but bubble gum and hard times and I'm fresh out of
bubble gum. . . .
Yes, I'm hemp the demp the women's pimp
Women fight for my delight.
I'm a bad mother fucker. . . . (Henderson 187–88; Gates 72–73)

Counter-signifying allows black men to create a range of positive black male subjects—the "bad man" in the quotation above—and it seeks to restore black manhood in the symbolic terms of the phallus and in terms of the more literal, physical, sexual function of the penis.[10] As another example below will show, the "man" and the "main man" are other categories of black male subjectivity that black male counter-signifying creates for the individual black male subject. The "bad man" above signifies on a black man among black men. He speaks in hyperbolic terms that coalesce with the white patriarchal phallic symbolization of power, prestige, and privilege; his account of himself shows the supernatural power to do and know things and the power and privilege to "roam the world" enforcing his will. However, some of his exploits are clearly the sexual exploits of the penis. (For example, he is the "womb beater" and the "baby maker.")

Also, he achieves the voice denied him by Calibanic discourse in white patriarchal culture. He uses language creatively, improvisationally, and open-endedly to develop the image of the "bad man" grounded in his sexual prowess and world-conquering power. In his black male context, at least, he humanizes himself. He is the "beast from the East" who plays the world; however, for him and other black men, his phallic and sexual exploits make sense in terms of a history of oppression. In his context, his virtuoso ability to use his voice to express himself, to tell his story, is concomitant with his intelligence and raises him far above—and makes him much more than—the uncivilized, bestial "gabbler" signified in Calibanic discourse.

Gates quotes another example of signifying.

Man, I can't win for losing.
If it wasn't for bad luck, I wouldn't have no luck at all.

I been having buzzard luck
Can't kill nothing and won't nothing die
I'm living on the welfare and things is stormy
They borrowing their shit from the Salvation Army
But things bound to get better 'cause they can't get no worse
I'm just like the blind man, standing by a broken window
I don't feel no pain.
But it's your world
You the man I pay rent to
If I had your hands I'd give 'way both my arms.
Cause I could do without them
I'm the man but you the main man
I read the books you write
You set the pace in the race I run
Why, you always in good form
You got more foam than Alka Seltzer . . . . (74)

This example of black male counter-signifying is less risqué because it is not explicitly sexual and is also more purely phallic in the symbolic sense of the signification of male prestige, power, and privilege. "Rap's Poem" does not necessarily antedate this form of counter-signifying; the phallic signification here is just as primary and important as it is in "Rap's Poem." The two forms complement each other, but the latter example better suits a more public forum because it lacks the explicit sexual statements of "Rap's Poem."

Phallic signification of male power, prestige, and privilege resides here in irony and subtlety of speech. The speaker figuratively creates the reality of power. But who is he complimenting, and who is he putting down? Is he serious in spite of his tone? The main individual in black male counter-signifying very often signifies his own subjectivity as a "man," "main man," or "bad man." So the speaker here may somehow be talking ironically about his own power. In the repartee and competition that is implied in this black male cultural setting, the respondent can establish his own category of manhood, and the side participants can share the created realities of manhood.

The individual in the latter example counter-signifies *and* leaves the "main man" his own space of positive signification *because* he is ironic. In the last nine lines, the speaker hyperbolically creates the "main man" by exaggerating his power and importance, and in the first nine lines, creates himself by exaggerating his lack of the same. However, the speaker's words sound ironic: He really talks about his own power and importance and speaks derisively about the "main man." Implicitly, the "main man," like the speaker, also has a creative voice, and consequently, the speaker's irony certainly leaves the "main man" space to show that he is a man. In Rap's counter-signifying in the first example, he allows the opponent to be a "man," and implies the same status for those on the side, while reserving the "bad man" status for himself. The speaker in the second instance of counter-signifying makes the status of man open-ended, and the respondent can show that he is a man. In what is explicitly stated and implied in both examples, the "bad man," "main man," and "man" demonstrate their intelligence and civilize and humanize themselves in opposition to Calibanic discourse by their virtuoso use of voice.

Even when it is below the surface, the reference to the sexual exploits of the black male subject is central to counter-signifying, just as phallic signification is. The speaker in the second example says, "it's your world / You the man I pay rent to." Signifying is constant improvisation, and many different plays and changes on lines exist, creating multiple connotations—often sexual ones. The speaker explicitly says what he says, but his words carry embedded within them the following line, which in turn carries a sexual reference: "it's your world / I'm just a squirrel tryin' to get a nut."

Black male counter-signifying disperses itself through the culture from concentrated forms like those above to less concentrated ones, including non-linguistic ritual forms and actions, and disperses itself to different forums or settings of the culture. Black men are conscious that they are "signifying" when they use the forms above; however, black male counter-signifying is unconscious because black men are unaware that they are responding to Calibanic discourse. Also, while being consciously witty and humorous, black male counter-signifying is always unconsciously serious because it responds to Calibanic discourse.

The need to signify a subjectivity that constitutes phallic and sexual power for the black male subject becomes very clear when one considers the pervasiveness and severe harmfulness of Calibanic discourse and the history of black men's sexual oppression by white men. Calibanic discourse is a pervasive, unconscious discourse that tells a negative story of black males. Black male counter-signifying includes a range of words, signs, and expressions; perhaps its surest sign, however, is the word "man." The word embeds all of the saturated phallic and sexual power of the two examples above.

Calibanic discourse pulls black male counter-signifying toward an intergradation and ultimately establishes hegemony; this happens in Wideman's *Hiding Place* (1981). In the following quotation, Tommy, a main character, convinces a black woman named Adelaide to have sex with him. The quotation refers explicitly to the church and to the pool hall and implicitly to a setting where Tommy counter-signifies in a group of black men.

Adelaide up there with the Young People's Gospel Chorus rocking church. Rocking church and he'd go right on up there, the lead of the Commodores, and sing gospel with them if he could get next to that fine Adelaide. So Thursday he left the pool room, *Where you tipping off to, Man? None of your motherfucking business, motherfucker,* about seven when she had choir practice and look here Adelaide I been digging you for a long time. I been knowing you for years girl, since your mama brought you in here and you wasn't nothing but a little thing in pigtails. Yeah I been digging on you a long time. Longer and deeper than you'll ever know. Let me tell you something. I know what you're thinking, but don't say it, don't break my heart by saying you heard I was a jive cat and nothing to me and stay away from him he's married and got a baby and he ain't no good and stuff like that I know I got a rep that way but you grown enough now to know how people talk and how you got to find things out for yourself. Don't be putting me down till you let me have a little chance to speak for myself. I ain't gon lie now. I been out here in the world and into some jive tips. Yeah, I did my time diddy boppin and trying my wheels out here in the street. I was a devil. I got into everything I was big and bad enough to try. Look here. I could write the book. Pimptime and partytime and jive to stay alive, but I been through all that and that ain't what I want. I want something special, something solid. A woman, not no fingerpopping young girl got her nose open and her behind wagging all the time. That's right. That's right, I ain't talking nasty, I'm talking what I know. I'm talking truth tonight and listen here I been digging you all these years and waiting for you because all that Doo Wah Diddy ain't nothing, you hear, nothing to it. You grown now and I need just what you got . . .

Thursday rapping in the vestibule with Adelaide was the last time in Homewood A.M.E. Zion Church. Had to be swift and clean. Swoop down like a hawk and get to her mind. Tuesday she still crying and gripping the elastic of her drawers and saying no. Next Thursday the only singing she doing is behind some bushes in the park. *Oh, Baby. Oh, Baby, it's so good.* Tore that pussy up. (64)

When the narration is both first and third person, and even when Tommy talks to Adelaide, the quotation always implies a counter-signifying scene among black men, and the counter-signifier and other black men are always present implicitly. In this form of counter-signifying, the speaker exalts himself sexually, not by primarily using hyperbole to tell how "bad" he is, but by reciting to the other men how he used his rap to "be swift and clean. Swoop down like a hawk and get to her mind." The narrator participates at the beginning as he sets the scene that switches from the church to the pool hall, where the narration presents the linguistic signs of counter-signifying: "*Where you tipping off to, Man? None of your motherfucking business, motherfucker.*" The section where Tommy talks to Adelaide is as much spoken to a black male audience—to whom he gives an account of his rap and recites his sexual exploits to show how "bad" he is—as it is to Adelaide. Tommy's rap to Adelaide clearly implies the speaker telling the story to black men and bragging to them. The last paragraph validates this point by making the implied black male cultural setting much clearer. Here, Tommy states the true intentions of his rap in the first person and clearly shows that he intended to prove his sexual virtuosity.

The quotation provides a perspective to view the dispersal of black male counter-signifying in various forms and forums. Forms of counter-signifying can be more than standard motifs on which speakers improvise, as my two original examples are. Reciting one's rapping exploits to constitute one's sexual virtuosity is also a form of counter-signifying. One can see how Tommy counter-signifies in much that he does, whether he is in the pool hall, in the church, outside the church, or on the street. This is true because the implication of a black male audience to which he proves his oral and sexual virtuosity is always there. Neither different forms and different forums nor the physical absence of black men alter the fact that Tommy is counter-signifying. As I will show later, this dispersal of black male counter-signifying is more phallic than sexual.

Tommy's need to show that he is a man of sexual virtuosity and power, prestige, and privilege develops in the context of Calibanic discourse's negative signification. Tommy wonders why he is so wild and always trying to express himself as he does: "What was there inside him that needed to be free?" (121). What Tommy does not know, and what other black men in the text do not know, is that they counter-signify in response to Calibanic discourse. As *Philadelphia Fire* shows, Calibanic discourse has the general, overall effect of a pervasive, unconscious discourse.

The hegemonic relationship between Calibanic discourse and black male counter-signifying implicitly reveals itself through the deconstruction of Tommy's manhood. Both Tommy and his wife Sarah, from whom he is bitterly estranged, capitulate to his signification in the terms of Calibanic discourse. Later in the novel, after Tommy's conquest of Adelaide, both of them unconsciously use terms of signification for Tommy congruent with Calibanic discourse. Sarah tells Tommy that he is not the man that she thought he was: "I thought I had a man but I didn't" (120). In fact, she reduces him to less than both a father and a man. She reduces him to the level of the Calibanic beast who is dangerous because he "fucks" and propagates himself. She tells Tommy that he is not the father of their child: "You're the one fucked him in me. That's all" (120–21). Tommy concurs that he is the "wrong nigger" male proscribed and prohibited in Calibanic discourse: "I was a wrong nigger. Sometimes I knew that I was fucking up and sometimes I didn't know. Sometimes I cared about fucking up and sometimes I didn't give a damn. Now that's a wrong nigger" (121). In spite of all his counter-signifying efforts, Tommy ends up (re)inscribing Calibanic discourse, especially Calibanic phallicism.

The confluence of the individual and the culture produces power dynamics that create societal reality. Tommy does "real life" things in the text, and Sarah judges Tommy and he judges himself based on these "real life" events. However, the creation of reality ultimately takes place in an unconscious discursive process initiated by Calibanic discourse. *Philadelphia Fire* shows that it is very difficult for black men to escape the pervasive effects of Calibanic discourse; in this context, the discursive power asserted by Calibanic discourse constitutes and determines Tommy and black men in deadly serious ways.

Calibanic discourse, in Foucault's terms (380), "excludes" the "possibilities" that counter-signifying creates for Tommy. Counter-signifying creates the "possibility" for Tommy to show that he is the sexual "bad man" in the quotation that I have examined. Counter-signifying disperses itself throughout the culture to produce phallic power, prestige, and privilege for Tommy and his friends. Tommy has also tried to constitute himself as the "bad man" by using his rap and counter-signifying virtuosity to scam a white man to attain the accouterments of power, prestige, and privilege—mainly money. For awhile, Tommy counter-signifies himself as both the sexual and phallic "bad man." However, after the scam fails and Tommy ends up in jail, he realizes that he is not a "bad man" but a "wrong nigger." In the terms of Calibanic discourse, Tommy has always been the "wrong nigger," "excluded" as a "possibility," instead of the "bad man" of power, prestige, and privilege. Like the rappers in the former two examples, Tommy, among black men at least, uses his virtuoso counter-signifying voice to demonstrate his intelligence, constitute his power, and civilize and humanize himself in opposition to Calibanic discourse. In the larger context, Calibanic discourse "excludes" and compromises Tommy's black male counter-signifying voice. In the hostile conversation with his estranged wife, apart from the context of black male culture, one can see how the signification of Tommy's black male body that "fucks" and the signification of the language in which he is a "wrong nigger" essentialize him and other black men.

Black men and their counter-signifying discourse are ultimately inseparable from the influence of Calibanic discourse, which forces black men (who willingly go) to the side to counter-signify, while its hegemony also draws black men and their counter-signifying discourse back to its story. This is how the counter-signifying response, in part at least, (re)inscribes Calibanic discourse. The individual subject and the group have "one point in common . . . the one at which they intersect at right angles; for the signifying chain by which the unique experience of the individual is constituted is perpendicular to the formal system on the basis of which the significations of a culture are constituted" (Foucault 380). The following figure extends this concept to illustrate my paradigm of American culture.

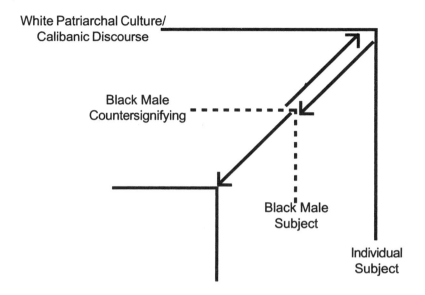

Calibanic discourse negatively signifies black male reality and elicits a response, which it contests and restricts.

The connection among the writers and novels in this study is their diverse expressions of Calibanic discourse within the thematic and structural process of the narratives. In chapter 1, I focus on *Philadelphia Fire* (1990), my main theoretical text. In this meta-narrative, paradox and ambiguity turn the attempt to define humane character, sexuality, and freedom toward (re)inscribing the opposing story of Caliban in *The Tempest*. The intersubjectively linked writers/characters unconsciously reveal their own unreliable voice, reprobate sexuality, and generally culpability even as they consciously invoke the liberating potential of (white) postmodernism and try to rewrite *The Tempest*. In essence, (white) postmodernism complies with Calibanic discourse. Contrary to the tenets of (white) postmodernism that express the potential for liberation through language, words torture the writers because Calibanic signification is inherent and fixed in them and in the writers' would-be liberating narrative. At the end, the text has shown that the writers probably cannot rewrite *The Tempest* and left the possibility of a story of liberation unclear.

Chapter 2 makes a transition to novels by Wideman and others in which

Calibanic discourse is only unconscious. These novels foreground postmodernist assumptions and try to tell a story of liberation, which reveals the unconscious influence of Calibanic discourse by (re)inscribing at least one of its identifiable characteristics. The second chapter deals with Wideman's *Reuben* (1987) and *The Cattle Killing* (1996). The character Reuben is another intersubjective figure who struggles throughout the narrative to define black male sexuality, humanity, and freedom through the "fictions" that he constructs. Although the definition of black male sexuality may be secondary, its dominant portrayal through the character Wally is negative. More importantly, the black male story of liberation is very much contested throughout the text, and the ending paradoxically associates black male fictions—particularly the one constructed by Reuben at the very end—with silence and abstraction. The power of the black male voice to construct a story that defines positively and liberates is questionable at best. *Cattle Killing* centers and foregrounds the story and the storytelling process even more. Another intersubjective character struggles nobly throughout the text to keep the story of the black quest for freedom alive, and his struggle ends ambiguously because he concludes that the story will continue, "If someone is listening" (208). In the epilogue, however, Wideman and his son Dan are writers intersubjectively linked with the main narrator, and they both implicitly and explicitly question whether the narrative has accomplished its mission of liberation. The writers specify the book's potential failure of voice.

The third chapter shows that Clarence Major's first five novels are a continuous quest by black male writers to define their sexuality, human self, and liberating voice through progressively self-referential narratives. In the first novel, *All-Night Visitors* (1969), it is very evident that Calibanic discourse, especially Calibanic sexuality, is in the language of the story of liberation, which (re)inscribes it throughout the text, in spite of the narrator's pretensions at the end. His role as a writer trying to tell a liberating story links the character in this novel to the other writers in the four that follow—*No* (1973), *Reflex and Bone Structure* (1975), *Emergency Exit* (1979), and *My Amputations* (1986). The quest to define a liberated self and sexuality takes place within the paradoxical space of self-referential narrative that increasingly silences it; in the latter novels, the self-referential narrative potentially negates black male voice. To the point that they are intelligible, the portrayals of black male human being and sexuality are ambiguous, and this ambiguous quality greatly suggests the bizarre and arcane. The negation of black male voice in the course of the narratives (re)inscribes an aspect of the Calibanic legacy to which Major's narratives clearly respond; the same is true for the ambiguous, highly bizarre black male characterization and sexual definition.

I analyze Charles Johnson's *Oxherding Tale* (1982) and *Middle Passage* (1990) in chapter 4. The multiple layers of Johnson's postmodernist project in ways make his narratives more complex and somewhat change the overall process of Calibanic discourse's (re)inscription. In these two novels, the secondary black male characters tell the story of liberation from their viewpoint as slaves. This is not the viewpoint of Johnson and the text, which accept slavery and oppression as parts of an ongoing, convoluting, intersubjective process that liberates by continuously breaking down and transforming identity and reality, including the reality of blackness and slavery. The black male slaves who express their story of liberation in racial terms are out of touch with the novel's underlying truth, and their negative portrayals reflect this. In Johnson's novels, Calibanic discourse is (re)inscribed in the overall process of telling a story that liberates the main characters by negating their black (male) identity, but a difference is that the text also presents the secondary characters' Calibanic signification more straightforwardly and uniformly throughout the narrative. The secondary male characters articulate their superficial perspectives and their opposition to slavery; they suffer violent, painful consequences only because they refuse to accept the novel's truth. This is clear and explicit throughout the novel. On this level, a response to Calibanic discourse and the more direct (re)statement of its characteristics theoretically comes from the characters—not from Johnson.

The power of Calibanic discourse to limit voice stands out because of contrast in black male texts based in the assumptions of (white) postmodernism, a discourse that theorizes the liberating potential of language, but Calibanic discourse also limits voice in black male texts that are modernist or that are not easily classified. The fifth chapter analyzes several texts to show this. One of them, Trey Ellis's *Platitudes* (1988), is clearly postmodernist, and the others are modernist or not easy to classify by form or theme. In addition to *Platitudes,* the texts discussed in this chapter are William Melvin Kelley's *A Different Drummer* (1962), Wesley Brown's *Tragic Magic* (1978), and David Bradley's *The Chaneysville Incident* (1981). Generally, (re)inscription works the same way in the structure and theme of non-postmodernist texts. The difference is that the would-be liberating potential of (white) postmodernism does not highlight its power through contrast. *Different Drummer* is especially important because it specifically names Calibanic discourse as *Philadelphia Fire* does. It is an additional way of focusing on the direct evidence of Calibanic discourse in black male texts; it is another example that makes the hypothetical concrete.

Calibanic discourse means obstacles to black male liberation in language and semiotics—in the words and non-linguistic signs that create reality in

American and Western culture; therefore, the influence of this discourse manifests itself in a broad tradition of black male writing. In chapter 6, I trace the literary roots of this discourse in black male fiction that manifests itself most strongly in contemporary postmodernist novels. This goes back to the time when the black male voice initially tried to express freedom fully in the context of realist/modernist/postmodernist fiction, which Richard Wright did in his 1940 book *Native Son*.

However, the main emphasis of chapter 6 is the connection of Ralph Ellison to the postmodernist fictions of Wideman, Major, and Johnson. It looks at *Invisible Man* (1952) and draws upon the critical discourse of both Ellison and the three writers to complete my analysis by establishing the background to the writers' work. As a critic and fiction writer, Ellison has been the greatest artistic influence on a large number of black male writers since the 1950s. Ellison's novel resonates with Calibanic discourse and with the (white) postmodernism of Wideman, Major, and Johnson, and the writers' critical discourse sometimes echoes his. Ellison is the most distinguishable artistic figure whose work is a precursor to Calibanic discourse in the contemporary black male postmodernist novel.

In the conclusion, I emphasize that the influence of Calibanic discourse is a defining aspect of the contemporary black male novel that is part of its overall depth and complexity. I want to put my foregoing analysis in a context that makes it clear that I think that these black males are excellent writers. My intent in this analysis is to show that on a usually unconscious level, black male texts thematically and structurally manifest cultural oppression that is embedded in language and semiotics. Analyzing black male texts from this perspective is not a criticism of black male writers and most certainly not a denigration of their art.

Generally, Wideman, Major, and Johnson do not get the credit they deserve—for their ability as writers, and for their attempt to deal substantively with black men and black culture. Wideman, for example, is one of the very finest writers of any nationality who has written since the mid-1960s, during which time he has published nine novels and three collections of short stories of high aesthetic quality. From his early career, *The Lynchers* (1973) is a great and powerful novel that relatively few readers know and appreciate. An impressive thing about Wideman is his ability to change and grow as a writer, which *The Lynchers* shows, and which his career since *The Lynchers* has shown. The Homewood Trilogy—*Damballah* (1981), *Hiding Place* (1981), and *Sent For You Yesterday* (1983)—takes Wideman in a different direction that makes black culture more centrally his interest. In the trilogy, Wideman also produces work of extremely high aesthetic quality. Since the trilogy, Wideman's fiction shows evidence of having subsumed the general aspects of his evolution throughout his career. *Cattle Killing* (1996) and *Two Cities* (1998) break new ground artistically; the former may be his very finest work of fiction. This is a remarkable achievement for a writer who has published twelve works of fiction in more than a thirty-year period. Wideman is already a major American writer of the second half of the twentieth century, and he should have many more years to continue to add to his body of work.

Clarence Major's achievement is radical, but he has made a great contribution to the African American tradition through his experimentation and through the range and variety of his literary works. Major has published a large body of poetry, nonfiction, and edited work, and has published eight novels. From the first novel to the last, Major's greatest contributions are perhaps his radical portrayals of black maleness in the context of experimental and self-referential narratives. Major's texts are often risqué—more risqué than usual—and maybe this is why he does not get greater attention and acclaim. But whatever the reasons, Major is under appreciated and unduly criticized. At the very least, he should get credit for what he has done, which is produce a significant body of work that, along with Johnson's work, takes the African American tradition in new directions.

Charles Johnson has set for himself the objective of breaking down the traditional expectations of the African American tradition in order to reconstruct it and to open new directions. To accomplish this, Johnson does and says things that are radical, and this makes him controversial. Johnson's willingness to experiment is part of his achievement, though; because of this, he presents so many provocative ways of thinking about reality generally and about black reality specifically.

Aesthetically, Johnson's writing is also of a very high quality; he is among the best writers writing today. In my analysis of Johnson in chapter 5, I discuss his work from the same central perspective from which I discuss the other texts. However, Johnson's radical approach gives Calibanic discourse a different slant and manifests it in complex ways that work in the texts' underlying levels. Calibanic discourse perhaps reveals itself in the most negative-sounding terms in Johnson's writing, but my analysis should not be construed as a negative comment about the overall aesthetic quality of the work. *Oxherding Tale* and *Middle Passage* have great power and aesthetic quality, but Calibanic discourse is part of the overall structure and theme of the texts that gives them their unique black male contours. I would like readers to keep this positive assessment of aesthetics in mind when reading what I say about the other writers also.

1

The Conscious and Unconscious Dimensions of Calibanic Discourse Thematized in *Philadelphia Fire*

*P*hiladelphia Fire (1990) depicts a negative, imprisoning Calibanic discourse about black men deeply embedded in the semiotics of American and Western culture; the discourse works both consciously and unconsciously, having virtually the same effect when conscious as when unconscious. Calibanic discourse challenges (that is, contests) and compromises (that is, restricts) the conscious response that it elicits just as it challenges and compromises the unconscious. It reveals how the challenge and compromise are embedded in language and implied non-linguistic signs, theme, and formal structure— embedded in the overall discourse of the text.[1] *Philadelphia Fire* is an example of the complicity of (white) postmodernism and its tenets, including its associated structuralist and poststructuralist principles, with Calibanic discourse to highlight the latter's limitation of voice through the former's contrasting liberating potential.[2]

The main character, Cudjoe, is a writer who tells the personal story of his adult relationships with his wife and children and with women generally. The specifics of the story clearly show that it is an unconscious response, a counter-story, to Calibanic discourse. Foreign islands are a center of the story. The story reveals Cudjoe's attempt to atone for his exile and dispossession of his American life and family and for the inappropriate sexual acts he associates with his predicament. Cudjoe unconsciously (re)inscribes his Calibanic legacy when he concludes that his dispossession is justified and when he duplicates Caliban's sexual signification by concluding that his own actual and symbolic sexual acts are reprobate.

A seemingly different Cudjoe, projecting his public persona as a writer and trying to carry out his responsibility to black people, also responds consciously by thematizing Calibanic discourse to make it explicit, to analyze its negative effects, and to break its hegemony. In this conscious process, he invokes *The Tempest* and the language of Caliban's pejorative inception and tries to write a counter-narrative that portrays Caliban as a character whom Prospero has victimized. However, the linguistic and non-linguistic signs (the non-linguistic being mainly the dreadlocked Caliban himself in this instance) significantly (re)inscribe the same story and meaning written in *The Tempest*. Cudjoe lacks the resources and the power to change the meaning that is so deeply embedded in the signs of American and Western discourse that everyone—white people, even black people, and everyone else—resorts to it without being aware of doing so.

Wideman himself is a character in the novel, and the realities of Wideman and Cudjoe generally conflate. The overall essence (and sometimes the specifics) of Cudjoe's story is also Wideman's.

This is the central event. I assure you. I repeat. Whatever my assurance is worth. Being the fabulator. This is the central event, this production of *The Tempest* staged by Cudjoe in the late 1960s, outdoors, in a park in West Philly. Though it comes here [part 2 of the novel], wandering like a Flying Dutchman in and out of the narrative, many places at once, *The Tempest* sits dead center, the storm in the eye of the storm, figure within a figure, play within a play, it is the bounty and hub of all else written about the fire, though it comes here, where it is, nearer the end than the beginning. (132)

In the quotation, Wideman is implicitly the conscious "fabulator," describing his creation of the text that thematizes *The Tempest's* Calibanic discourse and that simultaneously tells the story of the fire and of other disparate oppressive black realities related to Calibanic discourse; in the text, Cudjoe attempts the same conscious fabulation. The diffidence of the "fabulator's" voice presages the challenge and compromise of the writers' story.

At the same time, Wideman unconsciously responds to Calibanic discourse by trying to tell a story that liberates his real-life son, who is incarcerated and lost, and that liberates Wideman himself from his overall feeling that he is restricted and helpless. Because of Wideman's inability to free himself from these feelings, his inability to free himself of his feeling of angst-ridden responsibility for the lost son, and because he shows his unconscious internalization of Calibanic discourse through his deeply private thoughts about the son, this story is substantively the same as Cudjoe's story about his relationship to his lost sons. Calibanic discourse challenges and compromises the responses of both characters.

In the portrayal of his private thoughts in part 1, Cudjoe unconsciously internalizes and lives out Caliban's discursive legacy of the abusive, sexually predatory, irresponsible black male who justifiably suffers loss and dispossession. Like Caliban, Cudjoe's life is significantly centered on islands, where he tries to find relevance, meaning, well-being, and self-possession. In this context, Cudjoe thinks often about the loss of his wife and children, which forces his journey to the island of Mykonos. He feels that he deserves to have lost his wife and sons and virtually everyone else because he was abusive, irresponsible, and reprobate. Besides his angst about his abuse of his family, Cudjoe constantly broods over his surreptitious gazes at women and symbolic sexual violations of them, and he feels guilty, uneasy, and very self-conscious about some incidents.[3] All of this adds to his general feeling of unworthiness and the vague feeling, which goes along with the text's clear implication in light of its Calibanic imposition, that he, like Caliban, deserves loss and dispossession. Because of his marriage to a white woman and the betrayal of his children, he is "a half-black someone, a half man who couldn't be depended upon" (10). In many ways, Cudjoe's unconscious internalization of his own Calibanic inscription makes it a greater burden for him than it was for Caliban himself.

Cudjoe's recollection of one trip to an island well depicts his feeling that he has abused his family, sexually violated women, and lost almost everything and everyone important. The island "belongs" to Cudjoe's literary mentor Sam, who made a "gift" of it to his wife in part to make up for his transgressions and the life that they have lost as a result.[4]

In contrast to Sam's atonement and possession, Cudjoe only thinks about his actions on the trip to the island as manifesting his own transgressions and showing why he lost the life that he cannot possibly regain. He understands that he lost his family because he "found ways to positively, personally put a hurt on his sons and the woman [his wife, Caroline] he loves" (61), but through a close association of events, Cudjoe also connects his loss of his family and an even greater loss to his sexual licentiousness. He violates the naked body of Sam's eighteen-year-old daughter with his eyes while she is taking an outside shower in the moonlight.

Cudjoe hears himself trying to explain to his dead friend [Sam] why he's spying on his daughter. Bullshit about her being every woman and no woman won't go down. She is Cassandra, Sam's and Rachel's only child, eighteen years old. . . . He understands he's wrong to be stealing from her. Violating her privacy. Poaching the bloom of her young woman's body while she's offering it to the spirits of night. He shouldn't be at this window staring down at her, a hard-on extending his shorts in spite of the slew of classical allusions he rehearses to himself. Unable to be still, staying and leaving, as she plays in water warm as a bed. (63–64)

Removing himself from the watery view of Cassandra that creates the figurative warmth of a bed, Cudjoe strengthens the association with sexual violation by getting into his own bed and "masturbat[ing], careful not to wake Caroline, his back inches from hers, miles from her in a different place with a different weather, his face turned up to drink warm rain" (66–67). Cudjoe is remembering his loss and "exploring the connection. Missing his wife and now he finds himself missing the others. Sam and Rachel and Cassy" (68).

Cudjoe's legacy of violation of women, irresponsibility, and dispossession reaches to his "own" island of Mykonos, to the distant island of Haiti, where Caroline and his children now live, and to Philadelphia, where he comes to search for the lost boy Simba. "What was he looking for in women's bodies? Surely he'd have tripped over it trudging up and back those golden beaches on Mykonos" (27). Cudjoe rationalizes that a woman in Clark Park in Philadelphia is "new, Eve to his Adam . . . as he peered into the crack between her legs, the delicate pinks, soft fleece" (26). The symbolic violation sounds almost as real as a physical one. Cudjoe has violated Caroline in a very similar way: "When he sat reading with Caroline in the quiet of an evening, sharing the couch . . . why did she always close her robe or shut her knees if she noticed his eyes straying from his book, peering between her naked legs?" (56) Cudjoe feels Caroline's instinctive resistance to his violation, although he does not seem to understand fully why his wife resists the penetration of his eyes. He does, however, specifically associate this episode with his loss of Caroline, who after the trip to Sam's island leaves Cudjoe and moves to Haiti on the island of Hispaniola.

Many of Cudjoe's transgressions occur after Caroline has left him, but the actual chronology is unimportant because all of the sexual violations and irresponsible actions that he narrates, including those involving Caroline, connect in Cudjoe's story to produce his overall feeling that he causes and thus deserves the central loss and dispossession of Caroline and his sons. Cudjoe describes why his actions constitute a flawed, reprobate, bestial nature that cause him to lose everything important to him.

His sons were growing up like exotic plants on a faraway island he'd never visited. He knew them not at all. They spoke another language. They had another father. . . .
He'd removed himself absolutely from their lives. All or nothing is how he explained it to himself, to her. Left it on her to explain to the kids. A bastard.

He proved himself a cold fish of a bastard. . . . Run, Run. Never look back. A cry from the deepest recess of him, the part nurtured in forest gloom when he dangled from a tree by a three-toed claw. . . . Run. From the night hawk, the bear, the slithering lizard, the coiled snake. Run. Run. Run. (69–70)

Cudjoe remains unconscious of his own internalization of the Calibanic legacy, and he therefore never understands it well enough to free himself. He tries to rewrite and revise *The Tempest* in part 2, but in part 1 he fails to perceive that *The Tempest's* hegemonic legacy victimizes him. He never sees that what he and others, including Caroline, think of him is inseparable from an unconscious, hegemonic discourse that assigns his black maleness Calibanic qualities. He cannot escape his constitution by the culture: "[S]ince signification constitutes the matrix within which the subject resides after its entry into the symbolic order [of language], nothing escapes cultural value" (Silverman 165).[5] No matter what Cudjoe may have "really" done, he and others cannot constitute his subjectivity outside the "cultural value" of the unconscious Western discourse that makes his black maleness Calibanic.

On the level of *Philadelphia Fire's* conscious thematization of the writer's role, *The Tempest* controls the discourse about the fire and all the other seemingly disparate and scattered, generally oppressive and negative black realities in the narrative. The three parts of *Philadelphia Fire* show Wideman working with Cudjoe in an attempt to connect the hegemonic discourse of *The Tempest* to the text's diverse, seemingly disparate, oppressive black stories. Symbolically, the writer's text juxtaposes the destructiveness and watery death of *The Tempest* against the oppressive, destructive fire, suggesting that the former is, paradoxically in terms of its water motif, the source of the latter. Part 1 starts with this kind of juxtaposition. It begins with the story of the stormy, watery death of a man named Zivanias, called to his death by his legendary name, on the Greek island five thousand miles away from Philadelphia, and immediately breaks off after a total of about four pages to talk about the fire in Philadelphia and its consequences.

Part 1, like the other two parts, tries to piece together a narrative that makes sense and that liberates Cudjoe, Wideman, Simba, the young victim of the fire who is lost, and others. The fire attracted Cudjoe from the Greek island of Mykonos five thousand miles away to find "the child [Simba] who is brother, son, a lost limb haunting him" (7–8), and Cudjoe's description of his search in part 1 implies the relationship among *The Tempest,* Cudjoe's ruined life, the lost boy, the fire, and black oppression generally. If Cudjoe can make the connections and tell the story, he can liberate them all. The process begins by fragmenting the narrative voice to speak the disrupted, fragmented pieces of black narrative.

[H]e must always write about many places at once. No choice. The splitting apart is inevitable. First step is always out of time, away from responsibility, toward the word or sound or image that is everywhere at once, that connects and destroys.

Many places at once. Tromping along the sidewalk. In the air. Underground. Astride a spark coughed up by the fire. Waterborne. Climbing stone steps. To reach the woman in the turban [Margaret Jones, a victim of the fire], the boy [a victim of the fire for whom he searches], he must travel through those other places. Always moving. He must, at the risk of turning to stone, look back at his own lost children, their mother standing on a train platform, wreathed in steam, in smoke. (23)

In the context of its portrayal of him consciously carrying out his responsibility as a writer, the text depicts Cudjoe's attempt to show the relationship between *The Tempest's* story of Caliban and the fire and his attempt to write a story that connects Simba's loss to the discourse. The loss of Simba to the fire is also an integral part of Cudjoe's loss, but it is a loss for which Cudjoe understands the causes and for which he does not take primary responsibility. Cudjoe understands the primary role of white oppression and its effect on Simba and black people: "He'll tell Margaret Jones [victim of the fire and his source of information] we're all in this together. That he was lost but now he's found" (22). Cudjoe feels that he has a duty to black people and a special duty to find black male brothers and sons, like Simba, lost in the holocaust of white oppression. He lost sight of this important duty and drifted around after Caroline left him, and therefore lost part of himself that is like "a lost limb haunting him." If he can find Simba and free him from oppression, Cudjoe can also find and free himself.

Finding Simba is tantamount to finding his authoritative voice to write the book and make clear the responsibility for and the meaning of the fire, but Cudjoe lacks the authoritative voice to convince Margaret Jones that there is a silence and a story that needs telling in a book.

Do you know where [Simba] is?

I know where to find somebody who might know where he is. Why do you want to know?

I need to hear his story. I'm writing a book.

A book?

About the fire. What caused it. Who was responsible. What it means.

Don't need a book. Anybody wants to know what it means, bring them through here. Tell them these bombed streets used to be full of people's homes. Tell them babies bones mixed up in this ash they smell.

I want to do something about the silence.

A book, huh. A book people have to buy. You want Simmie's story so you can sell it. You going to pay him if he talks to you?

It's not about money.

Then why you doing it?

The truth is, I'm not really sure. (19)

Cudjoe consciously understands white oppression's primary responsibility and its grounding in discourse, but he cannot articulate the role that a "book" would play in disrupting, revising, and displacing the master narrative of Calibanism. The master narrative has an unconscious effect that compromises Cudjoe's conscious voice. Its source is a "book," *The Tempest,* that fabricates black male reality, but at the same time it inscribes it indelibly and unconsciously on almost everyone. This includes Margaret Jones, who cannot see how she helps deny Cudjoe a voice and cannot see that the source of black oppression and her denial of Cudjoe, whom she dislikes because of his irresponsibility as a black man (9–10), is discourse, discourse written in a master "book" of oppression. The master narrative produces its results and covers all traces of itself by dispersing its codes, signs, and cultural values through a system of cultural signification that since time immemorial, it seems, has become indelible, imperceptible, and unconscious—and therefore hegemonic. One does not have to experience the master narrative directly for its codes, signs, and cultural values to have their effect. Cudjoe cannot begin to tell Margaret Jones that it will take a liberating black "book," which raises this reality to consciousness and makes the necessary connections, to disrupt, revise, and displace the master narrative; he fails to explain and to expose the discursive source of oppression. In the final analysis, the master narrative causes Simba's loss in the fire, and because of the master narrative, Cudjoe cannot find the authoritative voice to locate Simba or tell his story.

Other black males in part 1, and in the text overall, also lack the voice and power (and sometimes the will) to free themselves and other black people. Timbo, Cudjoe's ally from the 1960s freedom movement, and now the slick attaché of the black mayor who ordered the bombing that started the fire, has abandoned his 1960s revolutionary principles. His creed is now a money creed, which aids oppression: "Answer's always yes. Yes, I'll take money. Don't care how much blood's on it. Don't care if it's my blood. Yours. I wasn't the one responsible. I'd prefer clean money but till clean drops down from heaven this will do" (84). On the basketball court, Cudjoe encounters O.T., the younger brother of Darnell, another one of his old friends, now in jail on dope charges. Cudjoe disbelieves O.T.'s story about his plans to return to school and play basketball after losing his scholarship for academic reasons: "Why couldn't he believe Darnell's brother? Why did he hear ice crack as O.T. spoke of his plans? Why did he see Darnell's rusty hard hand wrapped around his brother's dragging him down?" (38) According to Margaret's assessment, King, the leader of the black group burned in the fire, does have a voice of power:"[H]e was so sure of hisself, bossy, you know. The big boss knowing everything and in charge of everything and could preach like an angel, they called him Reverend King behind his back" (10). However, King's voice has no power against white culture's hegemonic discourse; the police burn him and his followers.[6]

Cudjoe never empowers himself any more than these other black men: As part 1 ends, he finally locates Simba and himself, and many others, in a nightmare vision of oppressive death that only yields its own terror and not the beginnings of a liberating fiction. Cudjoe tells Timbo of his dream of having his legs cut off and lying on the basketball court experiencing a horrible spectacle. The spectacle of black male mutilation and death is one of the main significations of Calibanic discourse.

I'm chopped on the ground, rolling around with half my legs gone but I'm also a witness, upright, floating, somehow staring down at the basketball court, screaming because a boy is lynched from the rim. A kid hanging there with his neck broken and drawers droopy and caked with shit and piss. It's me and every black boy I've ever seen running up and down playing ball. . . .

[Was it] Simba? The lost boy?

It could be.

Who killed him?

It was a dream.

Well make up something, then. Wake up and make up. Don't leave me hanging.

The dream stops there. Everything surrounding it's gone. I want to know the rest, too. Thought telling you might help. But it doesn't. I feel myself beginning to invent. Filling in the blanks but the blanks are real. Part of the dream.

Dream?

Yeah.

Shit, man. (93–94)

At the end of part 1, Cudjoe cannot invent a liberating fiction that gives answers and makes connections; the nightmare of oppression, which sounds too real to Timbo to be unreal, to be a dream, remains.

Part 2 thematizes Cudjoe's attempt to rewrite *The Tempest*. If he can rewrite *The Tempest*, he can attack the source of the oppressive discourse and thus change the oppression. This will change the fate of Caliban and his legacy, and it will free black males and black people by writing the reality of black oppression, and of the fire, out of existence.

Cudjoe tries to make clear how Caliban tried and failed to resist the word, the discourse, that would deny his existence and dispossess him and concomitantly committed the revolutionary act that inscribed his bestiality and dangerous phallicism. Cudjoe concretizes the trope from *The Tempest*—the "Abhorrèd slave" speech (*The Tempest* I.ii.422–36; *Philadelphia* 139)—that provides the basis for Calibanic discourse. He reads the trope.

The spurned woman speech. Clearly Miranda, not Prospero talking. . . . Testimony to her passion, her suffering to bring forth speech from the beast. Unbeast him. And what did she receive for her trouble, her risk? More trouble. Beastly ingratitude. She offered the word. Caliban desired the flesh. She descended upon him like the New England schoolmarms with their McGuffey's Readers. . . . Caliban, witches whelp that he was, had a better idea. Her need, his seed joined. An island full of Calibans. He didn't wish to be run through her copy machine. Her print of goodness stamping out his shape, his gabble translated out of existence. No thanks, ma'am. But I will try some dat poontang. Some that ooh la la, oui, oui goodness next to your pee. Which suggestion she couldn't abide. . . . He asked in short, for everything. She knew she was her father's daughter. . . . Daddy'd taught her not to give but to negotiate. . . . What's always at stake is the farm. . . . Keep your elbows off the table and your ankles crossed, knees together. Someday, when your prince comes, then you may people this property with property. (139–40)

The substance of what Cudjoe wants to show, and of what Caliban understands and rebels against, is that Miranda is central because Prospero uses her to take control and power over everything. He uses her to further his legacy with progeny like him; but even more importantly, she also perpetrates his words—his discourse—which stamp the rightness, goodness, and power of the father in its signs and codes while inversely inscribing Caliban, who does not fit the father's pattern. Miranda has a central place in a cultural process that dispossesses Caliban, and this process must villainize him to justify the dispossession and to protect the place of Miranda. Miranda turns out to be the father's pawn, a victim herself, but Caliban is the greater victim because he loses his island and gains the characterization of the uncivilized sexual beast through his attempt at sexual subversiveness.

In this context, Cudjoe hopes to rewrite the discourse of Caliban's warranted dispossession, bestiality, and danger: He wants to show that Caliban resists aggression and oppression and tries to make revolutionary change. The island rightfully belongs to Caliban, and he needs progeny to populate the island, carry his physical image, and speak his language to create a positive legacy that opposes Prospero's. Caliban's actions are understandable, and he definitely does not deserve loss, dispossession, and bestial characterization.

Rewriting Calibanic discourse violates what feels and sounds natural, because it is unconsciously signified;[7] Cudjoe's attempt to rewrite it ends up (re)inscribing it to a significant extent. Calibanism embeds itself deeply in the language and manifests itself in the institutions that maintain the white (male) status quo. Someone, perhaps Timbo, tells Cudjoe: "You can't rewrite *The Tempest* any damn way you please. . . . How's Caliban supposed to sass Miss Ann Miranda without him get his wooly behind stung good and proper by that evil little CIA covert operations motherfucker, Ariel? Round-the-Clock surveillance, man" (144). In his rewriting, Cudjoe can only write Caliban's "wooly behind" again, because Calibanism has already inscribed his bestiality, and he can only write Caliban's response to "Miss Ann Miranda" as "sass," because Calibanism has already inscribed his lack of an appropriately civilized voice.[8] The cultural enforcement agencies take over and punish Caliban when he validates his bestial, uncivilized linguistic inscription. The voice quoted earlier in this paragraph sums it up: "Prospero got that island sewed up tight as a turkey's butt on Thanksgiving. Play got to end the way it always does. Prospero still the boss. Master of ceremonies. Spinning the wheel of fortune. Having the last laugh. Standing there thinking he's cute telling everybody what to do next. And people can't wait to clap their hands and say thanks." Cudjoe has no chance of changing what has been, seemingly, so indelibly written.

In the final analysis in part 2, Wideman the character is as much unconscious of Calibanic discourse as he is conscious, and its hegemonic imposition works in both ways. Sections of part 2 portray Wideman setting his own oppressive black realities, his son's realities, and other black male realities against the Calibanic discourse of *The Tempest* to show how everything develops from this discourse. In the early pages of part 2, Wideman juxtaposes the fire, the life of his lost son, his failure to create a connection with his son, the motif of failed creativity generally, and the motif of *The Tempest,* and thus he tries to imply the connection among all these things. In parts of the story as it progresses, Wideman the conscious "fabulator" (132) makes a gradual and subtle transition and merges deeper into the world of his private angst about his own lost son; he merges into the world where Calibanic discourse unconsciously affects him, just as it does Cudjoe.

Because of the hegemony of Calibanism, Wideman, the black male writer and father, fails to use words, the privileged form of cultural signification (Silverman 164–65), to access and affect the reality of his lost, incarcerated son, which in turn leaves Wideman oppressed and lost. In the context of the novel, Wideman's son does have very serious problems that he and his father need to address. The greater challenge, however, is breaking the hegemony of Calibanic discourse that constitutes black males as subjects who are uncivilized, dangerous, and deserving of punishment. But words refuse to yield their saving, liberating potential to Wideman. Words refuse access to his son by refusing to connect and bond them, and thus he cannot tell the saving, liberating story that will free him and free Wideman. Given the hegemony of Calibanic discourse, Wideman's son can only be, like Caliban, the "Abhorrèd slave, / Which any print of goodness wilt not take. /. . .who hadst deserved more than a prison." Wideman, the character, never says this in the text, but the total context of part 2 and of the text shows that Wideman cannot tell the story of the son, because he cannot revise and displace the hegemonic discourse of Caliban.

In the second paragraph in part 2, the text presages the inability of Wideman to tell the liberating story of his son by questioning its own ability to imagine the fire out of existence and thus imagine a liberated existence for black people: "Pretend for a moment that none of this [the fire and its aftermath] happened. Pretend that it never happened before nor will again. Pretend we can imagine events into existence or out of existence. Pretend we have the power to live our lives as we choose. Imagine our fictions imagining us" (97–98). The text longs for the power to create a different reality, but it sounds very doubtful of itself.

The text cannot become a fiction that displaces the fire, a symbol of black oppression, and allows black people "to live our lives as we choose" because of the influence of Calibanism. Especially when oppressive acts involve black men, it is likely that the "grand jury [will determine] that no criminal charges should be brought against the public officials who planned and perpetrated the assault" (97). Because of Calibanic discourse, black men are dangerous criminals, and thus they deserve whatever punishment or retribution the state gives them. The grand jury will usually not indict in this society. Also, in this society the text does not have the power to imagine Calibanic discourse out of existence, and therefore lacks the power to imagine the fire out of existence and imagine a liberated existence for black people.

One paragraph after the tenuously imagined fiction, Wideman introduces the relationship between him and his son in terms of absence, silence, and separation that he cannot mediate with words. Wideman ruminates painfully about a call from his son.

> You were absent and the ring brought you back. To where? To whom?
> Hello.
> It is my son. . . . He is my lost son on the phone and I must answer before I don't have the power to say a single word. . . .
> I don't know what words mean when he says them. I don't know if he knows what they mean or knows why he says them. So we can't move beyond the ritual of greeting. To ask how he is opens a door into the chaos [of] our lives. Perhaps he's unable to tell me how he is. Perhaps I wouldn't understand how to take what he'd say, even if he tried to tell me. Words between us have become useless. Decorative. They can't furnish the empty rooms of our conversation. But the phone rings and he's two thousand miles away so all we have to work with are words. . . .
> Nothing is more painful than the phone ringing and finding him there at the other end of the line, except finding him not there. The sound of the phone call ending, the click, the silence rushing to fill the void words couldn't. (98–99)

Later, Wideman concludes that the words *father* and *son* do not hold the "possibility of salvation, redemption, continuity" (103). He reduces the words to a structuralist-like existence in a closed linguistic system that is both arbitrary and relational; that is, they relate, make sense, and create value and order in the linguistic system—and only in the system—because of their difference from each other. However, he cannot use them to affect the relationship between him and his son in the natural world outside the system.

> Think of these two words in natural order and sequence. One comes before the other, always, forever. And yet both must start somewhere, in order to begin one must break in, say one or the other, father or son, to begin. The mystery of their connection is that either word will do. I am the son of my father. I am father of my son. Son's father. Father's son. An interchangeability that is also dependence: the loss of one is loss of both. I breathe into the space separating me from my son. I hope the silence will be filled for him as it is filled for me by hearing the nothing there is to say at this moment. I hope saying nothing is enough to grip the silence, twist it to our need. Which is holding on, not letting go. My breath in him. This temporary contact fallen into silence, into listening for the other's silence. Not because it is enough but because it's all we have. (103–4)

Wideman's inefficacy reveals only a closed linguistic system that denies him any agency that will help his son. Structuralist Ferdinand de Saussure says in *Course in General Linguistics*: "Whether we take the signified or the signifier, language has neither ideas or sounds that existed before the linguistic system but only conceptual and phonic differences that have issued from the system. The idea or phonic substance that a sign contains is of less importance than the other signs that surround it. Proof of this is that the value of a term may be modified without either its meaning or its sound being affected, solely because a neighboring term has been modified" (120). In the "father/son" quotation above from *Philadelphia Fire*, Wideman largely sets forth a critique of language that says and implies much of what Saussure says; but unlike Saussure, Wideman obviously acknowledges the world beyond the system of linguistic signification—a painful, oppressive world. However, he has no agency to fabricate his and his son's "real world" reality into a story.

Wideman is obviously still the conscious writer/intellectual here, but also, as he goes deeper into the exploration of the pain associated with his lost son, he becomes more unconscious of Calibanic discourse and unconsciously (re)inscribes it through his inefficacy and the failure of his liberating voice. In spite of his intellect, Wideman unconsciously challenges and compromises his own response and (re)inscribes his Calibanic signification because he is the "speaking subject [who] is not really in control of his . . . own subjectivity" (Silverman 50).[9]

Calibanic discourse carries the "cultural codes" (Silverman 50) that dominate Wideman, the character and "fabulator," in the last quotation from *Philadelphia Fire* above. In the context of him being unconscious of the discourse and its effects, the words *father* and *son* only remind him of the pain and loss of separation; he does not seem to be aware of why this is true. Even more importantly, he lacks the agency to tell the story that will fill the void, restore the loss, and liberate him and his son, because the signification of Calibanism denies him human connection and liberating voice. Silverman says the "off-stage" voices determine significantly "what can now be said, written, or filmed." I would only add that these voices—of Calibanism in this case—also determine *who* can say some things. These hegemonic voices deny Wideman the qualities that will allow him to speak in a voice that will utilize the positive linguistic concepts of *father* and *son*, connect him and his son, and liberate them. The oppressive power of Calibanic discourse stands out above the opposing potential of (white) postmodernism as manifested in liberating fictions.[10]

Various fragmentary episodes throughout part 2 implicitly relate to the hegemonic imposition of Calibanic voices and values on Wideman to deny him the agency of father and artistic creator who can save his son. One short fragment depicts sculptor Alberto Giacometti looking at a person posing for

a sculpture and having all the other possible sculptures of the person inter-
vene until "[t]here were too many sculptures between my model and me. . .
.there was such a complete stranger that I no longer knew whom I saw or
what I was looking at" (103). There is an artistic inefficacy here similar to
Wideman's and a paradigm of Calibanism's hegemonic effect on him. Two
simultaneous fragments shortly after this make the point that "it was so
hard to write" (107). The first, from "L. Zasetsky recorded by A.R. Luria in
The Man with a Shattered World," depicts an author who has an idea to
express his injury and illness but has difficulty putting together as many as
three words to express it. Here, the injury and illness parallel the unconscious, imperceptible effects of Calibanism on Wideman. The next fragment
shows Wideman trying to finish the page proofs of his novel *Reuben* (108).
Wideman wonders: "[I]s it possible this morning to begin again, to find within
myself what it takes to meet and be met by whatever will be out there when
I have the mug of coffee in my hand, the papers and pens spread on the arm
of the chair, my eyes opening to the lake's stillness and quiet." This fragment
parallels the first in the implied inefficacy of the writer and the implied need
to find a ritual that will allow the writer to approach reality on terms of his
own choosing.

In part 2, Wideman fails to tell his lost son's story and to liberate him, or
at best leaves the attempt compromised; this parallels Cudjoe's failure to
rewrite *The Tempest* to liberate himself, all the other lost, dispossessed
Calibans—including Simba, Wideman, and Wideman's son—and black people
generally from the fire and a legacy of Calibanic oppression. Wideman's
words to his son at the end of part 2 recall the text's desire to "[p]retend we
can imagine [the fire] . . . out of existence" (97) at the beginning. He tells the
son that "[w]e do have a chance to unfold our days one by one and piece
together a story that shapes us. It's the only life anyone ever has. Hold on"
(151). Both the voice at the beginning and Wideman's at the end sound uncertain that the imaginative fiction or story will work. The admonition to
"[h]old on" suggests how compromised Wideman's son's story will be. Also,
very appropriately at the end of part 2, a two-day, two-night rain storm
washed out the production of his rewritten version of *The Tempest* staged by
inner-city black kids, thus symbolizing the hegemony of Shakespeare's "real"
or "natural" tempest over Cudjoe's "bogus" fabrication. For a time, Cudjoe
believed that somehow the kids would still stage his play. In his last words in
part 2, he says, "I wonder why I believed that" (150).

The end of part 3 depicts Cudjoe at a sparsely attended memorial service for
the fire victims, which represents the failure of Cudjoe to tell the story of the

fire and the other stories he needs to tell. Before this ending, part 3 focuses on J.B., a homeless black man who, similar to Cudjoe, fails to piece together a story that liberates by linking the fire to its source. J.B.'s section of part 3 prophesies a nightmare world where all of Philadelphia burns, the MOVE fire having created a second, larger fire through which the oppressed and dispossessed take their revenge. Homeless, outcast J.B. is also a Caliban like the text's other Calibans, "[s]tuck playing roles [they] have been programmed to play" (175), and like them, he lacks the clear perception and voice to tell the story of an oppressive nightmare reality that changes it. What J.B. sees unclearly, though, is that white oppression of black people will lead to a conflagration of oppression engulfing everyone in the city. Because of J.B.'s lack of voice to tell this story, the legacy of oppression of black men—J.B.'s legacy—that *The Tempest* has created will overwhelm everyone, not just black people. Part 3 focuses mostly on this larger reality but at the end comes back to Cudjoe and his inability to tell the story of the fire that makes the connections and liberates black people.

J.B.'s section of part 3 posits a cosmology in which the oppressive discursive codes of *The Tempest* have imperceptibly and unconsciously distorted and displaced the codes of a teleological Book of Life incorporating nature and human beings into an existence that gave everyone access to "Life's bounty, Life's sacred trusts and duties" (167). J.B., James Brown ("They teased him forever when the singer stole his thunder" [156]), gets the book after the suicide of a white man named Richard Cory.[11] Cory portrays himself as the one who distorted the codes of the book by translating them into a "grunting, rooting, snarling pig tongue" (167). He "planted incriminating evidence" on earth's "dreadlocked king" and "stranded my good brown brothers out on a limb." But Cory only vaguely understands the reality of what he has done: "Forgive me, brothers. I didn't know what I was doing. Still don't. Never will. Forgive me" (168). The effects of *The Tempest's* discursive hegemony are only imperceptibly and unconsciously present in what Richard Cory says and in most of part 3, but they insidiously manifest themselves in this oppressive nightmare world for which Cory blames himself.

By distorting the codes of the Book of Life, Cory has produced a distorted book in which a message of retribution has de-centered and displaced the original message of salvation.

The Tree of Life will nourish you. You need only learn how to serve its will. Its will is your best self speaking the truth to you. The seed of truth is planted in all of us. You only need to listen. Let it grow . . .

J.B. started reading somewhere in the middle a few lines at the top of a page. A block of writing cramped into a space not much larger than a postage stamp. Rest of the page untouched. Waste of paper, J.B. thinks.

He tries again. Lets the pages flutter. His finger leads him to this.

It's time, my friends, to reap what's been sown. The Children's Hour now. The Kiddy Korner. What have they been up to all this time we've left them alone? Over in the shadows with Buffalo Bob. Mister Rogers. The Shadow knows. But do we? Are we ready to hear the children speak? Ready or not we shall be caught. We are pithed. Feel nothing. Children have learned to hate us as much as we hate them. I saw four boys yesterday steal an old man's cane and beat him with it. He was a child, lying in his blood on the sidewalk. They were old, old men tottering away. (187–88)

The message of retribution clearly carries traces of the story of the child-Caliban Simba, burned in the fire, and thus the discursive hegemony of Calibanism works in complex ways of unconscious, imperceptible, and unintentional inscription and (re)inscription. Because of Calibanism, the white story of the MOVE fire can justify the fire that burned both King and Simba, adult and child-Caliban, respectively. By justifying Caliban's oppression, the white story (re)inscribes Calibanism at the same time that the discourse of Calibanism produces the white story.

This Calibanism that burns black children has dire consequences, however, for both black people, on whom culture inscribes it and who (re)inscribe it themselves, and for white people, who perpetuate and thus also (re)inscribe Calibanism. The society's soul becomes insensitive because of such horrible inhumanity, which extends all the way to black children like Simba. People in the society unconsciously and unintentionally neglect, and thus show their hatred for, all children—not just black children—because children seem defenseless and unable to command attention. The result is gangs of children, all kinds of children, marauding, threatening, and killing adults. Calibanism has certainly successfully oppressed black men and maintained hegemony over black people, which will have retributive consequences, but its processes also potentially encode the sickness that will cause retribution to spring from other places.

The following plot events take J.B. back to the symbolic source of the distorted book of retribution, of his own distorted vision, and possibly of his and the society's doom. J.B. wearies of trying to decipher the book and falls asleep, only to awaken on fire and to hear laughter and little feet running away. He runs toward the fountain in the square but realizes that the water has been turned off for hours at this time of the evening (188). In what sounds like another take on the same scene, J.B. does not know if he is watching cinematically, dreaming, or writing the nightmare he is living, but "here he was ha ha ha the pitter patter of little sneakers laughing, little white boys drenching him in kerosene and throwing a match ha ha ha laughing, running away pitta patta and he's shaking his fist but they have the Book . . . running away. . . ." He runs and flops into the dry center of the fountain (188–89).

The missing water symbolizes the unconscious discursive process that *The Tempest* has spawned, which holds such a powerful hegemony *because* it is unconscious and imperceptible; it becomes the remnant of *The Tempest* and its discursive hegemony that distort both the book and J.B.'s perception and that ultimately may doom society. On the symbolic level, the water paradoxically causes the fire, but J.B. cannot find it to put out the fire. The missing water leaves J.B. without an apparent source and leaves the book—the story of the fire—scattered, fragmented, and incoherent. At the same time, the water symbolizes the source that scatters, fragments, and confuses J.B.'s senses. He sees "possibilities, possible worlds" (188), but he cannot read the book or read or write a reality that will displace or revise that which is not even there, or at least that which appears not to be there. J.B.'s failure to understand and recreate seems to be his doom, and the same may be true for society.

Cudjoe's section at the end of part 3 carries ahead the themes of the society-consuming fire, the missing water that symbolically denies its complicity by being missing, and the failure of the word, the story, that will change and liberate.[12] As Cudjoe leans against the edge of a dry fountain (194), a speaker at the sparse rally echoes the theme of the retributive fire: "Fire Fire Fire. As you live. So you shall die. By fire fire fire. And those who kill by fire shall die by fire fire fire. And then there are no more words, only the power of the pounding drums, pounding heart, the fist pounding the anvil where fire burns and is transformed from word to force by this man's chant and curse and prophesy" (196). In the context of *Philadelphia Fire's* portrayal of Calibanic discourse, this dreadlocked, bare-chested black man is a dangerous Calibanic figure like the dreadlocked character Caliban in the text (120), but he also turns the society's acts back on it in a dreadful prophecy.[13] But it is not clear what these words mean in terms of the text's quest to tell a black male story of liberation.

In the last paragraph of the book, before he turns to face something rumbling ominously behind him, Cudjoe very tentatively projects the saving words—"*Never again. Never again*"(199)—that could be the root of the liberating story, but this sounds inadequate in the face of the text's portrayal of Calibanic discourse's power. Also, the sparseness of the crowd at the rally reinforces the idea that no one tells an adequate liberating story that includes the fire. Society may succumb to the violence that Calibanism inscribes on black men. The quest to tell the black male story of liberation never succeeds, however, and the potential success of this quest is not clear.

Everything considered, *Philadelphia Fire* presents a challenged and compromised response to Calibanic discourse at best through a complex relationship of structure and theme. Paradox in the narration of the black male characters' and the text's liberation quest becomes the locus for the (re)inscription of Calibanic discourse. As Cudjoe and other black male characters pursue their liberation quests, they sometimes represent their own internalization of the Calibanic qualities and proclivities from which they try to liberate themselves. Also, thematically, part 3 of the text presents an ambiguous conclusion that makes it sound as if the retribution of Calibanic discourse may be turned back on white culture through the wrath of both black and white children. At the end, though, the text never shows that Cudjoe can tell the liberating story and free himself and other black men from the legacy of Calibanic discourse. So the ending also leaves open the possibility for the symbolic (re)inscription of a main theme of Calibanic discourse— primarily that Caliban has an inferior voice and cannot tell a story that liberates him—from which the text tries to liberate itself and its characters.

There are other ways in which structural and thematic paradox and ambiguity compromise the black male voice of liberation. Structurally, the text shows the potential of black voice; its structure represents, and thus voices, the fragmented, disparate, hard-to-connect pieces of the liberating black (male) story. Thematically, the text reveals the reality of a fabricated white hegemony; the text's themes clearly imply that white people in power make up Calibanic discourse as a very important part of the Western culture's justifying myth. Calibanic discourse is no more natural, real, and true than other fabricated codes.[14] If white people can write Calibanic discourse into Western culture, Cudjoe can perhaps write it out.

However, the main theme and another implied thematic assumption of the text work against these aspects of structure and theme to make this uncertain. The black male characters, primarily black male writers, are ineffectual in breaking the discursive hegemony that can be broken in the context of other aspects of structure and theme. Implicitly then, readers must realize the possibilities within the text by analyzing what the text says about reality and piecing together a liberating story from its fragments. The text has raised an unconscious discourse to consciousness and shown that the white, Calibanic master discourse is only one fabricated reality. Knowing this, perhaps readers can still revise the master narrative and tell a story that liberates black people by drawing together the disparate, scattered pieces of black narrative.[15] What the text makes possible may not happen; readers may (re)inscribe Calibanic discourse. Clearly implied here, and more explicitly stated at other places, is a contrasting liberating potential of (white) postmodernism that highlights Calibanic discourse's limitation of voice.

2

The Thematized Black Voice in John Edgar Wideman's *The Cattle Killing* and *Reuben*

The thematized writer in *Philadelphia Fire* is intersubjective, many different writers at different times all at once, and "he must always write about many places at once. No choice. . . . First step is always out of time, away from responsibility, toward the word or sound or image that is everywhere at once" (23). Thematized, intersubjective characters who are writers, fiction makers, and storytellers also try to create the fictions and tell the stories that will liberate in Wideman's *Reuben* (1987) and *The Cattle Killing* (1996). The similar quest of writers/creators to tell the story of liberation connects Wideman's three novels.

Theme and structure undercut the story of liberation and (re)inscribe Calibanic discourse by symbolizing the inferiority and failure of black male voice in *Reuben* and *Cattle Killing*, respectively. Particularly in talking to each other, black men speak in a voice of liberation to tell a story collectively and individually that frees them by refuting the racist narrative of history and ideology that dominates Western culture's perception of them. The voice also takes on intersubjective dimensions through different black male characters who try to construct the same (or a very similar) story that traverses time and history. In the first instance, the voice fails to connect black men and counter racist ideology. In the second, it stops short of constructing a positive racial myth that arches over the past and opens the way to the future.[1]

In the relationship between Reuben and Wally, and generally in *Reuben*, the process of liberating storytelling among black men breaks down and ends in ambiguous results; by the end, the text's language, theme, and formal structure all interrupt Reuben's voice, cast doubt on his story, and threaten his identity as a lawyer and place as a comforter and healer in Homewood. Reuben tries to tell bonding and liberating stories in response to negative white fictions, but he lacks someone to engage in the important living process that will free him and give him voice and power—the living process of listening and telling and telling again, on and on, the process of creating "next and next and next."[2] *Reuben's* attempt to deconstruct white fictions implies the liberating potential of (white) postmodernism. However, *Reuben* leaves the title character and black people vulnerable to racist accounts of truth. The text does not utilize the potential of (white) postmodernism to construct liberating fictions, and it highlights the challenge and compromise of black male voice in the terms of Calibanic discourse.[3] Further, *Reuben* demarcates the breakdown of storytelling for black men from a more successful process among black women through which they connect and potentially liberate themselves.

Like the narrator in the later novel, *Cattle Killing,* Reuben is a medium who traverses time and place to make connections and to comfort and heal black people in the present time of Pittsburgh's black Homewood community. A lawyer of sorts, he listens to black people's stories to voice them in a way that will penetrate the hegemony of the law and deconstruct other harmful white fictions. When white reality threatens Reuben's existence, he finds no one has listened to his own story to retell it, empower him, and free him. In the section entitled "Reuben," the text asks questions and makes statements that point to Reuben's predicament at the end: "Who was Reuben, what was he? What work did he do?" (132) The text says further, "Loneliness is standing and testifying and no echo, no one bearing witness. Where are they? The lost ones who shouted: Oh, yes. We were there" (133). There is no one among the "lost ones" of black people, who are reminiscent of the lost in *Cattle Killing*, to bear witness and retell Reuben's story.

In the "Thoth" section, Reuben invokes the power of the ancient Egyptian God to make himself a powerful creator who ranges over time and place to invent identity and his own cosmology, which constitutes his personal reality of love and commitment that will empower him to take action for his client Kwansa Parker. Reuben imagines his separation from the perfect oneness of a brother at the beginning of some ambiguous primeval time (64). He imagines his life as a loving commitment to the lost brother, whom he calls Reuben II and makes a brass charm to symbolize (64–65). Through the strength of his creativity, Reuben generates the empowering virtue of love that subsumes evil in order to prepare himself to help Kwansa in Homewood's hateful world of evil white fictions. Unlike *Cattle Killing*, *Reuben* makes the preparation for action that will change lives most important, but like the speakers in *Cattle Killing*, Reuben must somehow tell the story that will free him from imprisoning white fictions and empower him.

The "Thoth" section begins with an imaginary encounter between Reuben and Eadweard Muybridge that implies the necessity for Reuben to find the living connection and process of storytelling that will liberate. Muybridge, the nineteenth-century photographer, tried to stop "time and unlock the secrets of motion" (63). To his chagrin, Muybridge learns that time is synchronous: "Everywhere and nowhere at once. . . . The same numbers on the clock face can tell today's time, tomorrow's, yesterday's. A clock's face registers every moment, past, present, and future" (62). He also says the following about time and motion: "I learned motion is like time in its invisible, indivisible plunge from one frame to the next. My pictures never caught it. . . . I created rows and rows of cells. Tiny, isolated cubicles with a pitiful little figure marooned in each one. Prisoners who couldn't touch, didn't even know the existence of the twin living next door" (63).

Reuben dismisses Muybridge at the end of this encounter because, instinctively at least, he knows that he must, like the narrator in *Cattle Killing*, become a medium who crosses time to engender a living, human process that connects, empowers, and liberates. He rejects Muybridge's cold, scientific approach, which tries to capture and control and leaves him frustrated with the discovery of time's synchronicity. Reuben tells himself a story that goes back in time to connect with this brother and empower Reuben through his commitment of love to the brother. He hopes that moving through time in the process of the story, as opposed to Muybridge's attempt to arrest time and motion, will prevent Reuben and his twin from being prisoners isolated from each other like the "twin" pictures in Muybridge's frames. The story that Reuben tells himself empowers him to make a magic charm through which he tries to utilize the timeless love and commitment he feels for his brother in the present to help him do his work for Kwansa (70–71). However, because he lacks a living connection and process of human interaction, Reuben's storytelling fails to empower him sufficiently. At the end of "Thoth," white fictions—"Mountebank. Charlatan. Fool. Witch doctor"—"[laugh] him out of existence. . ." (71).

The text's depiction of Reuben's relationship with Wally most vividly shows Reuben's failure—and black males' failure typically—to connect with each other through a living process of telling, listening, and retelling that will empower and free. Wally, a traveling college basketball recruiter much younger than Reuben, needs Reuben's existence to make his own existence real (113–14), but because of "abstract hate," Wally talks to himself much more than to Reuben, constantly telling himself the story of his "abstract" murder of white people.

Take your revenge [on white people] in the abstract, on principle. If you're a recruiter, your job keeps you hopping from city to city. . . . Which makes you kind of abstract in the first place. . . . In the second place, you got no ties. . . . You're a floater. People begin to see you that way. Which amounts to not seeing you at all. Invisible. Prince of the air. . . . You talk to yourself and ain't nobody answering but you. Now that's about as abstract as you can get. Put it all together and what you have is a situation where you can be whoever you want to be whenever you turn up in a new place. You are an abstract person, so you can test your abstract feelings. Release the abstract hate through an abstract crime. Murder one of the motherfuckers you wanted to kill ever since they killed a piece of you.[4] Nothing personal, you dig. . . . what you're really doing is working on the biggest problem: the abstract hate. That's what you're really killing. (117–18)

Then, Wally "watch[es] the old man [Reuben] for a reaction. You are so slick you're at least three places at once. Watching Reuben. Listening to the recruiter rap. Making it all up as you tell the story. . . . How many faces do you own as you construct an imaginary dialogue for an imaginary conversation you aren't conducting with anyone but yourself?" Wally's "abstract" conversation frees him to be several places simultaneously, like Reuben and the narrator of *Cattle Killing,* but this kind of conversation with the self is the antithesis of the living process of storytelling that potentially liberates in Reuben and *Cattle Killing.*

Specific encounters between Wally and Reuben show Wally's inability to listen to Reuben, retell his story, and perpetuate a positive tradition of love and commitment. In the final analysis, Wally's failure to engage Reuben in a liberating human process abandons the latter to the reality created by evil white fictions. In the "Flora" section, Reuben tells Wally the story of his tragic, painful relationship with Flora, but Reuben places the emphasis on his love for Flora in the story. Wally, however, is incapable of hearing the positive virtue of love amid white hatred and meanness in the story (93–95); therefore, he will be unable to retell a story of love that subsumes negatives and perpetuates this virtue. In the "Mr. Tucker" section, it takes a structural device—"[a] device in old movies for dissolving from one scene to the next" (201)—to free Reuben and Wally from an unproductive, deadlocked conversation; the scene goes off to the vacuous blue sky and happiness of Wyoming—"Yippee. I. Oh. . ." (202). Wally's failure to connect with Reuben and to hear his personal story in "Mr. Tucker" leaves Reuben humiliated and trapped by white newspaper fictions (202). At the very end of "Mr. Tucker," Reuben returns to his invented cosmology and the relationship with his lost brother. The last two paragraphs of the section, however, situate Reuben in a dream where one of his white tormentors from the Flora story is in control, and Reuben wonders if "his brother [would] ever be free" (205).

The two primary black women characters in *Reuben* do connect significantly by empathizing, physically touching, listening, and talking; being with Toodles and revealing her story to Toodles give Kwansa the power to speak affirmative words about herself and Toodles and to strengthen her in her search for her son, abducted by his father Waddell. In the "Big Mama" section, Kwansa goes onto the street to search for Cudjoe, her son, after the empowering experience of a night in bed with Toodles. She begins to tell a positive story about herself and her relationship with Toodles, and this affirmation conjoins new confidence and determination to find her son.

> I got time. Time's all I got. I can wait. She spoke the words aloud, to no one in particular, to anyone who knew what she was talking about. Like she'd told the world last night about Toodles. Spoke to nobody and anybody who wanted to hear because she was telling the truth. She was the one who knew. She was the one it was happening to. She was telling it like it is. Never mind you heard it before. Heard it different. She'd heard all about it too. But hearing was one thing. Being there another thing. And now she's been there and now she's telling it the way it really is and if you have ears it pay you to listen. You might learn something about Toodles's bed. About this empty corner and how long, how long I'm gon beat these hard streets till I find my son. (135–36)

Kwansa tells her story to "nobody and anybody who wanted to hear," which means that a listener is only suppositional, but very importantly, Kwansa believes in the worth of the knowledge that her story inculcates—"if you have ears it pay you to listen.[5] You might learn something about Toodles's bed."

In this section of the text, Kwansa goes on to set forth a narrative about her personal hardships and the history of the Homewood community that subsumes pain, suffering, and oppression with a perspective that holds the possibility for individual and community liberation. Kwansa tells the story to herself, but given her relationship to Toodles, Kwansa and her story of community life have the potential to be part of the human process of storytelling that is necessary for liberation.

Kwansa and her story oppose Wally's story of alienation, detachment, and abstraction as well as Reuben's more human story, because Reuben, unlike Kwansa, finds no one to engage in the important living process that will give his voice power and free him. The women in the text potentially find what *Cattle Killing* calls the process of "[n]ext and next. Always un-known. Always free" (182).

Women have more resources than men that allow them to tell their sto-ries and find their voice of liberation; like *Philadelphia Fire*, the text some-times essentializes black men and women in terms of deficiency of voice and sufficiency (or potential sufficiency) of voice, respectively. The male narrator in *Philadelphia Fire* describes the connection among the women in his family as he at the same time describes his own lack of voice.

There aren't words for what I think as I watch the oldest and youngest females in our family size up each other. Where they're going, where they've been is part of what they're learning, exchanging. Their conversation excludes me. As it must. As it should. A door opens and a wind sweeps over them sealing the moment, a silence and crystalline murmur too fast, too ancient to register anywhere but in the two pairs of eyes meeting. Neither will forget the moment. The baggage carried forward, the trip still to make. Words fail me because there are no words for what's happening. I am a witness. All I know is that everything I could say about what I'm seeing is easy, obvious and, therefore, doesn't count for much except to locate me outside, record my perplexity.[6] (118)

As in Kwansa and Toodles's relationship, the "conversation" among women in *Philadelphia Fire* is more than just their words, but clearly they connect and tell their stories in ways that men cannot.

In the penultimate "Toodles" section, *Reuben* brackets the black female lib-erating voice with imaginary voices that are apparently male and seemingly weak and ineffectual. At the beginning of the section, the character Toodles ritualizes words with seemingly magic effect: "Things have a way . . . Toodles said that. Things have a way of . . . Toodles repeated the words three, maybe four times before she formed the rest of the sentence saying, Things have a way of working themselves out" (206). The result at the end of this para-graph is that Kwansa and Toodles connect to exemplify the way that the virtues of love and commitment liberate by subsuming the negative in the storytelling process: ". . . Kwansa hurts for her, feels how bad Toodles feels. And Kwansa loses for an instant the pain she's carried. . . . Gives it up for Toodles' pain, which is hot and mean and different, yet a twist of the same knife buried in Kwansa's gut. She hollers for Toodles and forgets her own pain though it flickers in Toodles' eyes, in those bullshit words" (207). Yet, two paragraphs later, the text offers the following commentary on the women: "From a great distance, longer than the time it's taken all the voices that have ever told stories to tell their stories, in the welcome silence after so much lying, so much wasted breath, the *women's voices* reach us. Where we sit. Imagining ourselves imagining them" (207–8; italics mine).[7] References to distance, silence, and sedentary, abstract "imagining," seemingly by black males, twice removed from the power of the women's stories, make it unclear whether black male stories can liberate.

The ending to *Reuben* signals that it is a structural device, which goes back to the context of the structural "device in old movies for dissolving from one scene to the next" (201–2). The ending's title, "And," indicates that it is a structural device that opens the text up for more of the story, but the question is whether the ending keeps the liberating process going or opens the story up briefly to finish it superficially. The earlier "device from old movies" ends the failed, fruitless conversation between Wally and Reuben; that device provides a way to escape a situation that will produce nothing good and that can go no further positively. Perhaps the ending finishes the story and provides the same kind of escape.

The ending punctuates *Reuben*'s ambiguous, contingent, and uncertain development and process that, if anything, leave the black male voice of liberation more compromised than *Philadelphia Fire*'s. It begins with "[i]magine" (214), and thus very clearly associates itself with the seemingly weak, ineffectual black male imaginary voice telling the story in the penultimate "Kwansa" section. The association with the text's black male imaginary voice makes it possible that the ending cannot be part of a truly liberating black male storytelling process. In this context, the ending as a structural device cannot symbolically keep the liberating process going. The three-paragraph, less-than-one-page ending, in which Reuben picks up Cudjoe to take him home (214–15), is a way of closing the text with a superficially liberating act, but it remains unclear whether its imaginary voice can produce a story that liberates.

Particularly when juxtaposed to black women's voice and story of liberation, the narrative's portrayal of the restricted black male voice and story of liberation symbolically (re)inscribes an essential theme of Calibanic discourse: Black men lack a reliable voice that signifies their humanity and liberates them from oppression. Structural ambiguity and paradox and paradox and ambiguity in the narration of the black male characters' and the text's liberation quests are the main aspects of the story of liberation that move it toward (re)inscription.

Cattle Killing[8] continues the quest of writers/creators to tell bonding and liberating stories in direct response to negative white stories, but it focuses even more centrally on black male voice than *Reuben*. The black male writer at the beginning tries to "*step out the hotel door and into another skin*" (4), and in doing so, he moves into a spiritual world set apart from everyday reality for significant parts of the novel. In this context, he seeks to respond to negative white fictions with stories that will bond and liberate black men and black people generally. The liberating potential of (white) postmodernism is implied in *Cattle Killing* in much the same way that it is in *Reuben*. In the final analysis, the potential of (white) postmodernism will only contrast and highlight Calibanic discourse.[9]

The writer is a character in the text who is attending a conference in Philadelphia, where he grew up. He leaves his hotel with his current book to visit his father, who lives in the black section of town on the hill, with the intention of reading to him from the book. The writer talks about how he will find the position in time that will allow him to create the spiritualized seeing and spiritualist connection that the narrator and the narrative will use in an attempt to achieve liberating voice.

> *The boy shot dead [in the black neighborhood] on the hill last night. His ancient African lad [the narrator whom the writer invents] meeting his brethren as [the writer] thinks the meeting, as he unleashes himself from this time, this moment beginning the climb to his father [on the hill]. What is the name of the space they occupy now. All of them. The [dead] black boy always fifteen, the two boys [the fifteen-year-old and a fourteen-year-old, also shot] freshly dying, the long gone African [character of the seventeenth century whom the writer invents], his father.*
>
> *Was it a lie, a coverup to say they've all looked into the same sky, walked the same earth and thus share a world, a condition. Even so, given the benefit of the doubt, what kind of world is it. Why is it not weeping for everything lost. And why is he afraid of dying. And who is he anyway,*[10] *interchangeable with these others, porous, them running through him, him leaking, bleeding, into them, in the fiction he's trying to write. . . . (13)*

The writer turns the narrative over to the African narrator, who, like the writer, will become "interchangeable . . . porous" in a process that will attempt to recover what is lost and create a tradition that connects; achieving this is achieving liberating voice. From this special, spiritualized place of seeing and connection with the dead, the narrator and the narrative try to bear witness and create the tradition that liberates by transcending the silence of death. They try to tell the collective black story of the quest to spiritualize the world and live free of the demons conjured by white myth and the physical horrors and ravages of white imperialism and racism.

The writer's fiction and the narrator he invents try to become storytelling mediums who move backward and forward in time. Liberation resides not so much in actual freedom from the physical ravages and the mythic destructiveness of white racism, but in the process of telling the story that binds, heals, illuminates, loves, sustains, and maintains continuity. Liberation is the process that maintains a tradition and bears witness through the telling, listening, and telling again.

The narrator inculcates the liberating process of storytelling as he recounts and connects stories and fragments. The text makes the eighteenth century the prime location of the narrator, a preacher who converts to Christianity after his manumission from slavery as a young man. However, the narrator's supernatural vision makes three centuries synchronous and time amorphous and ambiguous as he tries to use his narrative to heal a sick woman. This narrative allows for an open-ended process of storytelling that goes backward and forward and never ends: This is liberation. But liberation also resides in the stories generated by the narrator's supernatural vision that breaks down mundane concepts of time and reality and allows the possibility to remake a world freed in opposition to the control of racism. These stories significantly constitute the narrator's Godly service to the world, a service that consistently tries to raise black people above evil and sin.

The narrator explains to the mysterious woman the open-ended storytelling that maintains a tradition: "I wanted to bring you [stories] as gifts, stories of my dead to keep you alive, to keep love alive, to keep me coming here each evening to be with you in spite of my dead, in spite of what was missing, lost, unaccounted for, never to be found again, in spite of the earth turning faster underneath us so each time I walk through your door there is less time and more time to be mourned, to be mounted in the stories I hope would bind us, free us so always there would be more, more" (206).

The narrative describes the vision the narrator has at St. Matthew's, a white church on the outskirts of Philadelphia:

St. Matthew's wooden walls turn down like Jericho's walls of stone, like pages of a book, opening upon a fantastical landscape. He could see as far as the ends of the earth in every direction. . . . The world, its far-flung wonders, contracted so everything could be encompassed by his vision. This world and a multitude of others whose existence had been hidden until the walls fell away and he found himself seated at the center of a disc upon which the universe was shrunken and arrayed. Nay, not shrunken. There was no diminishment of scale or distance. Better, its immensity rendered available. The miracle was that near and far had become interchangeable. Things close at hand, things separated from him by a continent, were blended. One. He roamed everywhere at once. At any moment exactly where he needed to be.

Instead of being overwhelmed by infinite vistas, he was flooded by peace. . . . First chance, he'd tell the others—when all your desires are granted, you have no desires.

But he had no wish yet to say anything to anyone. He was the others. They were thinking with his thoughts. Their thoughts were his. He lived uncountable lives. Breathed for all of them, dying and being born so quickly life never started or ended. It flowed. . . . he missed nothing but nothing halted his gaze either and the world was one sight, one luminous presence inventing his eyes. (68–69)

The narrator can see everything to be seen and knows everything that the "uncountable" living and dead know.

The narrator recalls a black preacher he had seen somewhere talking about the purifying light of the supernatural; the preacher goes further than the narrator toward explaining how this kind of supernatural seeing potentially remakes the world. He says "the mountains, the marble-pillared houses of government, have no more substance than taunts and whisperings and stares of the devil's agents sent to plague you. Phantoms. Ignore them and they have no power over you. Learn to look inside yourselves. Feed the light" (20).

This world-changing inner light of spirituality relates to both the process of storytelling and to the content and outcome of the stories about black individuals striving to be free. The inner light, manifested in more forms than the religious in the text, will never fail as long as the stories bear witness to its power; conversely, the narrator and his narrative try to use the inner light to continue the stories. The narrative containing the stories that the narrator sets forth portrays his own life, but at the same time, it tells the stories of many black individuals who strove to do much of what the narrator does—foster the light against the false appearances of racist evil in order to change the world.

The mechanics of the text's process of storytelling coalesce with its depiction of a multifaceted spiritualized seeing and spiritualist connection. The narrator can see and narrate many things backward and forward over time because his first-person point of view merges with the text's third-person to share the storytelling. Also, the narrator's first-person point of view becomes interchangeable and intercommunicative with the first person of another character, Liam, during significant parts of the text. Further, the narrator's first-person point of view allows him visual access to a spirit world beyond the mundane and earthly. And finally, the narrator's storytelling becomes synchronous to take up the lives of the unspecified dead, who "speak to [him]" (153), as well as to give the accounts of the specifically named characters.

The narrator talks about the storytelling in terms simultaneously describing its mechanics and implying his vision. In these stories, events happening for the first time can be "a return [to what has already happened]. To memory, possibility, life. As all stories are" (55). The narrator's inner light of spirituality is inseparable from the mechanics of storytelling in generating stories that create the possibility of changing the world and that bear witness to the power of the inner light. Part 1 mostly affirms the power of this spiritual light in an evil, racist world and the saving process of storytelling.

In part 1, the story that the narrator tells about the woman he meets on the road (36–37) depicts her miracle of goodness and the narrator's miracle of faith and goodness. The narrator sees the woman as he travels in the back country looking for "families unconverted to the truth of the light" (36), and finds himself guided and affirmed in faith by her. The narrator portrays the woman almost as mysteriously as he and the narrative portray the women to whom he tells this story, but he makes clear her love and sacrifice and that she can be redeemed and reborn out of her Godly act. The woman, seemingly the maid of a well-to-do white lady, treks slowly through the country with grimy, bleeding feet carrying a dead, white-looking baby. She and the narrator walk to a "quiet crescent of lake he was viewing for the first time. Perhaps no human eyes have seen it before" (44). The woman goes through a bizarre ritual, preparing herself and the dead child for renewal and redemption, and walks into the primeval-looking lake until the water closes over her head. There is "[n]o name for the time" (47) that the narrator waits for the woman to walk out of the lake, which she never does.

Her loving example and the narrator's failure of faith in not waiting long enough all work, paradoxically in the latter instance, to affirm the narrator's faith in the worth and efficacy of the woman's loving act:

I didn't wait long enough. I lost faith. Deserted her. She trusted me, asked me to help, but I didn't wait long enough. . . .
    She returned. I know she did. If I'd waited, I might have found you [the mysterious woman to whom he tells the story] sooner. Before it was too late.
    Perhaps its not too late. Perhaps it never is. (48)

One example of saving faith by the narrator might have inspired another, and the narrator might have found the woman "sooner" if he had shown more faith at the lake.

However, it is not too late, because stories such as this and the ongoing storytelling bear witness to the light. The stories can possibly save the mysteriously afflicted woman to whom he tells them, inculcating the process of storytelling as he does the telling, and she can possibly continue the stories and the tradition to save others. One cannot separate the content and outcome of the lives of the characters in the stories, and of the narrator's life that is also inscribed along with their stories, from the process of storytelling. The process, however, overarches the content and outcome.

The narrator's story of the woman moves synchronously in time—forth and back, back and forth, on and on—to encompass her and other bearers of the light, including the narrator. When the narrator later moves to Philadelphia, he hears stories told by others about the woman's love and sacrifice for the white-looking child during the outbreak of plague (49–54); these stories incorporate the lives of the tellers into the woman's life. The stories that the narrator hears *after* he met her also simultaneously take him back *before* he ever met her, making beginning and ending amorphous. He does not know "[w]here . . . my story [should] start, where end. . . . Nothing had ended. Mystery had deepened. . . . There I was in Philadelphia, the waters parting, her figure rising again" (52). For the narrator, the woman miraculously *returns again before he ever met her* in an equally mysterious but different woman from the spirit world. The narrator has a convulsion, and the woman from the spirit world touches him with water and brings him to life. She uses the same redemptive power of water that the woman walking into the lake uses to renew, redeem, and resurrect herself and the white-looking baby (74–76). This occurs in an episode before the lake woman experience, right after the narrative miraculously made all time and space one with the narrator's eye (69). The narrator also hears the woman's voice *again before he ever heard her* in the voice of Liam's wife (79), a white woman affected by black oppression because of her marriage to Liam and who bears witness to her own version of the light.

The narrator's forth-and-back/back-and-forth story of the women bearing the light includes Liam's story, which goes back to the African past of the myth of the cattle killing, which simultaneously dictates the oppressive future of African Americans. At the end of part 1, the narrator becomes intersubjective with Liam's stories; their first-person points of view merge: "I knew I must be in the Africa of Liam's stories. I was the boy he'd been before he was snatched away forever [by English slave traders]" (143). From this perspective, he sees the myth of the cattle killing, and at the very end of part 1, he watches the fiery death of Liam and his wife, their house torched by whites, which leads to his concession to the ineluctable power of white racist oppression: "Circles within circles. Expanding and contracting at once— boundless, tight as a noose. God's throat, belly, penis, cunt, asshole, the same black ditch. The people an unbroken chain of sausages fed in one end and pulled out the other. A circle without and within, the monstrous python swallowing itself, birthing its tail" (149) The narrator ends part 1 with this horrifying image of black oppression. This kind of horror will eventually force the narrator to stutter (205) and cause his storytelling voice to fail in part 2.

The text's overall development and process move toward ambiguity, uncertainty, and contingency. Both the narrator's story and Liam's story, which are in substantive ways the same, show this. A significant portion of part 1 testifies to Liam's struggle to find the good in the world, but Liam's story of his successful struggle is also inseparable from the story of his individual oppression, the destructive cattle killing myth, and the oppression of African Americans.

At the very end of part 1, the narrator's voice within Liam's African stories inculcates the synchronous process of storytelling, and before this, Liam's storytelling in the first person inculcates this liberating process at the same time that it depicts the story of the attempt to remake the world in the face of racism.[11] Before the narrator goes back in time intersubjectively to retell Liam's African story to the mysterious woman, the text depicts Liam retelling the narrator the stories he told his wife, and as always in the text, the narrator is retelling the stories to the mysterious woman. The "colors inside" (126) become Liam's more secular form of the inner light that will change the world. Liam tells the narrator that he tried to warn his future wife about the racism and brutality of the world; he tried to warn her through his stories about George Stubbs, his white master in England, an anatomist who attempted to use sketches to reveal the secret to life beneath the flesh and bone.[12] Liam says that "[m]y stories about Stubbs were not simply reminiscences. I was trying to warn her. About the future, our prospects for a life together in this New World. Crossing the ocean, I expected the colors inside me would be freed. I knew I couldn't tolerate anything less than what Stubbs granted himself. Not one life, black man and white woman in a cage others fashioned, but what was next and next and next" (126). The light inside Liam inspires his storytelling (and later his art of painting) that depicts his effort to remake a better, nonracist world and that at the same time teaches the narrative's liberating process, its "next and next and next."

Liam's stories about Stubbs show how Liam struggled to be free and to show "the truth inside us all" (127) in the racist white world that he symbolizes by the cattle slaughterhouse in England where Stubbs's father, his master before Stubbs, made him work. Liam sees the connection among Stubbs's traffic in illegal cadavers and his selfish dedication to dissection and sketching to reveal the truth of life, Stubbs senior's building of an empire through his brutal cattle slaughterhouse, and the African slave trade, of which he was a victim (127–28). The defining moment of Liam's time with Stubbs is a harrowing episode in which he attends Stubbs while the latter's white fellows list the nonhuman differences of a pregnant African cadaver. The words of the white men strip away the illusion of Liam's human identity and reduce him to frustrated desire and ineffectuality as he sees the reality of a world where racism objectifies all blacks with the most horrifying callousness and brutality.

> My legs trembled. I pressed my hands into the wall. I needed the stones for support. . . . The African woman on the table was my sister, mother, daughter. I slept inside her dark stomach. I was gripping her heart with both my hands and it was the world's heart, hard and cold as ice. . . . They'd find me cowering in the black cave of her womb . . . dead and alive, alive and dead. I wished for the fiery breath of a dragon, for tongues of flame to leap from my mouth and consume that terrible cellar where the auctioneer [selling the body] had already begun his obscene chant. (137)

Stubbs's art that pursues the truth does, however, inspire Liam to invent an "art . . . to expose the lie of the madness [of racism]" (127), and Liam escapes to America to pursue his art.

Liam's experience with the narrator shows the efficacy of liberating storytelling. In the American years before he met the narrator, Liam unsuccessfully "tried to find the light" and only "grew more and more silent"(126), separating himself from his wife. He did not realize that he had "[s]o many stories to tell. . . . till [he] learned [the narrator was] willing to listen" (131). Liam rediscovers his storytelling voice by telling his stories to the narrator, and he later discovers the art to paint his white wife in a style that symbolically eludes the trap of racism. Liam paints "[n]ot what [he] imagined or [the narrator] imagined or [Liam's wife] imagined, but what could come next. After this time. Next and next. Always unknown. Always free" (182). Liam can paint after he regains his storytelling voice, and his painting thus symbolizes the process of storytelling that liberates by bearing witness to Liam's and other black people's inner light and humanity that guided their attempts to make a just, humane world. On the level of structural correspondence to the symbol of Liam's painting, the process of storytelling liberates by sustaining a black tradition. He acts to make the symbol to free himself as he symbolizes the liberating process of storytelling.

The narrator retells Liam's stories, which leads the narrator to the African myth of the cattle killing. The cattle killing myth portrays the Xhosas perpetuating their own oppression and destruction by believing an evil spirit of despair that told them they must kill their sacred cattle, as the invading whites had already started to do, if they wanted to wipe out the plague of disease and white oppression and return to the sacred ways in a new world. When the Xhosas kill their cattle, they of course carry out their enemy's work. They "speak with [their] enemy's tongue. . . . fall asleep in [their] enemy's dream"; they "murder themselves" (147). The African girl who tells the story to the narrator, in a dream while he is in the Africa of Liam's stories, says that she will return to him in a happier dream where "our enemies [are] dead . . . the slaughter of our cattle, the slaughter of our children not dyeing our hands blood red with guilt. A love dream. Yours. Mine" (148). She offers hope that the descendants of the Xhosas can overcome their capitulation to their enemy's dream and their self-destructive prophecy.

The girl becomes a part of the positive storytelling process; the story that the girl tells about the evil destructiveness and the Xhosas' struggle against it will coalesce with a tradition of black storytelling that binds, heals, illuminates, sustains, evokes love, and maintains continuity. Implicitly, the teller and listener endlessly repeat the stories in a voice generated by virtue, always free from the confining hatred and oppression of the cattle killing myth, also encoded in the stories. In this context, the black storytelling tradition subsumes the cattle killing myth.

But at the end of part 1, the myth becomes the central construct that precipitates the narrator's realization of the vast power of racism and foreshadows the stuttering of his voice. The waking sight of Liam's house burning immediately conjoins the hopeful words of the African girl, and part 1 ends with the narrator's depiction of the "[c]ircles within circles" of ineluctable black oppression.

From this perspective, the black tradition may encode the cattle killing myth but not subsume it; it may be a prophecy against which the African American storytelling tradition cannot prevail. The myth's direct proximity in the text to the account of Liam's and Liam's wife's murder belies the positive effect of everything that Liam accomplishes. In light of the revelation of the cattle killing myth and the horrible view of Liam and his wife burning alive, the narrator believes that slave traders took Liam and his "African brethren . . . from the land of their fathers to preach false prophecies" (148). The storytelling "prophecies" of black people, concomitant with their moral acts, cannot change the horror, brutality, and oppression of their reality and the world, symbolized by the animal slaughterhouse of Liam's English experience. Also, the realization of the world's true racist horror can silence the storytelling voice, can stop the process and tradition. In the final analysis, the tradition may encode destructive evil as well as saving morality.

Part 2 depicts the horrifying evil of oppression that causes the narrator's stutter, symbolizing the loss of his storytelling voice and the potential break-down of the liberating process. Part 2 leaves the process and the tradition it creates ambiguous. The narrator's experience with racism in Philadelphia after Liam's murder and during and after the plague causes him to feel that it is "[t]ime now to give it up. This speaking in a strange tongue, [a] stranger's voice I struggle to assume in order to keep you [the mysterious woman] alive" (205); he feels the "language coming apart in [his] hands." The burn-ing of the black orphanage and of the black orphans of the plague forces the narrator to these depths of despair. Kathryn, a victim of rape by her white master during the plague, is part of the chronologically ambiguous collective group of women to whom the narrator tells his stories. She intervenes most directly to rescue the narrator and to allow the text at least an ambiguous conclusion to the quest to perpetuate a liberating tradition.

Kathryn hears and empathizes with the narrator's pain, and most impor-tant, she reciprocates his love—one of the main virtues of the tradition that frees the participants in the stories from hatred and oppression, which the stories also encode. Consistent with the text's emphasis on sustaining the process above the actual outcome of events in the stories, Kathryn encour-ages and affirms the narrator's efforts to tell stories even though they cannot change actual events: "something is terribly wrong and he can't do a thing, she can't do a thing to change it, so she says, No matter, no matter, it's fine, baby. You're fine. Letting him know she understands and it's all right. Either way. Everything. Any way. As long as you tried your best, baby. Fine. Fine. Fine" (205–6).

Kathryn becomes one with the synchronous, mysterious collectivity of women whom the narrator interacts with and tells stories to, and in spite of the narrator's stutter, the women's implied presence correlates with a struc-tural ellipsis that means a return to the process and tradition instead of an omission of words.

One day when it's time to tell the last story and I stutter because it sits like a stone in my throat and carries the weight of all the stories told and untold I wanted to bring you as gifts, stories of my dead to keep you alive, to keep love alive, to keep me coming here each evening to be with you in spite of my dead, in spite of what was missing, lost, unaccounted for, never to be found again, in spite of the earth turning faster underneath us so each time I walk through your door there is less time and more time to be mourned, to be mounted in the stories I hoped would bind us, free us so always there would be more, more. . . . (206)

The narrative has moved from Kathryn's specific encouragement and affirmation after the narrator stutters to the time when the narrator stutters when trying to tell the last story.[13] The stutter associates the latter scene with Kathryn, but the woman is not specifically Kathryn, because Kathryn always visits him in the morning instead of the evening, which is the time referred to here. Kathryn is here, not as an individual, but as part of an implied collective group of the women in the text. The "you" represents both the text's central mysterious individual and implicitly all the other women, including Kathryn, whom we cannot separate her from in the text. The ellipsis, along with the words just before it ("more, more . . ."), signals a return to the process. At this same point, the narrator expresses hope that he and the woman can connect and free themselves through the stories: "I hoped [the stories] would bind us, free us so always there would be more, more . . ." The presence of the women and the continuation of the process correlate.

The restored voice and process lead to freedom constituted in love, but this freedom is qualified. The paragraph after the ellipsis returns to the "[o]ne day" reference of the preceding paragraph, and the narrator announces that he will tell stories that include landmark twentieth-century symbols of freedom and places associated with them. This time the narrator does not say that it will be the "last story" or that he will stutter. The stories will be stories of love about the narrator's dead that give him life and express his love for the woman: He wants to "save you, save myself, tell you stories so my dead are not strangers, so they walk and talk, so they will know us and welcome us. Free us. To love" (207). The narrator concludes part 2 by saying that the storytelling process and its stories will save them—"If someone is listening" (208). The contingency at the end of part 2 makes the conclusion ambiguous, because at some point at least, someone may not be listening, and the process will break down.

Cattle Killing thematizes texts that attempt to attain the liberating process symbolically through structure. Both the opening section and the epilogue thematize the text that the writer (and in the epilogue the writer is clearly Wideman himself) is writing. Another important thematized text is the blind woman's book, which the narrator reads in part 2.

The blind woman's book mysteriously becomes the possession of the narrator, and it reveals much about Kathryn's oppression and abuse and about the lives of the black orphans of the plague who get burned up in the orphanage fire. *Cattle Killing* never makes it clear how the narrator gets the blind woman's book (perhaps he gets it from Kathryn). It only says cryptically that the "book [was] entrusted to him [and] he opened [it] and searched for clues only after he'd lost her [perhaps Kathryn but also any of the other women in the text] again" (198). The blind woman is Kathryn's white mistress, and she makes Kathryn the amanuensis who writes her story. In the process of writing the blind woman's story, Kathryn records her emotions too, telepathically it seems, although *Cattle Killing* does not specify how she writes her feelings into the book. Kathryn's emotions come from her rape by the blind woman's husband, the prominent Dr. Thrush, who plays an important role during the plague.[14] The blind woman's book also records, again seemingly through a kind of telepathy that *Cattle Killing* does not specify, the emotions and the oppressive plight of the black orphans among whom Kathryn and her mistress work.

On one hand, the blind woman's book, which she cannot see or write herself, and which she believes no one but Kathryn will ever read (163), speaks a truth that, ironically and figuratively, even the blind woman should be able to see. It speaks the pessimistic, terminal reality of the black lost and dead who are victimized by racism. The narrator uses the condition of the black orphans depicted in the blind woman's book to describe black reality: "We have lost them and they have lost us and that is why we are dead" (202). Just before this in the text, the blind woman's book influences the narrator to describe black reality in terms of a dismal figure of death. The narrator closes the book and tries to move beyond the lost, dead ones of the eighteenth century inscribed there to pray for the black unborn. This attempt only leads the narrator to utter despair, however: "the prayer might boomerang and fling him back to his own beginning and he would have to kneel there and open his mother's legs and see himself curled asleep, see everything in a blast of white light that also shouts *no no no* because surely as the light reveals it also separates. The seed of him shrivels. His mother moans. Both of them shot and tossed in a ditch beside the road" (199). This figure of utter death and destruction rivals the figure of ineluctable oppression at the end of part 1 (149) for pessimism.

On the other hand, however, one can read the significance of the blind woman's book much more positively: The blind woman's book produces the narrator's relationship with Kathryn (200), who, as I have said, reassures and perhaps saves him when he stutters, and in turn perhaps saves the storytelling process. The narrator looks in the book to find a connection to Kathryn and the other woman, both of whom are lost (198). The intimate communication with Kathryn—the "finding" of Kathryn in a sense—starts after the narrator searches the blind woman's book for "clues." For some, like the narrator and the author of *Cattle Killing*, the book as a structure and form is always a part of the storytelling process, and this nullifies for them the dead-end reality of the content of the blind woman's book. Whatever its content may be, the blind woman's book informs the narrator's and the author's perspective; they use it to keep the story going and to keep the storytelling process going, leading to the loving relationship with Kathryn, leading to the book discussed in the epilogue and its positive implications. The other interpretation of the significance of the blind woman's book contradicts this one, but *Cattle Killing* leaves open the possibility of both interpretations.

In the epilogue, Wideman's son Dan, who has just read *Cattle Killing*, finds a "real life" connection to *Cattle Killing's* fiction; Dan discovers the connection in letters from one brother to another detailing events in their lives that correspond to events in the lives of the narrator and his brother in the text. In part 1 of the text, the narrator says that his brother embarked for Africa soon after he purchased his freedom from slavery and never returned; the narrator implies that he was lost at sea (32). Searching the British Museum's African Archives, Dan finds letters from one brother, who left America, to his brother still in America; the letters depict events that match the dates and details of the lives of *Cattle Killing's* narrator and his brother. But the letters that Dan finds show the brother reaching South Africa and creating a life there for himself after he left America (211–12). The brother in the letters lived "fifty-some years" in South Africa (211) and worked with the South Africans in their struggle for freedom. In the letter quoted in *Cattle Killing*, the brother talks about the South Africans' struggle for freedom after talking about his perilous voyage and joy when he reached Africa.

The country is in turmoil. Decades of war have left the African people landless, starving, dispirited. A prophecy has arisen and many Africans follow its mad reasoning. They are killing their cattle. This desperate measure is intended to drive away the whites, magically return the blacks to prosperity and power. But the effect of the wholesale destruction of their herds is exactly the opposite of what the Africans intend and the prophecy promised. Deeper misery settles over the land; the children are dying. The Africans are destroying themselves, doing to themselves what British guns and savagery could not accomplish.

I do not know how it will end, but I know my duty. I will pray for these

noble, generous souls bewitched by a prophecy that steals them from
themselves. I will struggle beside them as long as there is breath in my body.
    This note, the others I intend to write, may never reach you, yet I am sure a
time will come when we shall be together again.
                                            Hold on, Your Brother (212)

    The epilogue emphasizes the importance of the structure of the text; through the letters and Dan's account, the epilogue opens up the formal structure of the text to a "real life" storytelling voice that will help to maintain the continuity of the tradition against the potential for failure that the text has shown. As Dan says to his father in his own letter, the brother's "letters are a continuation of [*Cattle Killing*]. A sort of happy ending, maybe" (210). Dan does not know if "my letters and your story are actually, factually connected" (211), but whether they are or not, the letters extend the text of *Cattle Killing* into the "real world." The "relationship between brothers in the 'real' world [mirrors] a relationship you made up for your book. Or vice versa. You call it." This implies an encompassing reality that binds both the fictional and "real" brothers with hope and love. The tradition maintains its continuity and ability to liberate through positive values, because the epilogue opens up the structure of the text to listen to and tell the "real life" story. This broadly encompassing listening and telling continues the storytelling process because it ensures the "[n]ext and next. Always unknown. Always free" (182).

    The letter quoted in the epilogue also goes back to take up the evil cattle killing myth to make it a part of the positive storytelling tradition. The cattle killing myth is archetypal in *Cattle Killing,* and thus this instance of its subsumption by the tradition could stand for all the other instances of the tradition subsuming racist evil. The brother promises a loving commitment for the South Africans that may allow them to overcome the cattle killing prophecy and fulfill the happy dream that the African girl spoke to the narrator about earlier (148). The words of the brother establish the nobility of the Africans in their struggle as well as the power of his own inner light of spirituality, which seems largely extinguished from the narrator in part 2 of the text's fictional version. The ability of the brother to visualize them together again and to put it in his story shows the power of the inner light to foster the storytelling tradition that subsumes the archetypal evil of the cattle killing myth. Through the process of the stories that he tells in his letters, the brother demonstrates love, commitment, faith, and other virtues against racist hatred and evil that enslave black people through negatives. The brother's example here symbolizes all other instances when black tellers and listeners will endlessly repeat the stories generated by a voice of virtue such as the brother's, always free from the enslaving hatred and oppression of the arche-typal cattle killing myth.

In many ways, the sheer richness and power of the text's narrative would seem to belie the symbolic (re)inscription of Calibanic discourse. Certainly, from one perspective this brilliant novel has as much powerful potential for voice as it has for restriction of voice. Characters who are intersubjectively connected try to tell a story of liberation that they may not be able to tell, but the characters' portrayal that emphasizes their spiritual quest, and some-times attainment, is also a strong statement of voice that would seem to mediate the negative symbolism.

Nevertheless, the epilogue opens up additional interpretations. Dan hy-pothesizes that no one would "buy" or "believe" the "real" story if it were incorporated into the text—even as the text incorporates it as part of its structure. Dan found the letters after his father published *Cattle Killing*, but his father would not have been able to use them anyway: "Even if I'd un-earthed them sooner, you wouldn't have been able to use the letters, because nobody would buy the spin they put on your story. The circle's too neat. Who would believe. . .[?] (210–11). Dan implies that people could become confused and refuse to believe because of the conflation of the "real" and fictional in the letters and the book. In this context, "no one will be listening."

Moreover, the epilogue does not complete the task that the narrative sets for itself at the beginning. Was the fiction that the writer was starting "*a lie, a coverup. . . . And who [was] he anyway[?]*" (13). What was his connection to the black boys on the hill murdering each other and to his father? Could he find the voice to write their story, connect them, and thus empower and liberate them? The questions imply the black male bonding and achievement of voice that are the writer's task. The answers to these questions are still uncertain in the epilogue, and it seems that the narrative may not go far enough.

The fictions written by the black male writers, the book by Wideman that Dan reads and the letter that the African brother writes to the brother in America, do not clearly attain voice and connect: The text reveals their po-tential failure of voice. The letter that the African brother writes says that "*[t]his note . . . may never reach you*" (212). Dan and his relationship to the text of *Cattle Killing* and to his father are more important, however. Dan is physically separated from Wideman in the epilogue, and though Dan's archi-val findings seem to complete Wideman's book, the book does not clearly speak to Dan and connect him to his father: "An engaging, intriguing book, as most of his father's books were for him. And as most of his father's books, this one also seemed inspired by something unsaid, unshared, hidden. Silent at the core. Stuff maybe his father couldn't say. Full of silence and pain at the core. The same shit they could never get to, let alone deal with when they talked. What often kept their conversations brief, on the edge of tense, even when they both were clearly happy with each other, pleased to be playing ball or talking books, enjoying a meal, whatever" (209).

The black male writer of *Cattle Killing* can definitely write a very powerful fiction, but it is also a fiction that names its own possible failure. At the end, *Cattle Killing* brings its narrative back to a world of black men where, paradoxically, the very powerful fiction does not attain voice, empower, and liberate. Paradoxically, the black male writer and the black male text lack sufficient voice. This is where paradox and ambiguity most clearly enable the symbolic (re)inscription of Calibanic discourse in the text's liberation quest, and challenge and compromise the black male voice and story of liberation.

Fritz Gysin concludes his essay on *Cattle Killing* with this: "[W]e, as readers, challenged and fascinated by complex postmodern narrative strategies, never succeed in establishing clear-cut connections among individuals, communities, and spiritual essences; the significant insights we gain, lose, and regain as a result of our constantly shifting stance, provoke a perpetual bonding and unbonding with the text, a ritual action that only good texts encourage, and outlive" (Gysin 627). Gysin suggests the greatness of the novel and the power generated when its story of liberation is contested and restricted in the context of its postmodern potential.

3

Clarence Major's Quest to Define and Liberate the Self and the Black Male Writer

Clarence Major is in many ways a unique black male writer because of his extensive use of postmodernist and poststructuralist themes, forms, and approaches. In increasingly pessimistic terms, his novels focus on the liberating potential of discourse. In his first two books, black male characters purportedly liberate themselves through the subversive use of language and the fictions they construct. Over the course of several novels, however, it becomes more and more evident that discourse is hostile and imprisoning, and the texts progressively make discourse synonymous with arcane self-referential narrative. This narrative becomes the place of articulation of the black male story of liberation. The story of liberation is also arcane, but it is not unreadable during significant parts of the first five novels.

Although *All-Night Visitors* (1969), Major's first novel, appears to be different from the other novels, textual evidence in all the novels reveals a central, connecting effort to tell a black male story of liberation. Specifically, the features of the story of liberation in the texts are the quest to attain an empowering voice that liberates from racism generally, to define the self humanely and positively, and to portray positive black male sexuality. In the first novel, the black male writer veils his identity—revealing it only twice—and uses vulgar, sexual language subversively to define his sexuality and liberated human being. After *All-Night Visitors,* more and more fully thematized black male writers create narratives to free themselves, but the narratives refuse any definition except the self-referential. The writers become trapped in these narratives and tell the story of liberation within and in opposition to the hostile, imprisoning reality of self-referential discourse. The story of liberation increasingly merges into the self-referential. However, there is always the presence of the thematized *black male writer* who tries to define his and his characters' freedom against the reality of the self-referential. Finally, the black male story of liberation is practically silenced when it becomes virtually the same as self-referential narrative.

The discursive quest in Major's texts is continuous, and to understand it in one text one must look at them collectively. The body of texts reveals that they collectively and individually respond to Calibanic discourse. In *All-Night Visitors*, it is clear that the main character tells the story of liberation in the same language of Calibanic discourse that represents him negatively; on this level, this language directly (re)inscribes Calibanic discourse. Overall in the novels, ambiguity and paradox support the restriction of voice in each text and in the collective body of texts. After *All-Night Visitors*, restriction of the story of liberation and its concomitant definition of positive voice, character, and sexuality in the esoteric narrative of the black male writer's liberation quest (re)inscribe Calibanic discourse. In the individual texts, both the story of liberation and the connected (re)inscription of Calibanic discourse become less clear as the narratives become increasingly metafictional, but elements (and later, vestiges) of both are in all the texts.

Generally, the influence of Calibanic discourse in Major's texts works in the way that it does in Wideman's. It is inherent in the language. Largely through ambiguity and paradox, liberating character portrayals turn toward affirmation of Calibanic qualities, and liberating narratives structurally and formally symbolize Calibanic discourse by undercutting the voice of liberation during the process of their development. Specifically, Major's texts (re)inscribe Calibanic discourse through character portrayal and through the restriction and, finally, the virtual silencing of voice. The relationship between (white) postmodernism and Calibanic discourse is also generally the same and specifically different. The liberating potential of (white) postmodernism clearly highlights the oppressive power of Calibanic discourse in the underlying narratives of the first two novels. In the next three, the thematized writer's attempt to tell a specific black male story of liberation still takes place within the context of the postmodernist potential to create a liberating fiction, although the larger self-referential narrative virtually silences voice.

Briefly, the plot of *All-Night Visitors* depicts Eli Bolton, the main character, growing up in an orphanage in Chicago and experiencing its insensitivity and savagery.[1] He has an even more horrible experience fighting as a soldier in the Vietnam War. Later, he falls deeply in love with a white woman named Cathy and moves from Chicago to New York, where Cathy leaves him. As a result of the traumatic relationship with Cathy, he moves into a flophouse,

The Other Side, and lives the sad life of a dope user among addicts and prostitutes. Upon his return to Chicago, he witnesses a fatal stabbing on the street. The novel ends with a symbolic act of humanity through which Eli tries to rise above the brutality and inhumanity of his life experience.

Through its discursive process and development, Major's *All-Night Visitors* reveals the challenge and compromise of the black male story of liberation as well as any text. It portrays the hegemonic signification of the main character in the terms of Calibanic discourse—a specific, foregrounded Calibanic phallicism in this text—through its graphic racial and sexual language; the main character's attempt to deconstruct this signification, sometimes by speaking in this same graphic language in order to signify positive sexual definition and a humane character; the (re)inscription of Calibanic phallicism as the main character tries to use the graphic sexual language of his Calibanic portrayal to deconstruct it; and the society's discursive reenactment/reinforcement of Calibanic inscription. The "good" ending of *All-Night Visitors* is superficial, because it cannot produce the positive conclusion that it purports to produce. Eli creates liminal spaces of freedom for himself, at best.[2]

Philadelphia Fire's critique of Calibanic discourse fits Eli. Wideman's *Philadelphia Fire* (1990) quotes Miranda's "[a]bhorrèd slave" speech (*Philadelphia* 139; *The Tempest* I.ii.422–36) that defines Caliban's uncivilized nature and bestiality. Prospero has control over Caliban, and the language that Miranda gives Caliban is the only one available to him to redefine himself. Caliban can only "curse" when he tries to redefine himself, because the language essentializes him and prevents redefinition. *Philadelphia Fire* shows how Calibanic discourse is unconscious. As such, it is "buried" and "unmentionable" in the language, but "nonetheless signified in the small-print forever-after clause" (*Philadelphia* 141). Prospero's positive character and Caliban's negative character have become, basically, indelible in the language over time. Eli, like Caliban, is responding to his negative signification in the same language that signifies him, because it is the language available to him. Eli tries to use the very words of his negative sexual signification to deconstruct the power of those words at their source and to redefine himself, but because the words are part of an unconscious discourse that carries his essentialized signification, he only (re)inscribes this signification.

A series of relationships with Cathy and other women, through which Eli tries to define his humanity and positive sexuality, provides the substance for my analysis of this text. The discourse of Eli's encounters with women is both vulgar and offensive because of its graphic sexual terms and purportedly descriptive of salvific human emotion and commitment; it implies that culture signifies Eli in terms of Calibanic discourse, from which he must liberate himself by using language subversively.

Very early in the text, Eli uses graphic sexual language that evokes his Calibanic portrayal in phallic terms to draw attention to the inauthenticity of his inscription.

My dick is my life, it has to be. Cathy certainly won't ever come back. I've stopped thinking about the possibility. Eunice [another woman with whom he has a positive, loving relationship] has . . . gone . . . and I'm taking it in stride. My black ramrod *is* me, any man's rod is himself.

This thing that I am, this body—it is me. I am it. I am not a concept in your mind, whoever you are! I am *here,* right here, myself, MYSELF, fucking or being driven to the ends of my ability. . . . whatever I happen to be doing, I am not your *idea* of anything. (4–5)

There is a suffering person here who has lost his relationship with Cathy, a human being whom he dearly loves.[3] His emphasis on sex and his phallus is a sign of painful loss and wounded humanity focused in the senses of the human body—and not the Calibanic signification that is an unconscious "*idea*" or a "concept in [the] mind" of American culture. Eli signifies that he is deeply human and is not the Calibanic beast.

At places in the text, Eli more explicitly signifies his opposition to Calibanic signification and indicts the society for it. In talking about his despair and desperation that makes him fantasize about killing Cathy to keep her, Eli says the following: "But I kill for love, and I sense the matchless alarming hatred you already have for me. Just because I, in the wealth of my strangely emolumental nightmare, *know* that I cannot go on living without having at least a fragment of my spiritual bride, my white-limbed mistress, my quiet Cathy with me, you already consider me a cranky demented black butcher, a rapist. If I too, [*sic*] think of myself in this way it is only at the most superficial level of my inscriptive mind" (20–21).[4] Eli states his opposition to Calibanic signification—"demented black butcher, a rapist"—by relegating it to the "most superficial level of [his] inscriptive mind." Later, when the police take him to the station to place him in a lineup after the murder, his question specifically indicts society for its signification of black men: "Was a black man always a renegade or what in hell was going on in this society?" (122).

Eli tries to get completely beyond social signification, but the linguistic signs for his body and its sexuality dominate him. He attempts a deconstructive project: He seeks the "large and natural" in life, to look "up into Life, the Beginning, raceless beginning, of everything deeper than anything social"

(8–9). The deconstructive project is reinscriptive, though; he signifies his Calibanic bestiality—the black male whose "dick is [his] life," who is always "fucking" a white woman—at the same time that he tries to use these signs in a discursive process to signify its opposition.

Eli's (re)inscription of Calibanic discourse is inseparable from his own unconscious internalization of it. He says that if he sees himself in the society's negative terms, he does so only superficially. However, the text shows that voicing his own Calibanic signification makes it possible for it, and that of black men generally, to exist at a deeper, more substantive level.

Black signifying/dozens playing rituals at the orphanage are an example. The "more manly" boys at the orphanage challenge the "less manly" Junior, who "is trying to prove he's brave and heartless, just to be accepted" (88), to kill a dog to prove his manhood. Eli participates with a mind divided between horror and fascination, the unconscious voice of conformity breaking through into momentary consciousness: "'Yeah, motherfucker,' I say, 'its cold. Give me that knife. I'll show you how to do it!' somebody in me said, a conforming lineage god of insanity, with buckteeth" (89). The signifying later reaches a higher pitch as others participate: "'If you don't take your knife right now!—and do it—your mama's a coal miner with a funky ass-full of coal dust; for drawers she wears overalls. . . .' Meanwhile everybody is falling out with bloodthirsty laughter, some of us running around in circles, holding our stomachs, malicious and deformed by our devilment. . . . 'Damn Leroy . . . you sho know how to signify!'"(91). After Junior kills the dog, Eli thinks that "Nothing is real! Nothing has any meaning! What have we done to each other?" (92).

The episode shows that Calibanic discourse determines black men from inside and from outside their own culture. Black male culture, the culture within American culture, carries Eli and others along in its unconscious compulsions to signify black manhood in response to Calibanic discourse. On a level that pushes slightly beyond the unconscious, they at moments realize— in some very vague way at least—that in enacting their manhood rituals they have acted like animals and thus (re)inscribed and internalized their Calibanic signification, which becomes particularly clear in black male signifying rituals. Calibanic signification dominates because black men will continue to be largely unconscious of it, and the culture will unconsciously read it in everything that they do.

Eli goes beyond the attempt to deconstruct Calibanic discourse by using its specific overt, phallic terms, the vulgar terms that foreground race and sex. Particularly during part 2, *All-Night Visitors* moves through instances of discourse where Eli tries directly and explicitly to inscribe his humanity; he emphasizes his humanity through language that expresses compassion and concern. He de-emphasizes the language of sexual lust. Thus, in another way, he tries to tell a story of liberation. Cathy is Eli's favorite woman, and he expresses himself most humanely with her in two "Cathy" episodes in part 2.

Through these episodes, Eli tires to evoke his humanity on a highly refined level. He uses his sexual feeling for her to transport himself to an alternative world where he can realize human compassion: "The best thoughts, like the best feelings, are always born passionately—especially compassion itself. I felt it for her, this moment profoundly, and later, and always. 'Come here, Cathy'" (127). Later in the text, while listening to Cathy's story of abuse by her stepfather, Eli's words take him to this alternative world, where he tries to express his and Cathy's human essence: "She suddenly looked at me, her face so filled with gorgeous colors beneath the snow milkiness banana-yellow streaks, with an interplay of scarlet touches, of gold yellow around her temples. . . . All of those tones, washes, tints, blends, were always there in the raw and warm structure of her face, but it was only at this moment that the kaleidoscope of it hit me; deepening levels of my own sensibilities for some sudden unconscious reason, expanding and enhancing her essence as well as my own" (189–90). Through this discourse, Eli tries to define his true reality, which sets him far apart from the Calibanic phallicism that he (re)inscribes and internalizes when he attempts to use language subversively.

Eli also states for himself a role as a writer with the gift of language that he can use to constitute his true reality in a similarly refined way and to free himself to experience the peaceful essence of human existence. He suddenly breaks forth in the text with a reference to the discourse of the "master writer" that embraces him and that serves as a symbol of his human liberation:[5] "I had a daydream of a man's arm washing up on the shore. Where had that come from? A cluster of motionless boats on the horizon, birds crying over them. The lyrical words of the black master writer who saw the *human* condition as a poet, embracing me! There would be no breakfast, I knew. I wasn't out here [in Peekskill] for formal things like that. The peace, the quiet existence of growing things standing or moving in their time. That was why I was here" (169). Eli's reference to being a writer here is the first in the text, but he later reveals that he was a student writer of great reputation at Roosevelt University (183), implicitly one who could define his reality and human existence in these terms.

However, in spite of Eli undertaking various discursive projects and assuming various discursive roles, the text reveals that it unconsciously (re)inscribes Calibanic discourse in the process of telling the story of liberation. The reaction of the white man who discovers Eli "raping" Cathy on the street (28), Eli having gone temporarily insane because she is leaving him, shows how the text's foregrounded Calibanic phallicism is the immediate, basic unconscious sexual signification of a black man. The white man immediately responds with "Ku Klux Klan babble" that has an "Americanism in [its] melody and tones."

The "Americanism" discursively reenacts/reinforces Calibanic inscription; it is a linguistic fragment that is the essence of a discourse. It challenges and compromises the black male story of liberation because Eli *is* the essentialized *"nigger raping a white girl"*—even as he has sex, even as he later goes about the discursive process of describing his sexual self, and particularly his sexual body, that is liberated from sexual proscription. The language and semiotic system—which includes the black male body—will not allow him to be anything but the stereotype, the "raping nigger," that he tries to use them to counter. The black male body is, in essence, "nigger." "Nigger" is "rape." "Rape" is "nigger."[6]

The ending is a superficially "good" conclusion to Eli's story in light of his "American" signification as the "raping nigger," and thus presents a paradox that supports the overall unconscious (re)inscription of Calibanic discourse. In the concluding sections, Eli describes his best times with Cathy when he most clearly expresses his compassion and love for her (179–94). He also begins the very last section of the text, "Mama Mama," by talking again to Tammy, the woman he uses the most vulgar sexual language to describe early in the text, and distances himself from this vulgarity. He now remembers the encounters with Tammy, apparently the same ones in which he tried to deconstruct his Calibanic signification, differently: "I am remembering all those sorrowful moments of the distorted codes and dispatches of herself to me" (198). He ends the novel with the symbolically humane act of giving up his apartment to an indigent Hispanic woman and her children (199–202). According to Eli, this act makes him "firmly a man,"[7] and at the end he stands awaiting daybreak, "vibrantly alive" (202–3).

The ending sounds very positive, but it has to be superficially positive. It has to be superficial because it concludes the text but does not produce the change that it purports to produce. Eli's position is still liminal and problematized, because his and the text's process of telling the story of liberation (re)inscribes Calibanic discourse more than it makes him "firmly a man," which he claims.[8] He lives within the liminal space by constantly signifying against Calibanic discourse. Implicitly, Eli must continue to find instances and moments of discourse–liminal, problematized spaces—to define himself in opposition to a culture that defines him Calibanically. More explicitly than any other character in this study, Eli "curses" like Caliban.

Major's project in *No* (1973) is much the same as it is in *All-Night Visitors*. In the later text, he is only moving a step closer to making clear how the quest for black male freedom is, for Major at least, basically one undertaken in and through the discourse of his narratives. Through its arcane, esoteric form, the discourse of *No* produces a paradoxical, ambiguous, and uncertain black male voice of liberation that is substantively similar to that of *All-Night Visitors*. In both texts, a writer/creator works within language and discourse to tell a story of liberation. However, *No* is the first text in which the writer overtly makes discourse synonymous with arcane self-referential narrative.[9] Arcane self-referential narrative becomes the place of the articulation of the black male story of liberation, which is also arcane, but readable in the terms of its identifiable characteristics. After *No,* these characteristics become harder to read as the narratives become increasingly self-referential, but vestiges are still readable within the pattern of the arcane. Ambiguous representation of liberating voice, character, and sexuality in this pattern restrict the story of liberation and are the sporadic symbols of Calibanic discourse in the self-referential narrative.

The first two paragraphs of *No* sum up, or certainly foreshadow, much of what *seems* to happen in this unusual novel, which does not work primarily according to concrete plot details. Moses Westby, the father of the main character of the same name, killed his wife Veronica, his son Moses, his daughter "Gal," and himself when the children were young. (It is impossible that he literally killed himself and his family, of course, if much of the life that his son lives and the story he tells, which includes old Moses and Gal, returned from the dead also, takes place after the murder. At any rate, the novel defies "realistic" explanation in this way, and young Moses's own murder provides part of the defamiliarized landscape and bizarre texture of the narrative.) Moses and Gal lived with other people after the murder and among many other very strange things, experienced the life of the "penal colony," which is young Moses's name for the imprisoning white society from which he constantly tries to escape during the novel: "It wasn't really a prison except in an abstract social sense and also in a very personal sense. In truth no one ever really could point out where it began or ended, and it wasn't limited to one country. When Oni and I went away together to Latin America, we were still in it. That's how elusive it was; and it was always shifting. It had so many levels and there were so many ways you could define it. Many people never even once thought of it as an actual prison" (3–4). On the trip to Latin America with Oni, a childhood associate and then a girl-friend, Moses ended up in a bullring where he touched the head of a bull that gored him. This experience gave Moses a sense of "how *naked* my presence in the world really is. How absolutely unsafe I'll always be" (3). However, at the end it freed Moses to fly away on a plane to what he "believed to be a new beginning" (207).

Moses implies his role as a writer through barely veiled references to it. As a writer, he infuses his discourse with arcane, defamiliarized thought and with bizarre sexual references and episodes, and structures it through para-graphs that constantly and arbitrarily change shape. In a process that relies heavily on the writer's spontaneity to create both theme and structure, Moses tries to define his human self in the context of arcane counter-narrative.

Perhaps Moses most clearly implies that he is a writer through his self-consciousness about language. He says the following at various places in the text: "The things that happen below the level of speech are like real with the atomic weight and energy of radioactive isotopes" (52); "Even to *invent* a circus, I think, is painful. The futility of it, y'know. Words. Your pleasure, my obsession" (75); "I had the terrible feeling that if I were not careful I could bury myself beneath spoken words and lose touch with myself and the particular areas of reality I had so far been lucky enough to stumble on" (194). Moses expresses an apprehension about language because it is self-referential and obfuscates as much as it signifies. *No's* narrative is one in which the writer supposedly finds freedom at the end, but already words have started to be self-referential in a hostile way.

The writer's quest is consistent with the attempt to construct a liberating postmodernist form. In this context, Moses calls society a "penal colony," and Major has said in *The Dark and Feeling* (1974) that in *No* he was "try-ing to show the shifting elements of the so-called self" (141). Implicitly, Major is trying to define a de-centered, postmodern self that society's social codes, the greatest manifestation of which are abstract, cannot confine and con-tain. Major says further in *The Dark and Feeling* that he "regret[s]" the Freudian influence on *No* (137). The following quotation demonstrates this influence in the text.

I moved northeast slowly, it possibly took years. Also, while all this physical activity was taking place, who and what I am was also in flux; anyway, it was around this time that I began to consciously feel that I was at least on the road to self-determination.

> Also, if I were living more consciously than unconsciously I wanted to come to fully understand that middle land between the two as well as the other two. But what I truly suspected was I was

> somehow suspended in a kind of pivot between the two, conscious
> and unconscious. I felt like a creature unable to sleep *and,* at the
> same time, unable to wake. (143)

In spite of the fact that Major says he "regret[s]" the Freudian influence, his
focus on its fragmentation of the self is consistent with his idea of the "shifting elements of the so-called self," and all of this broadly and generally
conflates with the attempt to create a narrative with liberating potential. The
writer creates the potential narrative space of freedom to tell the story of
liberation, and although it happens to a lesser extent than in the later novels,
the text undercuts liberation in many ways.

No is formally as radical as anything that Major has written; it fits a
general pattern of his postmodern works and of postmodern black male novels. It implies the failure to appropriate (white) postmodernism and voice it
in black terms that articulate a black male story of liberation. The book's
arcane counter-narrative is fundamentally postmodernist. However, the story
of liberation written within the counter-narrative implies the need to use
postmodernist liberating potential to construct a black male fiction that refutes white racism. But the text cannot utilize words and postmodernist narrative form to carry out this agenda.

The following extended example of the text's discourse shows the efforts to liberate the self in the face of the abstract conditions of the society,
which are no less confining because they are abstract. Moses's discourse attains a level of substantive abstraction and abstruseness commensurate with
the abstract, "elusive," ubiquitous bonds of society. Moses tries to define his
human freedom and his sexuality through his ritual actions within the recon-
dite terms of the narrative. As far as plot is concerned, I will only say that the
following is, apparently, an episode among the characters in which a woman
named Lucy has fled from the men and is hiding in the cornfield.

> My knees were aching from squatting so long but I could not
> conceive of moving. I was frozen in a nightmare where I should run
> but couldn't. Suddenly, I saw Fisheye stand the bottle (click) on the
> porch. Sigh. A half yawn; then, lean back on his left elbow, and with
> his right hand, dig into his pants pocket. He brought out a stiff
> oblong object that looked like a dead robin. I squinted to make sure;
> and it *was;* and it was about ten inches long. The light was good
> enough so that I could see the chestnut-red breast. Well, naturally, it
> seemed odd that a *grown* man should be carrying around in his
> pocket such a thing; and yet, somehow I thought I understood it.
> The only thing that worried me a moment was: what would he do
> about the possible problem of the tiny pest that lived at the root of
> the feathers, in the bird's skin. He probably hadn't thought about it,

especially if they hadn't yet begun to reach and crawl about on Fisheye's own skin. I looked at B.B. for a reaction but he didn't seem interested in Fisheye's possession. B.B. looked at the thing, then twisted his face the way he does when he's bored; then looked toward the embankment where Nasteylipp was last seen.

I found it impossible to hold back my question. I said to Fisheye, Can I see that?

Sure thing. Come take a look.

My knees cracked as I stood up and inside the house I heard Grew giggle and began laughing. It was good to hear that sound. Maybe Slick John was telling him jokes about the many wild incidents of his experience as a tax collector in the penal colony.

I stood at Fisheye's knees smelling his enormous sweaty odor blended with the stink of the booze. I knew what it was, nevertheless, I asked, What is *it*?

It's my bird.

What does it do?

Fisheye didn't answer me because at that moment Slick John Flower came out, the screen door banging behind him. He had his right hand extended before him, palm up, and in it, he had something carefully balanced. I thought it surely must be something quite precious because of the awed expression on his face. His eyes were focused on the . . . it was something oblong but slightly smaller than the bird. Slick John stooped beside Fisheye, and they both began to grin. B.B. slowly drifted over, obviously not wanting to, but to see what was happening. Suddenly it became clear to me, what the object was. I recognized it as Grew's peter.

Isn't it nice? said John.

Here, said Fisheye, put it in.

Fisheye was holding open a deep long slit in the robin's chest and it was obvious that the bird was hollow inside. Carefully, like a surgeon working on a heart transplant, Slick John eased the spongy, shrunken thing down into the crevice, and Fisheye ceremoniously closed the sides over it.

A moment of silence was observed, then Fisheye spoke. How is he?

Fine, fine. I left him playing with Lucy's straightening comb. He's going to be *just* fine!

B.B. suddenly started laughing uncontrollably as Fisheye patiently reinserted the bird in his pocket. And at that moment, from the cornfield, we all heard a loud and beautiful, almost sensuous, sneeze! . . .

He threw up Lucy's dress and the moon glowed on her fat belly. She wore no underclothes; she never wore any underclothes, which is why her thick bush was not a new sight to my eye. I'd seen it many times at times when she stooped to pick up something or sat carelessly in a chair. I often dreamed of her in a way that I was scared to dream of Veronica, though, I had, by accident also seen Veronica's bush a number of times. Such incidents always fascinated me because I never really had had sex with a woman or a girl; and the babysitter episode didn't count as sex and even *then* I knew it.

> Why were they taking so long? I was anxious to see the act. A twig snapped somewhere and the night wind blew softly. The Fisheye apostle was digging in the pocket where he'd put the bird. But what he brought out was a two-ounce white tube of polymer acrylic; holding it between the shaking thumb and fingers of his left hand, with the other he uncapped the pigment, and squeezed a little up from the airtight tube. For a moment my eyes shifted to Fisheye's tense face: he was nervously chewing his bottom lip. His dimples showed dimly. Nasteylipp twisted and cursed and Slick John groaned impatiently. Fisheye shifted the tube now to his left hand and squeezed it; I watched it emerge snakelike, glossy and red, onto the tip of his right index finger. Satisfied with about an inch of it out, he ceremoniously began to smear it into the thick matted hairs around Lucy's hole.

Shit, Fisheye, snapped John Slick, that's not *enough*!

Nasteylipp Lucy screamed, HELP!

Scream all you want, said John, call the Governor of Chicamauga, if you wanna, call *anybody*! Nobody can help you!

> Meanwhile, Fisheye had squeezed out a much longer portion of it and was vigorously applying it to Lucy's nappy nest.

The stuff drys fast, said Fisheye, *too* fast!

Slick John barked impatiently, *Just work faster*!

And a moment later Fisheye was done. He leaned back and looked squintingly sideways at the painted cunt. Appraising his work like a real mastercraftsman.

> You finished?

Yeah, John. And she's as beautiful as a shark. (35–38)

The black male story of liberation is written within the esoteric narrative: As the creative artist, Moses tries to explore and authenticate the sources of his human feeling and sexuality and of his human creative potential through his ritual actions. The narration does not "mean" anything as much as it allows the exploration of self and being on a metaphysical level commensurate with the broadly encompassing power of the society to confine. The entire text is constructed in this fashion.

Nevertheless, the story of liberation may (re)inscribe Calibanic discourse. Perhaps the signs of black male sexuality grounded in the discourse suggest how it is problematized. What do the ritualized sexual acts mean, and what does the whole bizarre episode mean, particularly in light of the sexual acts? Is Moses's sexual interest and action tantamount to negative sexual portrayal? What is the sexual definition and overall self-definition that comes out of this episode? There is no question that Moses is trying to define his sexuality and human self. However, the text raises questions—unsettling ones—about Moses and black maleness as it tells the story of liberation. The discursive process that would liberate turns upon itself ambiguously and confusingly. The text perhaps (re)inscribes Moses as rapist and sexual beast as much as anything.

Like the ending of *All-Night Visitors, No*'s ending is a superficially "good" one that presents a paradox supporting the overall (re)inscription of Calibanic discourse. Moses calls the act of touching the bull a symbol of his freedom: "I touched [the bull's] head and in a strange and beautiful way that single act became for me a living symbol of my own human freedom" (204). It means that he "was no longer a victim. . . .[and allowed him to] decide if I wanted to go on living" (203). Regaining consciousness an hour after the bull gores him, he "began to put the pieces of [himself] together again" (205). In the last sentence, he flies "toward what [he] believed to be a new beginning" (207). In this "new beginning," will he continue to signify his freedom by telling the story of liberation in the same way? This almost contradicts his belief that he will live freely because the story of liberation and the action which purportedly concretizes freedom do not clearly free him. It is hard to say that he has signified a liberated "new beginning."

The "good" endings to *All-Night Visitors* and to *No* are both superficial, because each one's purported positive conclusion is inconsistent with the text's overall discursive process and development. The endings cannot concretize freedom in any definitive way, which they seem to indicate that they do, in the face of the preponderance of the text's discourse—its language and implied signs of black male sexuality, its theme, and its formal structure. The ending of *No* is problematized in an additional way: Moses concretizes his freedom by situating it in an experience that allowed him to "decide if [he] wanted to go on living," and that left him unconscious for an hour and in a state in which he could have died. Given this, one could read Moses's escape at the end as his death. That is, the escape could be figurative as well as literal. The "flying away" at the end literally could be death. Moses's only freedom could be death? (This reading takes on resonance when one remembers that the text opens the boundaries between life and death at the very beginning because Moses Westby Sr. killed the family when the younger Moses—his son and the narrator—was a child, before much of what "happens" in the text actually happens. In a sense then, the narrator tells the story from the realm of death.)[10]

Reflex and Bone Structure (1975) is a self-referential narrative in which the author, the main character, tries to control his own story, which threatens and defies him but refuses to allow him to stop writing it at the same time. The text goes a step further than *No* because it foregrounds and thematizes the role of the author and his discursive quest, thus making them fully explicit. It also makes it clear that narrative is self-referential and hostile to the author. By the end, the author apparently fails in his attempt to control his story and his characters because of the defiance and hostility of the story's own language and semiotics. The author's story traps him and his characters.

The black male author does try to tell a story of liberation, but the story and its failure of voice are more diffused into the self-referential narrative. The author constantly tries to define the self and concomitantly his sexuality and sexual expression as he tries to make his writing referential. The black male self and sexual identity are ambiguous because the text is arcane, but clearly the author is crude and vulgar in some ways. The clearest thing is that the text silences the black male story of liberation.

The text thematizes a discourse constituted by language and a range of modes of symbolization, including the media, specific media events, and other cultural forms that define reality through popular and historical events. Generally speaking, the text's discourse produces characters who lack form and substance and who at the same time vex the author because he cannot control them. Their uncontrollable reality bothers the author so much that he constantly tries to blow the characters up. In the final analysis, he cannot shape their reality into a successful story, and he cannot blow them up, or at least get rid of them (145). Another reason that they exist beyond his control is the (white) postmodernist qualities that refuse to allow the author a controlling voice in shaping reality.

Many times in the text, the author explicitly states his understanding that the properties of language deny him a controlling voice in shaping reality. The following describes the author's feelings abut his relationship to language: "You're on a train moving along the countryside in a foreign land. . . . A lady sleeps with a frog on her lap. Who are you? You're the author. You're writing a letter to Dale: 'If you are only a word then Cora was alone when she died [in one of the many explosions that the author pretends killed her]. If explosion and death are only words then nothing happened'" (88–89).[11]

This is the reality of the self-referential narrative. But written within the counter-narrative are identifiable elements of a story of liberation that (re)inscribes Calibanic discourse in the text's process and development and/ or become virtually the same as self-referential narrative. (White) postmodernism highlights the failure of the story of liberation because words still allure the author to use them to define himself and his characters positively and successfully, but he cannot use words to construct a liberating fiction. The narratives of freedom created by the writers in Major's novels increasingly lose their liberating potential.

In this more restricted setting, the author often watches, virtually helpless, as different media or media events take over the reality of the text and threaten him or make him uneasy. In the following quotation, the sequence of realities spawned by *Gone with the Wind* poses a tantalizing, if not deadly, threat to the author and Cora: "For kicks Cora and I go to see *Gone With the Wind*. But something is wrong. It's about the Lindberghs trying to escape the swift G-men of the FBI. Suddenly it changes. It's about World War I. A scene where tiny bombers are dropping bombs on thousands of babies in cribs. We leave the theater. The screen follows us. It moves along a few yards ahead, still showing the same movie. The scenes keep changing. A million people are wiped out in a snow storm. A policeman stops us. We're arrested" (53). As is true throughout the text, the author never clearly understands the source of the threat created by the discourse, but the danger does seem to materialize when the reality of the discourse "arrests" the author and Cora.

Three quotations from different parts of the text suffice as examples of the discourse's more aggressively hostile defiance of the author's control of his characters and defiance of his attempt to tell the story that makes sense of what goes on between them. The last quotation ends the text as the author fails to eradicate the characters' reality when he cannot control it.

> I have a terrible time understanding precisely what goes on between [my characters] and myself. It is extremely hard work. I try to see how they speak to each other and listen to their words, but they keep tricking me. All I feel I can successfully do is *look* at Cora. Fill my senses with her loveliness. She is just there. I'd try to force her to do anything [sic]. Yet I force her all the time. I keep annoying her, trying to get her to open to me, really reveal herself. The split trunk of a tree. Her spit drips on my neck. (47)

> I stand in front of [Cora] and she smiles. I can imagine how she looks beneath her stylish red dress. Red shoes. A red ribbon in her dark thick hair. I

can see in my mind her soft mound, the lips damp and slightly puffy. She needs variety. She still dreams, daydreams. She thinks of the terrible prince from her childhood and she seeks him. What can I do. I can't tell her: you're wasting our time. I'd drive her farther from me. I can't afford that. I'm already barely hanging on to her. Please, Cora, come back to my reality. Start a new way. (63)

I suck [Cora's] tongue and lick her hairline. I bite her neck and run my tongue into her cunt. Up the crack of her ass. This way I know she is still living. She strokes my hair and whispers, "Oh, Canada, oh baby."

Canada has melted into an abstraction. Even so he is still concrete. Dale was never anything but a word. I'm fed up. I want to get rid of them.

Cora wanted to get out of herself. She is sleeping. I kiss her ear. Lick the hair under her arm. She is running away across a desert. The sand is hot. The sky is black. She is almost out of herself. She falls on hands and knees. Dale arrives on a camel with a message from Canada. He reads it through a loudspeaker: "As you run, remember, a shadow settles over my spirit. You understand that, Cora, and you understand how I will move through it to the clearing I seek. If only I could wrap wet towels around the broken pieces of the shadow. But that might not do it. If I could deal with the beginning and the ending a little better. Still that might not do it. Even to invent another name for myself won't do it. It's strange, the clearer things get the less it matters. Even the shadow doesn't matter."

Dale gives Cora a hand. At the edge of the desert they step into the city. They step into a house. It explodes. It is a device. I am responsible. I set the device.

Canada calls me. With the phone an inch from my ear I listen: "Once you stop [writing] there isn't likely to be any thing left. Otherwise it would not be time to stop."

With my bare hands I break the phone. Canada is still talking to me through the pieces. I throw them on the floor and kick them. (145)

Canada's conundrum captures the author's predicament in his own discourse: "'Once you stop [writing] there isn't likely to be any thing left. Otherwise it would not be time to stop.'" The author cannot stop, and he must stop simultaneously. He must not stop because this discursive space is the only place where he can potentially be free. The potential seems more limited than it is in *No*, however; the arcane and defamiliarized discourse in *Reflex* seems to afford scant space for liberation. In fact, it seems that he must stop writing because the hostility in the discourse threatens his existence.

As is true with Moses in *No*, the author may (re)inscribe his Calibanic sexual signification as he tells a story of liberated sexual expression. The author contends with Canada and Dale for control of Cora, and he depicts this struggle in terms of his attempt to have a satisfying sexual relationship with Cora, thereby possessing her and taking away his feeling of insecurity. Quotations from *Reflex* that I have already used portray his relationship with Cora. The following are additional disparate examples that are typical: "I . . . go behind the gym. . . . [to] fuck [Cora] in the grass" (84). But knowledge that Cora has sex with Dale seems to mortify him: "Cora kisses Dale's neck—because they obviously get together and fuck like animals. Such acts break down my will to communicate. I lose faith in the key. And I begin to dislike kissing" (51). What is the effect of the author's language in these examples and the effect of his portrayal of his sexuality in his discourse throughout the text? He may raise unsettling questions and (re)inscribe a negative sexual portrayal.[12] Clearly though, the black male story of liberation is silenced as the self-referential narrative silences the author.

Emergency Exit (1979) continues the author's misadventures with discourse, showing more clearly than *Reflex* that he cannot control it. Major associates himself with the author by placing his own photograph and photographs of his paintings in the text.[13] As in *Reflex,* the author tries unsuccessfully to define himself through his portrayal of his characters and his relationships with them, including his sexual relationships with women.

Throughout the text, the author tries to escape the characters and to escape the hostile discourse, and at the end, he attempts the text's final "emergency exit" through a series of twenty-three narrative descriptions, as one of his female characters, who is now his wife, watches him. A selection of these numbered narrative fragments follows.

10. So he made his way across the threshold not only barefoot but half naked. A few hundred interested characters in this very novel stood around in his neighborhood waiting for this earth-shaking event. Drama was taking command! he was coming out.

11. Directly in front of the house there was open warfare. One army was on the far side of the highway and the other on the near. The highway itself was the battleline. A stray round of bullets ate a circle in the porch wall near his head. He stopped moving.

12. These are the hostile armed forces he said aloud to himself. Yet he would not turn back. He'd come this far and sunlight was only a few feet away. Only a coward would retreat. He did not know the issues they fought over.

13. The soldiers did not know the issues either.

19. Drama looked back at [the dead soldiers] and realized that the dead ones had gotten up and rejoined the fight. Perhaps they were all using blanks. Just playing a game of fiction.

20. Through the gunfire he heard his wife calling him.

21. To hell with her.

22. He continued.

23. The minute he reached the warm light of the sun he began to burn. First the right arm then his face and left arm. Also part of his chest not covered by the nightgown. Little flames began to leap from his face and arms. But he did not stop. (256–58)

It is hard to connect the author's ambiguous and perhaps unsuccessful escape with a failed black male story of liberation, with anything black, or with anything but the words and the narrative itself. It is true that *Emergency Exit* draws "attention . . . inward toward the novel being made, rather than outward to a world in representation. *Emergency Exit* is therefore its own reality, one that the reader helps construct with each constituent part" (Klinkowitz 61). On the other hand, the text does specifically identify the author as a black male and relate him to Major. Although the black male voice moves closer to being the same as self-referential narrative, the author still tries to define his characters and define and liberate himself. The text may not reach "outward to a world in representation," but written within its self-referential narrative is the experience of a black male trying to define himself in the terms of a black male story of liberation. In this context, the "reader . . . construct[s] each constituent part" in a setting informed by potentially negative signs of black maleness. Also, the virtual silencing of black male voice is a symbolic (re)inscription of Calibanic discourse.

My Amputations (1986) is another text about a writer (Mason) whose life and experience disorient and fragment him, thus causing his "amputations." The following quotation from the very end of the novel is a final example of discourse in Major's work. The quotation shows the metafictional qualities of *My Amputations*, but clearly a black male voice that dubiously attempts to define and liberate also speaks here and throughout the text.

Inside, he couldn't see anything—at first. Then, by candlelight he saw that the room was packed with people sitting on the ground in a circle; all wore wooden masks. An old man in a red robe came in. He told Mason to sit. Mason sat. The old man then sat on the ground next to him. . . . The old man spoke: "The envelope, please." Mason pulled it from his pocket and handed it over. The old man ripped it open and read aloud: "*Keep* this nigger!" He then looked with calmness at Mason. "Are you the person referred to here?" Mason didn't think to hesitate. He chirped. He felt the gravity of the situation—the serious presence of the circle of wearers of masks. . . . He thought he recognized the flicker of an eye in a slit, the gesture of a body, the turn of a head, the shape of a set of breasts, the curve of a big toe. But he couldn't be sure. . . . Then the old man said ". . . You, my son have come to the end of your running.". . . It was hot and muggy. The hut smelled of, of, cow rocks, turtle piss and smoke. (204–5)

In this quotation, the black male story of liberation is silenced by self-referential narrative, and the silenced black male voice of liberation is symbolic of the (re)inscription of Calibanic discourse. However, from a different perspective, the black male story of liberation still speaks within the narrative's metafictional self-reference.

My Amputations refers to many different writers and texts, both white and black, but in the quotation, it specifically evokes *Invisible Man* and *Cane,* which portray black male liberation quests.[14] The quotation is perhaps more reminiscent of aspects of *Invisible Man* than anything else, though. The masking and "running nigger" motifs of the Invisible Man's quest for freedom are definitely represented here. *My Amputations* is evoking a black male story of liberation, but it is doing it within a self-referential narrative that, at this point at the end, is naming what takes place in other books.

This is another example of the black male story of liberation becoming virtually synonymous with self-referential narrative. The clear black male voice of liberation that speaks in *All-Night Visitors* and in *No* is silenced here because the narrative refers to a world of texts where everything is intangible or unintelligible. Or everything is almost unintelligible: Mason is still a black male writer whom the text defines in terms of liberation motifs from other black male texts.[15]

When read and analyzed in order, Major 's first five novels show an ongoing exploration of black male self-definition and liberating voice that goes deeper and deeper into self-referential narrative. The language and narrative of the novels continue to manifest the signs of black maleness—but with decreasing clarity and specificity—and attempt to define the self and to speak in a liberating voice. In this context, Major's last three novels all still respond to Calibanic discourse as the first two do: They attempt positively to define black male voice, character, and sexuality. However, it is also true that the black male story of liberation is hardly distinguishable from the self-referential and arcane, which virtually silence it. It is indeed probably only traceable by connecting the later novels to the broader related context. In this context, there is a clearer, more definite process in which the texts try to tell a story of liberation that silences voice and (re)inscribes Calibanic discourse through character portrayal, theme, and symbolism. In this context, it is possible to see the same thing in *My Amputations* and *Emergency Exit.*

No is the transition novel to the more thematized discursive quest in the next three novels that subsume the response to Calibanic discourse within their postmodernist, metafictional modes, whose liberating potential becomes progressively hostile and oppressive. Seeing the discursive and thematic development from the first to the fifth novels allows one to see that the quest to define the self and to speak in a liberated voice is the same quest throughout the texts. The increasingly thoroughgoing metafiction in the later texts takes Major further into postmodernist, self-referential modes than any black writer has been. However, these self-referential modes are also sites where the writer attempts to find voice; they register a progressively stronger challenge and compromise of the voice of self-definition and the black male story of liberation generally.

I will close my analysis of Major's works with an addendum relating to *Such Was the Season* (1987) and *Dirty Bird Blues* (1996), the sixth and eighth novels, respectively, that supports what I have said about the previous texts.[16] In *Such Was the Season,* Major escapes the trap of self-referential narrative through a black woman's voice that constructs a more straightforward, less threatening narrative. I use an interview of Major by Jerzy Kutnik and Larry McCaffery to make my point. In an introductory section, the interview says that "Major's novels nearly all focus on men whose lives are either coming apart or never had achieved any unity in the first place" (122). A main emphasis in the interview itself is that *Such Was the Season* is the first novel to achieve a stable, unifying voice. Major says the reason is that he feels "more secure—secure enough at least so I don't feel the need to ask the same questions that drove me to create characters like the ones you find over and over again in *All-Night Visitors* and *No*" (125). "Juneboy [a main character] [is] presented through this folksy, down-to-earth woman's point of view." "[O]verall I'd say my own presence is so diminished in Juneboy's identity that he is at best a catalyst rather than a true persona" (126). "[F]rom the outset I felt more secure with the woman's voice I was using in *Such Was the Season.* I didn't have to think about inventing that voice because I'd grown up hearing it, I knew its rhythms from the way my relatives in the South speak. It was already there, so all I had to do was just sit at the computer and correct the voice by ear, the way you would write music. If the rhythm were wrong or the pitch off, I knew it instinctively because I'd lived with that voice all my life" (127). "The voice is what is innovative in [*Such*]. I wanted to give that voice such a commanding presence that it would, in fact, become the main subject matter of the novel. I wanted to make it impossible for readers to stop thinking about the voice once they had started reading the book, to make that voice always uppermost" (130).

The narrative of *Such Was the Season* is not a self-referential one in which the author tries to actualize the liberating potential of language and discourse, thereby contrasting and highlighting the power of Calibanic discourse in the context of my analysis of its relationship to (white) postmodernism. However, Major's words indicate that *Such* clearly fits the overall pattern of unconscious symbolic (re)inscription of Calibanic discourse. Symbolically at least, he negates the presence and voice of the black male persona, and through this negates his presence and voice as a black male writer. The black woman's voice in which the text speaks may be an ambivalent one (Bell, "Major's Homecoming Voice" 94), but Major seems to think that it is solid and "down-to-earth," "secure," and "commanding." Major himself feels more secure, but finds security in a black woman's voice.

Dirty Bird Blues, the most realistic, concretely descriptive, non-postmodern novel that Major has ever written, comes back to the point of view of a black male, Manfred Banks, and shows the same insecurity of male voice that Major talks about in the interview. Manfred is a blues singer who articulates his life experience in a blues voice, but the story of his life that he tells does not make him feel secure and protect him from his self-destructiveness or stop him from being harmful to others. And the same is true in the text for all black men. The following exchange with the wife of Solly, his best friend, whom he fights violently near the end, sums up the generally unfavorable portrayal of black men.

"Why is it yall [black men] can't act right, Fred?"
He laughed. "We jes trying to live. Thas all, Holly. I think Solly want to do the right thing, you know. But he gots to live too, you know. Be himself. Do things." He stopped himself, feeling odd about defending Solly, the one clearly in the wrong. (264)

Manfred's defense is half-hearted, and he does not believe it. He, Solly, and other black men are always "clearly in the wrong." At the end, the only thing that keeps Manfred alive, literally, is that his wife does not leave him, although she should because he mistreats her. He lives precariously, hopefully having gotten beyond the alcoholism and the potential for physical abuse, which he got from his father, which will drive his wife away from him and kill him.

What does the representation of black male character and voice in these two novels imply about the voice of the black male writers throughout the first five novels who struggle to tell a story of liberation? It implies that black male voice cannot adequately define and liberate. The first five novels restrict male voice, just as Major says *Such Was the Season* restricts it and as *Dirty Bird Blues* does.

4

Charles Johnson's Response to "Caliban's Dilemma"

In *Oxherding Tale* (1982) and *Middle Passage* (1990), Charles Johnson tries to avoid "Caliban's dilemma." Ashraf H.A. Rushdy points this out in a reference to Johnson's *Being and Race*.

> [Johnson says that] [t]he art of writing for those who discover that the history of language and fiction "is *not* sympathetic with their sense of things" becomes an art of writing against a tradition—indeed of contesting the "antithetical vision and perspectives of our predecessors" [*Being* 39]. While recognizing that this is the situation of all writers in a minority tradition (including women of all cultures), Johnson employs the name *Caliban's dilemma* to describe it.[1] . . . The answer to Caliban's dilemma in Johnson's career as a writer has been to write a theory of intersubjectivity into his [novels]. ("Phenomenology" 374–75)

According to Johnson, "Caliban's dilemma" sets the black writer in opposition to a white tradition that negatively portrays blackness. Johnson, however, implies that a liberating compromise can develop. The "solitary black writer sitting in his or her room to express a [black] experience [which is the manifestation of 'Caliban's dilemma'] is, at the very instant thought coalesces into word, thrown suddenly into the midst of a crowd . . . and what is expressed is inevitably a compromise between the one and the many, African and European, the present and past" (*Being* 40). Johnson's compromise and answer to "Caliban's dilemma" is his "theory of intersubjectivity" or intersubjective paradigm that precludes it.[2]

On the primary level of his novels' conscious meaning, the intersubjective paradigm changes everything by affecting all traditions; it combines a traditional black perspective with all other perspectives, thus "liberating perception" by subverting the dominance of any perspective.[3] To "liberate percep-tion," the texts often show the tragic from a comic perspective and make possible what one would not think is possible. For example, the narrative of *Oxherding Tale* equally accepts the tragic and comic. The story of Andrew Hawkins's father's troubles and eventual murder by the slave catcher (the character named the Soulcatcher) is as funny as it is serious. George Hawkins's problems start both with his slavery, which gives the white master power to mandate with whom he will have sex as well as to take George's wife sexu-ally, and with fear of his mystical, spiritual wife Mattie.[4] After an evening of drinking Madeira wine with George, Master Jonathan Polkinghorne, in a quirky mood, forces George to agree to go upstairs to the master's wife and bed and to let him go to bed with George's wife Mattie in his cabin. In spite of the funny twist, this can happen because of the deadly serious fact that the master controls the slave sexually and even determines his life destiny. When "George gave [the master] a look" (5) after the latter states his proposal that they change places, Jonathan compels George to do his will: "'George when-*ever* I advance an idea you have a most annoying way of looking at me. . . . No good will come of this. Goodnight. . . . I'll see you at breakfast.'" George has conceded that he cannot go home drunk to Mattie anyway (5), so he goes to the master's bed. George has sex with the master's wife in a humor-ous scene, she conceives Andrew, and the master sends George from the house to work in the fields, which leads to his rebellion against slavery and murder by the Soulcatcher.

A "liberation of perception," for Andrew and for the reader, takes place through Andrew's narration of this story and its associated events and through the lesson of intersubjectivity that he learns.[5] And hypothetically, a libera-tion of all the characters occurs when they merge into the intersubjective process, thus "liberating perception" for them, too. In Johnson's novels, intersubjectivity *is* liberation.

His novels add a different dimension to the unconscious writing of the story of liberation and Calibanic discourse; the traditional story of libera-tion voiced in terms of "Caliban's dilemma" responds to Calibanic discourse. In the multiple layers of Johnson's novels, the unconscious story of libera-tion is a black male story told from the characters'—not Johnson's and the texts'—traditional viewpoint opposing slavery and racism. The story of lib-eration is, then, portrayed through "Caliban's dilemma," which the texts avert through the liberating narrative of the intersubjective paradigm.

Calibanic discourse and its story of liberation are still inseparable, but there is a difference. In a sense, the challenge and compromise of the story of liberation are more uniform and consistent with the story itself throughout its narration. The direct evidence of Calibanic discourse is the symbolic and explicit (re)inscription of its identifiable features as a result of the texts' ongoing process and development *and* the more consistent and uniform representation of its identifiable features that stand out above the story of liberation within the text. (Re)inscription of Calibanic discourse depends on ambiguity and irony in the ongoing process and development of the story of liberation. However, Calibanic discourse often speaks on even terms with and supercedes the story of liberation. Calibanic discourse represents itself more straightforwardly overall, at the same time that the story of liberation (re)inscribes it as a result of the narrative's ongoing process and development. This more direct representation of Calibanic discourse is particularly evident in the characterizations of black males trapped in the fixed perspective that is "Caliban's dilemma." (Nate McKay is the best example.)

"Caliban's dilemma" is a place of negative opposition in Johnson's and the texts' perspectives, and this may be the reason that the texts more straightforwardly represent Calibanic discourse through characters positioned there. However, the identifiable elements of Calibanic discourse are also written throughout the texts in the intersubjective paradigm and its preset conclusion, and the intersubjective paradigm connects to "Caliban's dilemma" in a relationship of opposition.

Specifically, the challenged and compromised story of liberation represents and (re)inscribes black male failure of liberating voice, bestiality, slavery, and punishment associated with slavery. *Oxherding Tale* shows this better than *Middle Passage,* but both texts represent and (re)inscribe Calibanic discourse in the process of liberation. In *Oxherding Tale,* for example, black men are paradoxically dispossessed, remanded to slavery, and treated as slaves, even as the text "liberates perception" and frees Andrew. Also, Johnson's intersubjective paradigm is a process with a preset conclusion that essentially negates a black male quest for freedom and a black male voice of liberation.

Johnson calls his intersubjective theory phenomenology, but clearly its multilayered, liberating form is postmodern.[6] I have talked about the implied need for a black voicing of (white) postmodernism in Wideman's and Major's novels. *Black* liberation is not the texts' and Johnson's goal, and the thematic contours of Johnson's texts are different. Therefore, the need for a black voicing of (white) postmodernism is expressed differently, is less directly implied in the texts' convoluted levels of theme. On the level of intersubjective experience, Johnson negates the unique qualities of blackness, which negates the need for a black voicing; on another level, he critiques and criticizes the black male quest for identity and freedom, showing that the characters who pursue it are enslaved in "Caliban's dilemma." The need for a black voicing of (white) postmodernism is still implied from the perspective of Calibanic discourse's unconscious influence on the texts. "Caliban's dilemma" is so clearly a confining compartment or place for those who pursue a black (male) identity, while liberation very clearly takes place— or potentially takes place—among the layers of postmodern intersubjectivity. From this viewpoint, it is perhaps even clearer in Johnson's texts than in Wideman's and Major's that the liberating potential of (white) postmodernism highlights the oppressive power of Calibanic discourse in an underlying level of discourse.

Part 1 of *Oxherding Tale* sets up "Caliban's dilemma" by making black opposition to white oppression one of its main themes, and Andrew Hawkins's portrayal is central here. In part 2, Andrew averts "Caliban's dilemma" by "passing" into the "White World" and by achieving an enlightenment ("Moksha," the title of the last chapter) that allows him access to the intersubjective reality that negates black identity and breaks down black opposition.[7] Freedom for Andrew at the end is negating the black male identity and quest for freedom that place him in opposition to white oppression. This is the main place of the novel where the attainment of intersubjective experience symbolizes the (re)inscription of Calibanic discourse. However, part 1 also shows the influence of Calibanic discourse in its thematic focus on the "construction of [black] masculinities," which emphasizes a "shared nihilism or 'absence of life-assurance'" (Byrd 554).

The text's intersubjective paradigm changes the perspective on black men, particularly on the possibility of black male sexual acts. But at the same time, within the construction of maleness, it symbolically and explicitly (re)inscribes and represents Calibanic discourse because black men remain slaves living a dehumanized existence *as long as they remain black men;* they cannot attain a voice of liberation that subverts "nihilism" and gives them "life-assurance." In this context, at least one black slave, Nate, is bestial, and the slave culture punishes black men by their sexual thralldom in the culture, their constant pain and suffering, or their death. Andrew's condition in many ways represents the condition, or the potential condition, of other black males: Andrew "remains, for significant periods, either a sexual slave or a fugitive slave seeking meaning and safety in a culture and economy that would deny [him], at every turn, such fundamental needs of human existence" (Byrd 552). The text puts the primary emphasis on Andrew's struggle against slavery, but several other black males live lives focused by their struggle against slavery or their struggle to find "meaning and safety" as black men living in opposition to the "White World." George, Nate, Moon, and Patrick are examples.

Nate's characterization is the clearest specific instance of Calibanic discourse speaking on even terms with and superceding the story of liberation. However, the overall portrayal of black males represents Calibanic discourse in this fashion because it presents their failure of liberating voice, bestiality, enslavement, and concomitant punishment very straightforwardly. George's characterization depends more on ambiguity and paradox for resolution, and is thus more of an example of the (re)inscription of Calibanic discourse in the ongoing process and development of the narrative.

Oxherding Tale may be a "canonical text" in the "study of the construction of black masculinities" (Byrd 554), but it also depicts the deconstruction of black masculinities and the destruction of black male agency and corporeality. Again, the text works simultaneously on the levels of its intersubjective paradigm and the (re)inscription and representation of Calibanic discourse. In the context of the former, black male deconstruction and destruction take place in the process that both consumes and conserves everything, including evil and death, and obliterates distinctions. In this process, "all is conserved; all" (176) to produce the "profound mystery of the One and the Many"— which means "the One [that is] the Many." In terms of Calibanic discourse, black male deconstruction and destruction occur when black males either lose their identities or get punished for their very identifiable sexuality. I focus on the text's portrayal of a lack of sustaining, liberating agency (a fraternity that would give "life-assurance") and voice among black men at Leviathan, one of the two slave plantations in the text, and its portrayal of the mutilation of black male bodies and genitalia.[8]

The most remarkable example of black men's failure is Reb's insufficient support of his son Patrick. Reb, the Allmuseri and Leviathan's coffin maker, acts as the central figure in Andrew's progress toward understanding intersubjectivity.[9] Reb "bellowed like a steer" (56) at Patrick's funeral, but he also accepted Patrick's death and ended the matter when he nailed him in his coffin. He later answers Andrew's question about whether he blames him, Patrick's rival for plantation owner Flo Hatfield, for Patrick's death: "'I put his casket in the ground a month ago. You the one still carrying it around'" (61). The death of his son, along with everything else, is acceptable to Reb because all things are acceptable in the all-encompassing perspective of the intersubjective process. His response should help to inculcate the lesson of intersubjectivity.

However, the silence between Reb and Patrick is also a part of a pattern of symbolic failure of liberating voice among black men, and of concomitant black male deconstruction and destruction that more explicitly represent Calibanic discourse. Although the text does indicate that Reb talked to his son once (47), it never indicates that he spoke to him paternally or supportively. In reality, there is a "great gulf of silence between Reb . . . and his doomed son" (Byrd 554). This "gulf of silence" represents the general lack of voice, fraternity, and agency among Leviathan's black men (except for Reb and Andrew, whom the text brings together in Andrew's progress to intersubjectivity and divestment of black male identity). Reb's voice fails to function as the source that will give his son "life-assurance" and free him from the despair that kills him, and other black men fail to support each other because they are silent or hostile.

The community of black women at Jonathan Polkinghorne's plantation, Cripplegate—the only community of black women portrayed in the text—clearly has liberating, sustaining powers that give the women "life-assurance" against the transgressing black men and potentially against the ravages of slavery. At Cripplegate, Nate is a slave who philanders, and Addie is his wife. After one of Nate's escapades, the "Prayer Circle would meet at Addie's cabin, fifteen women seated in a circle of chairs, an article of Nate's clothing in the center, and their combined thoughts and common prayer—a power like electromagnetism" (103). The communal power of the women does not change Nate, but it enables Addie to punish him. Conspicuously, the communities of black men at Cripplegate and at Leviathan lack the fraternal voice and connection that would support, sustain, and potentially liberate them in this fashion.

At Leviathan, black males die and their bodies take agonizing, disfigured shapes; this destruction of black male bodies is part of the pattern of more explicit (re)inscription of Calibanic discourse.[10] The death and postmortem description of Reb's son Patrick is an example. Patrick eviscerates himself in a painful, grotesque killing that would satisfy a lynching party. Andrew describes the scene: "I remember seeing the slanting floor, a laky fluid, smudgelike shadows, [Flo's] stained throw rugs soaking in blood, her bedsheets, then her mattress where Patrick lay naked with his long legs twisted in the red blankets, both dark hands frozen on the shaft of the butcher knife buried in his belly" (51). In the context of the intersubjective paradigm, the passage suggests that Patrick's body dissolves polymorphically toward fluids, smudges, shadows, and stains. However, this graphic, painful evisceration is also a brutal destruction of black maleness that is punitive in the terms of Calibanic signification.

Later, Andrew describes the body of Moon, who is Flo's former lover and whom the Soulcatcher has caught and killed after he ran away.

[Moon was] pulped, reduced—in nature's grim perversion of democracy—to liquifying tissue, his head smashed like a melon, chest and belly splintered from gas building like boiler steam in his abdomen, his flesh the color of cooked veal. . . . Was this horror the coda of pleasure? There was, it seemed to me, something especially hideous in this end to enlightened hedonism, for the johnson (as we say—pronounced *yawn-sun*) of the lover expanded to Rabelaisian proportions, the testicles bloated bigger than coconuts, as if death mocked man's single distinguishing feature by enlarging the genitals, exploded and powdered them green with bread mold: a nest for maggots. (69)

The Vet, a white male character, sums up the significance of Moon's body in the context of the intersubjective paradigm: "'He's no one now. . . . On the market, he's worth about ninety-five cents in chemicals—five pounds of minerals, one pound of carbohydrates, one-quarter of vitamins, a few pounds of protein.'" Moon's death erases his individuality and starts a process in which he dissolves polymorphically into chemicals, a "grim perversion of democracy" that represents the text's intersubjectivity. However, Moon's body and genitals shattering, swelling, and putrifying in a death ritual connects it to the description of Patrick's body, and makes it part of the text's overall pattern of deconstruction and destruction of black males and failure of black male liberating voice.

The account of the death of Ezekiel, Andrew's white tutor, and the post-mortem descriptions of Moon and Patrick's bodies make an interesting comparison. Like the description of Patrick's death and especially Moon's, the account of Ezekiel's death (93–94) is a lesson, of sorts, about intersubjectivity. However, it is also markedly dissimilar. Ezekiel enters the farmhouse where he expects to find the woman (Althea) for whom he has paid four hundred dollars to save her from her irresponsible father:

The farmhouse had not been inhabited for years. Ezekiel looked in the kitchen, the study, the sitting room; no Althea. Only this toadstool smell floating over black-dark furniture. Broken lanterns. Roots bursting through the floor. Birds nesting on the chimneypiece. . . . He sobbed . . . dropped the flowers, then his cane, and crumpled at the room's center, his back against a barrel, the shadowy house quiet now, a bony ruin where the only movement was blood pounding in his temples, his heart overheating—searing pain in his chest, and then even the work of this bloody, tired motor went whispering to rest, his spirit changed houses, and dropped into the solitary darkness like stone. (94)

It is clear how the account of Ezekiel's death both complements the intersubjective paradigm and contrasts the portrayals of black males. Ezekiel "thought he would be transformed [by the act of altruism that causes his death] . . . he would enter, he believed, into a life of clarity and law" (93). Instead of being "transformed" in this fashion, Ezekiel suffers, in literal terms, a heart attack from the shock of disappointment and falls spiritually—"his spirit changed houses"—"into the solitary darkness" that destroys "clarity and law." Overall, the text depicts the process in which Ezekiel falls into the seeming polymorphic disorder that resembles the intersubjective paradigm. The portrayal is somewhat ambiguous because it emphasizes both the physical and the spiritual, but it emphasizes the latter more. While Ezekiel suffers a "searing pain in his chest," which is certainly a physical pain, he also experiences a spiritual change, which is not painful and punitive.

The fact that Ezekiel is an educated white man and that Patrick and Moon are slaves subject to the fate of slaves accounts somewhat for the difference in portrayal. However, when one looks at the difference of portrayal in the context of the overall portrayal of black men in the text, then it becomes evident that the influence of Calibanic discourse is possibly a reason for the difference.

The overall pattern of failure of black male liberating voice continues in part 2, even as Andrew liberates himself and "liberates perception." Throughout part 2, Andrew passes and becomes more comfortably assimilated as a white man, and in the last chapter, "Moksha" (enlightenment), he liberates himself symbolically by negating his black male identity, black quest, and black voice, which is at the same time the text's primary symbolic (re)inscription of Calibanic discourse through the intersubjective paradigm's process. But in part 2, Andrew also continues the text's pattern by physically separating himself from other black men as he attains his freedom, thus emphasizing their continued slavery and "shared nihilism or 'absence of life-assurance.'" (During part 2, Andrew even separates from Reb, the embodiment of the intersubjective paradigm. The Soulcatcher tells Andrew that Reb's escape catalyzes his freedom at the end, but Reb is not present when Andrew gains freedom.)

Significantly, the body and spirit of a black woman become an integral part of Andrew's liberation, and the black woman's physical presence inspires Andrew to free her in his fictive imagination, giving her freedom as a black woman that black men do not have. The "life-assurance" that Andrew accords the black woman, Minty, connects logically with the liberating power of the community of black women at Cripplegate, which includes Addie, Minty's mother.

A sequence of events and thematic developments from chapter 9 to chapter 12, the last chapter, makes the point. Andrew separates physically from black men, gains freedom by giving up his black identity, and frees Minty. The last sentence in chapter 9 reads: "And then, without looking back, the Coffinmaker stepped outside" (134). Reb leaves Andrew here, never to return physically. In chapter 10, "The Call," Andrew marries a white woman named Peggy Undercliff and "passes" deeper into the freedom of white life. At the very end of the chapter, Andrew discovers Minty being sold at a slave auction. "The Call," therefore, is to save Minty and free her. Chapter 11, "The Manumission of First-Person Viewpoint," manumits the slave narrative from a limited first-person perspective. This manumission coincides with Andrew's: "Having liberated first-person, it is now only fitting that in the following chapters we do as much for Andrew Hawkins" (153). Andrew's manumission, in turn, coincides with his "call" to free Minty. At the end of chapter 12, "In the Service of the Servant," Andrew frees Minty by creating the fiction in which she "stand[s] as a freewoman" (167) just before the beginning of the last chapter, where he symbolically gives up his black identity and attains enlightenment and intersubjectivity.

Minty's suffering, decaying body is a metaphor for the intersubjective paradigm, but more importantly, Andrew gives her "life-assurance" during her physical ordeal near the end and envisions her physically free before she dies. This is where Minty's portrayal differs from that of Moon, Patrick, and other black men in the text, and this is another way that the text manifests its overall pattern. Upon taking her from the auction and seeing her condition, Andrew assures Minty soon after he identifies himself to her: "'I've purchased you not to put you to work but, as I promised years before, to buy your freedom'" (157). Andrew later assures Minty again after looking at her body and realizing that she will die.

As I live and breathe, her bare legs . . . were hideous. *Hideous!* Incredible, the clarity with which I remember those pustules and bleeding sores like spots of flame. Above and below her knee, the skin was scaly, reptilian, peeling like old house paint, seamed with festering fever blisters, a few of which had burst, and secreted down her thighs a green and yellow fluid so clayey, and protoplasmic, it made my stomach clench. Lumpy veins crisscrossed her legs. Old boils had left black places where they'd dried. Despite myself, I felt dizzy. She would die soon. Who could doubt this? I shuddered to think of it. Cells in me, corpuscles in my blood, spoke before I could reason out a reply:

"I will see you through this." (158–59)

Andrew gives Minty her final "life-assurance" just before she dies and before he imagines her a free woman. Andrew tells Minty that he will take her to freedom in Boston and that he loves her.

> Her right hand reached out, tentatively, touching my face. She licked her lips. Something in Minty relaxed.
> "You said Boston. . . ."
> "Peggy knows someone there."
> My chest, I felt, was on fire. "We're leaving tonight." Undercliff, Wife, and, I thought, a third figure, stood in the doorway; I knew that without turning, felt their pressure shift the room's pressure. "As soon as you can travel. . . ." I remembered, at that moment, how Wife spoke of eastern beaches, their colors, which I knew had been planned at the instant of Creation to complement Minty, blues and browns to contrast the warm hues of her skin; and I saw her there, washing herself clean of the petroleum stench of the marketplace. She would have children—I'd never approve of their father, no man was good enough, and I'd nag whomever she chose—children all stamped with her strange beauty; I saw her stand a freewoman, washing her hair, then she stepped lazily back. (167)

Minty dies after this, but she dies free in "a world where no [slave] catchers, no driver's pistol-cracking whip, would ever caa her into darkness again" (164).

The intersubjective paradigm, the theory that women are superior because they are "more essential to Being" (30), and the reality of the slave system play roles in determining the fates of *Oxherding Tale's* characters. Anna, the white woman, "grew . . . in vitality" (158) at the end, and Minty, the black woman, died free with "life-assurance." The text leaves Jonathan, the white man, paralyzed and bedridden after an attack by George during the slave rebellion at Cripplegate (158).

However, in a text that is primarily about avoiding "Caliban's dilemma"—that is, liberating blackness by negating opposition to white perception—black men consistently remain slaves who lack liberating voice and agency; the text's discourse on black men is an underlying pattern that creates a different reality for them. In this pattern, the story of liberation (re)inscribes Calibanic discourse. The case of George is graphic. The Soulcatcher places a gun to the back of George's head and kills him in the last chapter (174–75). George "fell into West Hell to precisely the reward all black revolutionaries feared: an eternity of waiting tables" (175).[11] George's life ends in terror and pain, and he is still a servant after death. This is in stark contrast to Minty, who dies and attains freedom. (George's death also compares interestingly to Ezekiel's nonviolent death.)

Another way that the intersubjective paradigm "liberates perception" is by portraying a conflicted, confused fear/fantasy of black men in slave culture that generates sexual acts with white women in episodes and scenarios that have both comic and horrific results. The intersubjective paradigm avoids "Caliban's dilemma" by breaking down fixed perspectives on black male sexual acts and sexuality. Hypothetically, it creates a portrayal of black male sexual acts and sexuality that incorporates the humorous, the horrific, and everything else into one perspective that constantly changes form and shape and represents black viewpoints, white viewpoints, and all viewpoints. The text, however, also paradoxically (re)inscribes Calibanic discourse in the process of "liberating perspective" in this specific aspect of the intersubjective paradigm. Ultimately, the text still manifests the same underlying pattern in which black men lack liberating voice and "life assurance" and suffer physical punishment and destruction.

The sexual episode between George and Anna, the master's wife, early in the text is the first evidence of the confused, conflicted fear/fantasy of black men that generates seemingly unlikely sexual acts and connections between black male slaves and white women. As George slips under the sheets, Anna surprises him: "Sleepily, Anna turned and soldered herself to George. She crushed him in a clench so strong his spine cracked. . . . She talked to George, a wild stream of gibberish, which scared him plenty, but he was not a man to leave his chores half-finished, and plowed on. Springs in the mattress snapped, and Anna, gripping the headboard, groaned, 'Oh *gawd*, Jonathan!'" (6). Sobered and chastened by his wife Anna's rejection of him later, Jonathan asks Anna a question: "'Anna, you *wanted* George, not me, to be there [having sex with you], didn't you?'" (8). Jonathan gets silence in response to his question because the answer, apparently, is "yes."

Anna lives in a world where she experiences a fear/fantasy about George contrived by the slave culture's attitude to his sexuality, and it leads to this humorous episode. Anna's silence when Jonathan asks whether she wanted it to be George implies that she was expecting Jonathan to be there and sleepily fantasizing that it was George. She even speaks in the "wild stream of gibberish" that, in light of her silence when Jonathan asks the question, seems intended for George. She awakens to the fear side of her fear/fantasy dichotomy when she discovers that George is present physically.

The text is humorous, but the episode precipitates George toward the dead-end enslavement and death that characterize black male experience in the text. George acutely feels the "helplessness of black men before masters and Modern Women" (26). Talking to Nate McKay, Addie's husband, about doing right and being responsible, he later sums up the condition of black men living in a world where whites enslave them and black women misunderstand them: "'Then how do we do hit? Hold our families together when they kin sell us any minute, when it ain't clear what's right or wrong, and one li'l mistake'll destroy everythin' you been workin' fo? . . . Mattie, she don't understand none of this. I feel like a daid man gettin' hup ever' mawnin'—there ain't nothin' to hope for, work toward. How kin you go on, knowin' that?'" (105). George's only hope for freedom would be to give up his black male identity for intersubjectivity. Instead George continues his quest for black relevance and finally rebels, for which his punishment is death.

Jonathan sends Andrew to Leviathan to work for Flo Hatfield: "'This letter will see that you get work with one of my old acquaintances in Abbeville. We have not corresponded in years, but I believe she will put you to work.' He said this woman—Flo Hatfield—would see to all my needs (he didn't say what needs), and keep me busy (he didn't say how). . . . 'Now go and tell George and Mattie where you're off to'" (19).

Leviathan, Flo Hatfield's slave plantation, emblematizes a "country" that brings to realization a central fear/fantasy of black men that leads to their perpetual slavery and death. The black phallus enslaves Flo Hatfield (Byrd 553) in a frenzy of sex with black men separated from the aegis of white men. Flo, however, plays the controlling role of "white man" by enslaving black men in a counter sexual thralldom, sending them to the mines (a punishment worse than sexual slavery), and precipitating their deaths. In the process of all this, black men find no significant fraternity among themselves and find no liberating voice to give them "life-assurance."

Flo's personal fantasy that she realizes at Leviathan is also a part of Jonathan's and the culture's fear/fantasy. The text describes Flo's fantasy lover: "The lover of Flo Hatfield's fantasy was polymorphous: husband, ravager, teacher, Galahad, eunuch, swashbuckler, student, priest, and, above all else, *always there*" (61). Flo demands that her lover be "always there" and that he play many roles for her to define her own self through sensation; through her lover she feels her "'own pulse. [Her] own sensations. . . . [She has] a pulse everywhere'" (53). Flo and the black men at Leviathan live a "wheel-spinning life of desire" (71) that is a "male fantasy . . . with both Flo and [black men as] victims enslaved to an experience—a part of the masculine ego—that neither . . . truly wanted." The white male ego projects a world in which the fear/fantasy of black male sexuality is loosed in a frenzy of sex on a narcotized white woman.

Flo's life is the inverse of the intersubjective paradigm, and Andrew's experience with her represents it more directly. She reverses *Oxherding Tale's* intersubjective paradigm in which the black male subject negates the self and black male identity—the "Me" that is all important to Flo. However, Flo's quest for sensation to fulfill the self also instructs Andrew in his progress toward intersubjectivity. Through Flo's quest to fulfill the self, Andrew learns to "[e]xtinguish the ego" (64), a very important lesson in his progress toward intersubjectivity that allows him to lose the identity of self in the welter that is polymorphous experience.

Generally, there is a "liberation of perception" in the twists to which Flo gives reality and in the possibilities she creates in carrying out her fantasy. Flo has responded to the "emptiness of ego" (75) that male-dominated culture prescribes for her by, according to Reb, "learn[ing] to think like men" (62). In a sense, she becomes the "masculine ego" that would consume her, and she consumes in turn. As a white woman, she frees herself by enslaving/consuming black men, and she turns the white-generated fear/fantasy against the culture by openly demanding that black men continuously perform sexually for her in her own private space. This is what happens in the context of an intersubjective paradigm that theorizes itself as one constantly changing perspective that accepts all things and possibilities.

My point, however, is that in the terms of Calibanic discourse, the possibilities for black men as black men remain constant and do not change; this is written into the text's underlying discourse. In this context, Flo's black male slaves perform prodigious sexual acts at her demand; however, she always punishes them. She causes the mutilation and destruction of the black male body, or she sends them to the mines, which she does to Andrew, forcing him to "pass" and extinguish his black male identity to free himself. Unlike black women, white women, or white men, black men cannot retain their identities as defined by gender and race and attain freedom, and they can scarcely retain their identities and remain alive and whole in their black male bodies.

A main emphasis of the appropriated Caliban trope is the "Abhorrèd slave, / Which any print of goodness wilt not take, / Being capable of all ills! . . . who deserved more than a prison" (*Philadelphia Fire* 139; *The Tempest* I.ii.422–36). Two of *Oxherding Tale's* primary black male characters, Nate and George, conform to the appropriated Caliban trope in their character traits. George is by no means as fully irredeemable as Nate, but the text does show that in spite of mitigating factors, George may deserve the misery and ultimately the death and continued servitude that he experiences after death. Their portrayals relate to their failure to give each other "life assurance" and to their failure to speak in a liberating voice.

Nate is trapped in "Caliban's dilemma" by his opposition to white people, which he states (104–5), and his characterization is the clearest specific instance of Calibanic discourse speaking on even terms with and straightforwardly superceding the story of liberation. Nate is George's only friend, and theirs is, as Mattie calls it, a "friendship of lepers" (102) because of George's banishment from house to field slave and because of Nate's incorrigible badness. Nate terrorizes the black community with his vicious, evil sexuality; as he tells George, "'I'm a *physical* man, you understand, with powerful drives. It's only natural that when the wife's bleeding I should have somebody on the side'" (104). Nate mainly preys on the black community, but he also displays a general recklessness. He discovers that one of his "side" women has given birth to his son, and to protect himself from responsibility, he "threw a torch into her master's window, then placed the matchbox on her porch," causing her to be sold "[w]ithin the week." When George asks Nate why he acted as he did toward Delphine, his "side" woman, Nate says he did so because he did not need another mouth to feed and because he wanted to punish her for trying to trap him (104– 05).

Nate tries to give George solace through his friendship and counsel, but Nate's attempt to voice a liberating "life-assurance" for both him and George fails when the "Black World," primarily black women in the case of both, and the "White World," implicitly in Nate's case and explicitly in George's, punish them and deny them liberation. When Nate leaves home for extended periods to be with other women, his wife Addie and a group of black women gather to bridle his freedom and draw him back home for punishment (103). The black women's communal voice has a power that black men's voices lack, and they indeed pull Nate home, where Addie hides his food and she and the children fight him physically (104). After the fight, Nate has to search for his food, which he often finds "cold and fouled by farm animals in the barn." Nate ends up "[f]inger-feeding himself in the darkness, [and] hunched over his plate, he swore each woman's hand was a glove that concealed Satan's claw." George even breaks his connection to Nate, the man whom everyone else "wanted to shoot" (105), when Mattie implies that Nate comes around because he has a sexual interest in her—"'He isn't safe'" (106). In the final analysis, George's break with Nate leaves George by himself to "feel like a daid man . . . [and that] there ain't nothin' to hope for" (105). Nate, too, must live alone, lacking the freedom and "life-assurance" that he tried to give George through his counsel.

The humorous circumstances surrounding his actions, his attempt to be responsible, Andrew's love for him, and his overall portrayal in the terms of the intersubjective paradigm mitigate George's characterization. However, Andrew also states that George is "determinant for his life" (142), and thus implicitly creates his own negative fate, which is his murder by the Soulcatcher and descent into hell and continued servitude at the end (164–75). The following quotation exemplifies the multilayered presentation of George's character in which the intersubjective paradigm is the vehicle of the primary theme that (re)inscribes the text's underlying Calibanic discourse of black men.

[Andrew] rejected (in George) the *need* to be an Untouchable. . . . the rituals of caste would, regardless of law, live centuries after the plantations died. My father kept the pain alive. He *needed* to rekindle racial horrors, revive old pains, review disappointments like a sick man fingering his sores. . . . he *chose* misery. Grief was the grillwork—the emotional grid—through which George Hawkins sifted and sorted events, simplified a world so overrich in sense it outstripped him, and all that was necessary to break this spell of hatred, this self-inflicted segregation from the Whole, was to acknowledge, once and for all, that what he allowed to be determinant for his life depended on himself and no one else.
But I loved my father. . . . (142)

George misses the point of life because he fails to yield himself to the potential liberating wholeness of intersubjectivity. However, in the consistent, underlying discursive pattern that gives black men, in their gender/racial roles as black men, a different reality within the text's theme of intersubjectivity, he is a black man who hates, and most importantly, suffers brutal murder and eternal servitude in hell at the end. Andrew loves his father and sees the conservation of his father's love in the symbolism of the Soulcatcher's tattooed body in the penultimate paragraph (175–76). But still, George—in his black body, as a black man—suffers because he hates, and dies when he tries to liberate himself, only to suffer further servitude. George's portrayal is paradoxical, and his lack of liberating voice and deserved enslavement and punishment is an aspect of the paradox that (re)inscribes Calibanic discourse.

Middle Passage exhibits the same intersubjective paradigm as *Oxherding Tale,* but the influence of Calibanic discourse is less clear and conclusive and less direct and explicit. It is, however, subtly but substantively written into the text. Both *Oxherding Tale* and *Middle Passage* thematize themselves as hybrid texts, and the latter embeds the signs of Calibanic discourse deeply in its hybridization, which is another form of intersubjectivity.

The text of *Middle Passage* is an intersubjective process that symbolically (re)inscribes Calibanic discourse in the same way as the portrayal of its main character, Rutherford Calhoun. The text attains a hybridization that involves it in a palimpsestic process among other white texts and traditions.[12]

The hybridization of the text allows it to participate in a "communal dimension of language" (*Being* 39) that averts the opposition and the "antithetical vision" to whiteness that is "Caliban's dilemma" (40). The text gains voice at the same time that it loses its black characteristics, just as Rutherford attains true identity when he negates his black male voice and identity. In this context, Rutherford either constrains his black maleness (or perhaps civilizes himself beyond it), renders it innocuous, or changes it into a nonentity—or perhaps all of these. Hybridization encompasses the black text and its black male reality in a "middle" space that negates their unique black qualities, which is synonymous with Rutherford's experience of intersubjectivity. Hybridization is a negation of black male voice that parallels this same theme in Calibanic discourse, and the text also manifests this discourse's more direct and explicit signs within the pattern of negation. The thematized process that attains intersubjectivity, averts "Caliban's dilemma," and "liberates perception" cannot be separated from the influence of Calibanic discourse.

Rutherford's father is a character whose portrayal suggests the same direct, straightforward representation of Calibanic discourse as the portrayal of black male slaves in *Oxherding Tale*. The following quotation describing Rutherford's father parallels the description of George's murder and incorporation into intersubjective reality at the end of *Oxherding Tale*:

[H]e fought his family and others in the fields, chafing under the constraints of bondage, and every other constraint as well: marriage and religion, as white men imposed these on Africans. Finally, in the light of my slush lamp, I beheld his benighted history and misspent manhood turn toward the night he plotted his escape to the Promised Land. It was New Year's eve, *anno* 1811. . . . [he] took himself to the stable, saddled one of the horses, and, since he had never ventured more than ten miles from home, wherefore lost his way, was quickly captured by padderolls and quietly put to death, the bullet entering through his left eye, exiting through his right ear, leaving him forever eight and twenty, an Eternal Object, pure essence rotting in a fetid stretch of Missouri swamp. But even in death he seemed to be *doing* something, or perhaps should I say he squeezed out one final cry wherethrough I heard a cross wind of sounds just below his breathing. (170–71)

The text then describes the Allmuseri god that symbolizes intersubjectivity and includes Rutherford, his father, and everything else within its wholeness. This is the context in which the father is "*doing* something" as Rutherford "heard a cross wind of sounds just below his breathing."

The murder of Rutherford's father shows the liberating possibilities of yielding to intersubjectivity. However, the account of the father's life and death also implies an underlying discursive pattern that, although less fully developed, is similar to the one in *Oxherding Tale:* The black males who are American slaves lack liberating voice and "life assurance," and their bodies get mutilated when they attempt to escape slavery.[13] Although all other slaves do not hate him as they hate Nate in *Oxherding Tale,* the father has philandering characteristics that make him widely hated; even his own wife hated him because his "word" had no more power than a child's (169–70). The language and the description in the quotation—the "benighted history and misspent manhood" that are his life and that "turn toward" his escape and murder—sound like an indictment and punishment of the father. Also, within this context, the description of the father's death, like George's in *Oxherding Tale,* sounds punitive because of its brutally graphic details: the slave catchers "put [him] to death, the bullet entering through his left eye, exiting through his right ear." The father's struggle as a black man only achieves a "Promised Land" of eternal objectivity, not the black subjectivity that he wants.[14] Clearly, he lacks liberating voice according to the thematic pattern in *Oxherding Tale.*

Generally however, the underlying pattern of Calibanic discourse is less clear in *Middle Passage,* because the text largely develops in a linear fashion that emphasizes Rutherford's progress toward and affirmation of the intersubjective paradigm. *Middle Passage* presents Rutherford's conceptualization of "home" at the beginning; the concept of "middle" replaces, displaces, and redefines his concept of "home" during the text; and Rutherford returns "home" hybridized, changed, and integrated into intersubjective reality at the end.

At the beginning, Rutherford portrays himself in terms that reveal his character as a thief who violates and possesses women's bodies and other people's property. In describing his perception of New Orleans as "home" for a thief and "social parasite" (2) who lived off others, Rutherford emphasizes his voracious sexuality: "[New Orleans] was if not a town devoted to an almost religious pursuit of Sin, then at least to a steamy sexuality. . . . [It had] the most exquisitely beautiful women in the world, thoroughbreds of pleasure created two centuries before by the French for their enjoyment. Mulattos colored like magnolia petals, quadroons with breasts big as melons—women who smelled like roses all year round. Home? Brother, for a randy Illinois boy of two and twenty accustomed to cornfields, cow plops, and handjobs in his master's hayloft, New Orleans wasn't home. It was Heaven."(2). Isadora tries to make Rutherford marry her and to abandon his acquisitive pursuit of physical beauty, which is attendant to sexual stimulation and pleasure. She chastises him for wanting "someone [you] can show off and say to the world, 'See, look what I'm humping!'" (17). Instead of abandoning his old ways, Rutherford abandons Isadora and his "home" of New Orleans to become a stowaway on the *Republic,* a slave ship.

Although Johnson signifies briefly on the *Republic* as a world of men where an outrageous "masculine imperative" (41) turns them into caricatures of masculinity, he ultimately portrays the space of the *Republic* as a "middle" space that liberates Rutherford from any contained, fixed identity (Scott 665). The "middle" changes and hybridizes Rutherford. He is on the ship with all the other men, but he takes no sides during the mutiny and longs for the security of "home." After the mutiny, he tells Cringle: "'I'm not on *anybody's* side! . . . I don't know who's right or wrong on this ship anymore, and I don't much care! All I want is to go *home!*'" (137).

Rutherford's experience of intersubjective reality changes his concept of black identity and of "home." Seeing the Allmuseri god (168–71) destroys Rutherford's belief in black identity; he realizes that "the (black) self was the greatest of all fictions" (171). Deconstructing the "(black) self" is tantamount to making his black male human being a nonentity. This being done, Rutherford can conceptualize "home" as a place that restricts and confines black men.

> Then, as before, I desperately dreamed of home. . . . [Home] was a battlefield, a boiling cauldron. It created white rascals like [*Republic* captain] Ebenezer Falcon, black ones like [racketeer Papa] Zeringue, uppity creoles, hundreds of slave lords, bondmen crippled and caricatured by the disfiguring hand of servitude. Nay, the States were hardly the sort of place a Negro would pine for, but pine for them I did . . . for the strangeness and mystery of black life, even for the endless round of social obstacles and challenges and trials colored men faced every blessed day of their lives, for there were indeed triumphs, I remembered, that balanced the suffering on shore, small yet enduring things, very deep, that Isadora pointed out to me. . . . If this weird, upside-down caricature of a country called America, if this land of refugees and former indentured servants, religious heretics and half-breeds, whoresons and fugitives—this cauldron of mongrels from all points of the compass—was all I could rightly call home, then aye: I was of it. (179)

Rutherford's experience in the "middle" redefines "home" as a place where he accepts racist restriction of "colored men" because of the "triumphs" that balance it. Brian Fagel says that the "middle" spaces of *Middle Passage* reduce "[h]ome [to] an empty signifier": "The Middle Passage has left an indelible imprint on Calhoun's psyche, a haunting reminder that home and roots no longer have meaning. . . . Calhoun's sexual longing for Isadora, like his longing for home, has been consumed" by his experience in the "middle" (628–29). However, "home" has a different, redefined meaning instead of "no longer having [any] meaning." Further, besides taking away his "sexual longing," the "middle" experience takes away his racial identity and identity as a black male.[15]

As is true in *Oxherding Tale*, intersubjectivity changes the traditional portrayal of black male character and sexuality, giving them a slant that is sometimes humorous, and in other instances paradigmatically eliminating them. This is also the symbolic (re)inscription of Calibanic discourse. Beneath this, Rutherford as a black male, before he accepts intersubjective reality, exhibits Calibanic qualities more explicitly: He is a reprobate sexual philanderer and a thief. It is, however, what the text says and implies about Rutherford's father and other "colored men" that may be more important in terms of explicit and symbolic Calibanic portrayal. His father is a slave, who lacks "life assurance" and liberating voice, and the father's own life and choice to try to liberate himself seemingly lead to his death and eternal objectivity. In the final analysis, Rutherford hypothesizes that, in light of "small" "triumphs" and the "mystery of black life," "colored men" should "pine for the endless round of social obstacles and challenges and trials [they] faced every blessed day of their lives."[16] The latter statement by Rutherford works in the context of the assertion that the black self is a fiction—something that is not uniquely black and not actually real. If not a (re)inscription of Calibanic discourse, this kind of negation that accepts oppression is an obverse manifestation of it. It is significant in terms of the portrayal of black men in *Middle Passage* and the overall portrayal in both *Oxherding Tale* and *Middle Passage*.

5

Calibanic Discourse in Postmodern and Non-Postmodern Black Male Texts

This chapter addresses Trey Ellis's *Platitudes* (1988), William Melvin Kelley's *A Different Drummer* (1962), David Bradley's *The Chaneysville Incident* (1981), and Wesley Brown's *Tragic Magic* (1978). *A Different Drummer* is a non-postmodern novel that consciously uses the Caliban trope and unconsciously (re)inscribes it, and *Platitudes*, *Chaneysville Incident*, and *Tragic Magic*, a postmodern and two non-postmodern novels, respectively, show further that black male novels in both categories tell stories that conform to the pattern of the challenge and compromise of the story of liberation in the texts in the first four chapters.

To begin, Ellis's *Platitudes'* overall project as a novel thematizes and formally symbolizes liberation in postmodern terms; it creates an opposition between the liberating potential of its postmodernist form and the unconscious (re)inscription of Calibanic discourse. Parody is its dominant mode; ambiguity is its primary device. In general terms, the parody is a metafiction that exposes the self-reference of narrative and liberates the thematized black male writer (implicitly Trey Ellis) from the traditional constraints of narrative mimesis. Dewayne Wellington, the thematized writer within the larger context, creates a number of inchoate, potentially readable, potentially liberating fictions in the welter of ambiguity during the course of the parodic structure; he tries to define his character and reality through these fictions. At the very end, a humanizing, sexually empowering fiction evolves from the various fragmentary linguistic forms and voices that he has used throughout the text. However, the fiction has taken on the voice and influence of the black female writer who has contested his writing from the beginning, and it remains ambiguous whether the black male writer has the indigenous voice to define reality and character. It is particularly unclear if he defines character beyond the questionable sexual desires and expression as represented during the novel. Ambiguity turns the narrative toward expressing the failure of voice and toward negative character delineation. This is symbolic (re)inscription of Calibanic discourse through thematic development and (re)inscription in terms of more direct character portrayal. The thematized black male writer's attempts to use (white) postmodernism is the difference between *Platitudes* and the other three texts, which do not thematize writers and postmodernist modes. Calibanic discourse's restriction of voice and character in the underlying narrative stands out in the process of these attempts as the thematized writers consciously write to achieve voice and liberating character portrayal.[1]

A *Different Drummer* focuses on Tucker Caliban's efforts to free himself from a legacy of racism engendered by his naming and thus specifies *The Tempest* and its discourse as the source of the oppressive racist inscription of black male character, just as *Philadelphia Fire* does. The latter appropriates, transforms, and critiques the Caliban trope, showing that it is the central source of pejorative discourse about black men, the most substantive effect of which is unconscious. *Different Drummer* embodies both the conscious and unconscious influences of Calibanic discourse, because it names (but does not critique) *The Tempest* as the source of an oppressive Calibanic legacy, and then it shows the discourse's unconscious challenge and compromise of the black male voice of liberation in the underlying substance of its purportedly liberating narrative.

The manifestations of Calibanic discourse in *Different Drummer* further specifies what is unconscious in the other texts throughout this study. *Different Drummer's* combination of the conscious and unconscious is a key to making Calibanic discourse clear in the other texts, where aspects of it are unconscious. By referencing *The Tempest* and its legacy, *Different Drummer* is naming that which is broadly determinant in the portrayal of oppression in black male texts. From one perspective, *The Tempest's* legacy is unconscious in other texts, but the other texts (re)inscribe it like *Different Drummer* does during the process of telling the story of liberation that responds to it. From another view, *Different Drummer* names the legacy that is unconscious in other texts, and then unconsciously (re)inscribes it when responding to it like these other texts do.

Although there is no thematized black male writer or postmodernist mode, Calibanic discourse manifests itself in *Different Drummer, Tragic Magic*, and *The Chaneysville Incident* in a way that is generally similar to the texts in the other chapters. The three texts have in common the external manifestation of liberation and/or achievement of black male voice and a deeper, more substantive thematic manifestation of the challenge and compromise of voice and of the black male story.[2] *The Chaneysville Incident* unconsciously responds to Calibanic discourse with the portrayal of a black male character, John Washington, who counters slavery and racism with narratives that construct a black male voice of liberation and a liberating story. Among the characters in the texts, John is the closest to being a thematized writer in postmodernist terms. He constantly reads and tries to interpret texts left for him by his ancestors, and he tries to construct his own oral version of history from these texts. However, John is not the writer consciously struggling to make written words, and language in general, say what he wants them to say as he tries to write his own text. He struggles for the human feeling that will give him imaginative voice to tell his story, but he does not consciously write with the intention of freeing himself and his characters through his writing. *Tragic Magic* is more clearly a surreal modernist text, which unconsciously responds to Calibanic discourse and echoes Ralph Ellison's *Invisible Man*. It tries to counter racism by telling a story that positively defines an individual voice of freedom for the main character, Melvin Ellington, a collective voice and a community of freedom for black men, and positive sexuality and human(e) character for Melvin and for black men.

In the four texts discussed in this chapter, Calibanic discourse and the responsive story of liberation are largely inseparable. Often the direct evidence of Calibanic discourse is the (re)inscription of some of its essential elements while the text is telling the responsive story of liberation, which Calibanic discourse elicits. *Different Drummer* is not exactly the same, but it is similar. In *Different Drummer,* the direct evidence of Calibanic discourse is both the text's specific reference to it and its unconscious symbolic (re)inscription of its identifiable elements—the silencing of black male voice and the attendant portrayal of black male mutilation and destruction.

Platitudes' Thematized Black Male Writers and Calibanic Discourse's Narrative Opposition

The question throughout *Platitudes* is what is the direction and point of the narrative: What happens in the text as a result of the writerly acts of the thematized writers, and what is the result of their personal interaction? On one hand, the text (and implicitly Trey Ellis) starts by making clear its own reference to other texts and ends with a "dedication" that seems to show that the narrative has been a lark or a game. Between the beginning and the "dedication," Dewayne Wellington, the black male writer who is the main character, continues to play and parody serious narrative. On the other, Dewayne seems to reach a serious conclusion in which he overcomes his problems and manifests his humanity by becoming closer to his antagonist, female writer Isshee Ayam.

The epigraph and the "dedication" show the text's overall parody. The epigraph, which includes three footnotes, follows:

Brian O'Nolan[1] once wrote that the modern novel should be largely a work of reference.[2]

That sounds very well, gentlemen, said Lamont, very well indeed in my humble opinion. It's the sort of queer stuff they look for in a story these days. Do you know?
Oh, we'll make a good job of this yarn yet.[3]

1. A.K.A. Flann O'Brien and myles na gCopaleen.
2. "The entire corpus of existing literature should be regarded as a limbo from which discerning authors could draw their characters as required, creating only when they failed to find a suitable existing puppet. *The modern novel should be largely a work of reference.* Most authors spend their time saying what has been said before—usually said much better. A wealth of references to existing works would acquaint the reader instantaneously with the nature of each character, would obviate tiresome explanations and would effectively preclude mountebanks, upstarts, thimbleriggers and persons of inferior education from an understanding of contemporary literature. Conclusion of explanation." (italics mine) (*At Swim-Two-Birds,* Flann O'Brien, New York: Plume, 1966, p. 33)
3.Ibid., p. 245.

The "dedication" at the end of the book reads: *"For my mom and dad, wish you were here."*

The tone and form of the parody represent the freedom of Dewayne and Trey Ellis. The parody refers to narrative convention and to its own structure, and these references reflect the freedom of the writers to say and do anything they want. The epigraph apparently exemplifies less than O'Brien's serious intention to incorporate layer upon layer of literary texts into his own text.[3] In the context of what follows, *Platitudes'* epigraph's one italicized sentence, which is the writer's (implicitly Trey Ellis's) emphasis, would seem to imply the pastiche of materials, forms, and popular culture references that disrupt narrative mimesis throughout the text. Dewayne Wellington (and implicitly Trey Ellis) includes almost anything in the pastiche—a Preliminary Scholastic Aptitude Test, a Friends School Sexuality Survey, photographs, the description of a movie screen showing and announcing the preliminaries to the main movie, portions of the novel that Dewayne is writing as *Platitudes* unfolds. The writers apparently do it because they can and still call *Platitudes* a novel, when there is no contiguous narrative line or traditional narrative form. The "dedication" at the end, which Trey Ellis implicitly writes, and which relates clearly to nothing before it, contributes to the idea that the writer writes his own freedom. He writes to liberate himself from the traditional constraints of writing. And the liberation of the writer is black liberation in the context of Ellis's definition of a New Black Aesthetic constituted by hybrid forms in which "anything (good) goes" ("New Black Aesthetic" 243).

The construction of the novel within *Platitudes* (which Dewayne entitles "Platitudes") is an aspect of the parody's disruptive pastiche and signification on narrative mimesis; it is also an aspect of the text's symbolic (re)inscription of Calibanic discourse through thematic development and (re)inscription through character portrayal. The question, which is a really serious one in the text's underlying structure, is this: Can the black male writer tell a liberating story about black people that at the same time portrays acceptable sexual attitudes and responses by black males? The answer is unclear; Dewayne by no means shows that he can.

Dewayne describes his failed attempts to tell a story:

Things were going pretty well for a while, then somewhere along the line I got sidetracked again. I don't know. It's been almost twenty years since I was a teenager, but I thought it would all come back to me. I was also trying to remember my ex-nieces and nephews (my ex-wife's sister's children)—bourgeois, materialistic miscreants to the one, but I must have blocked them forever out of my mind. I swear that whole family is worth at least a thousand-page historical novel. Summers on the Vineyard, liposuction, tennis, analysis, golf, BMW's, and the Bahamas. If I were the black John Jakes I'd be laughing all the way to my made-for-TV-movie deal. (14)

He goes on to make a public appeal and asks: "Which Ones [of my characters] Do I Kill?" Isshee replies.

"Which ones do I kill?" you so needlessly and smugly ask. My answer shall be as brief and as precise as the turbulent storm of my incensed thoughts will allow.

Yet I will not answer with the word you probably expect—"Yourself." Nay,

instead I say all the women in your grotesque menagerie should be "killed"—
liberated from your sweaty and pitiful grasp.

No, we women of color do not need your atavistic brand of representation,
thank you.

Isshee Ayam

P.S. Here is how you should have commenced your "work." (15)

Within the context of the parody—and from this specific perspective
Trey Ellis is the hypothetical writer—Isshee shows that she has voice, and
Dewayne demonstrates that his is questionable. The story that Isshee tells in
installments following the above quotation is a parody of her and of itself.
However, it is a story of affirmation, and the most important thing may be
that Isshee believes her own story and refuses to question her own voice.
(And here the name Isshee Ayam is both a part of the parody and a representation of her own belief, which makes her strong and certain about her story.[4])
The parody would seem to undercut all narrative representation and particularly to ridicule the "Afro-American glory-stories" (19) featuring black
women that Isshee writes. However, within the parody and in opposition to
it, Isshee's "glory-stories" about black women have a clear message about
black women and freedom and about the negative qualities of black men.

The implication, then, is that within the parody Trey Ellis affirms the
black woman's story and voice and restricts the black male's. Isshee's story
about Earle, "Cornbread," and "Bassmouth" in effect caricatures the glorious portrayal of black women but also portrays black males in a more substantively proscriptive way. "Bassmouth" says the following to Earle and
"Cornbread" about persuading a girl to have sex.

"Well, let's say she says she don't want to 'cause she knows you's just gonna
skididdle on her and the baby and she'll be all 'lone wid dat youngin' in
Lowndes while you's ovah in Memphis or some such place with dem tree-
dollah hoores or up Norf all rich and fat, and she be on relief all her life 'til
she die. Wail, if she ups and says all dat gibbledypie, you just tells her a big old
bumblebee done stung your weeniewanker and kilt all yo' sap!" Bassmouth
laughed and laughed, his face twisted into a hideous death mask of ugly
stupidity as the other two hesitantly chuckled, just vaguely understanding
through the near-impenetrable cloud of youthful, hormonal ignorance that
something just might be amiss.

The muted gong of an age-old, time-worn skillet being beaten [by his
mother called Earle home.] . . .

. . . And there she was, as he would always remember her, looking out over
their barren yet triumphal paltry acres, her thick, kind hand saluting the
horizon as she scanned the woods for her only son, one thin wisp of sweet-

smelling smoke streaming out of the tall, noble chimney forever skyward, a telegraph to heaven, his mother always said, and behind her his glorious sisters, unrelenting breakwaters between him and the vagaries of a society he had never invited to come and agitate his gloriously simpleminded though priapic cosmos. (45–46)

In spite of its caricature of speech and everything else that mocks the story, it still manages to suggest sexual qualities and qualities of character related to sexuality that proscribe black males in the context of Calibanic discourse. The negative portrayals of black male sexuality and character stand out from the caricature of black female portrayal.

Dewayne's story is particularly hard to follow, in part because he speaks with his own voice telling one story at the same time that his voice takes on Isshee's influence and tells another. At first, Earle becomes sexually infatuated with a young white woman named Janey Rosebloom, and then Isshee's black character named Dorothy becomes more Earle's interest as the story moves closer to Isshee's. From the beginning, the story is a series of sporadic, hard-to-decipher fictions that loosely deal with Janey; the fictions do, however, exhibit what Isshee calls the "sweaty and pitiful grasp" of Dewayne's "atavistic representation." At one point, Earle is despondent, "seeing he wasn't now going to bang old Janey Rosebloom or nothing" (55). From this perspective, although the text mocks Isshee's ridiculing words about Dewayne, he verifies what she says by his own descriptions of sex and attitudes toward sex and through his tentative, fragmentary, diffident voice. As Dewayne moves closer to Isshee's influence and voice, he tells a more intelligible, less sexually oriented story about Dorothy. However, near the end his story still returns to sexually prurient descriptions of both Janey and Dorothy after Isshee skips her promised meeting with him in order to meet another man. Finally, Dewayne apparently empowers himself sexually through his interaction with Isshee and humanizes Earle's character portrayal.

Dewayne writes the following after Isshee disappoints and hurts him. The account takes up the story as Earle works with Dorothy's mother Darcelle:

Where is [Dorothy]?
Oh, I thought she told you. She says she sick. . . . that girl better be laying up in bed [at home]. . . . Here's the key.

The Cub Detective Series Presents
The Case of the Flexible Dancer

Chapter 49

She meets him, leaves her old boyfriend, stops seeing her girlfriends, sees only him. They ice-skate, go to Coney Island, ride through moonlit Central Park, she touches him often. He gives her a rose. She kisses him right on the lips. *Question:* Does she like him as more than just a friend?

Answer: Earle unlocks the building's front door, enters, then pushes it relocked. . . .

TA-dum! he proclaims.

Richard, the model, opens his eyes, closes his mouth, looks into Earle. In front of and below Richard the model's exposed white waist, a relentless brown buttock hinges a brown body, down to grab its own ankles, nose pressed to its knees. . . . A quarterback and his center.

TA-dum! TA-dum! TA-dum! Just a little more and I'll TA-dum too! she cries beneath her rhythmic and inverted dress. Only gradually does she understand the silence. (159)

After depicting Dorothy in this way, Dewayne retaliates further by describing a sexual encounter between Earle and Janey: "She holds his raven penis, insinuates it into her snowy self. . . . Her pearl hands pad his inky shoulders; she raises, lowers herself onto, off of him. . . . As her rhythm increases, her thighs flex, relax around him, her white stomach flexes, relaxes too, her wine nipples *are* warm erasers, she *does* moan as he presses her breasts. Cries rise from her mouth but start somewhere much deeper. She now curves back, her fingers squeeze her hair, her elbows high, riding no-handed, cries now short and quick. Then slow"(168).

After Isshee apologizes, explains that she knows what he has done and why, and gives him a final installment of the story, Dewayne reconstructs Earle's character compassionately and humanely in a love scene with the apologetic Dorothy, before Dewayne can get an erection to have sex with Isshee.

Now her kisses the warmth on his neck, a warmth that rises to his jaw and chin and he kisses her lips which are salt-watered and again and again he kisses short to prove he can, kisses her cheeks to her eyes down to her nose to her lips again, he can, and she kisses back too, *just* as much, and then he's aware that his heart's crazily banging because it's never felt this before, no fire drill, the real thing, and he wonders how he had ever lived so long without it.

Now that [Dewayne's penis] presses the underside of the desk, he will go wake Isshee. (183)

The "dedication" that I have referred to immediately follows this on the next page, and it reaffirms Trey Ellis's liberating postmodernist play with narrative form and tradition that began with the epigraph and that throughout the text has constituted an aspect of structure and theme. But the text "Platitudes" that Dewayne writes within Ellis's *Platitudes* fails clearly to define his liberating voice as a writer in his own right and to portray him and Earle positively in their own right.

Because she moves closer to Dewayne, Isshee humanizes the portrayal of Earle as a lover, thus showing that Dewayne influences her also; however, more importantly, Dewayne only seems to feel empowered to voice Earle's and his own humane sexual expression after Isshee does it. A quotation of the last installment of the story that Isshee gives Dewayne reveals that he draws heavily from her in creating his supposedly humanized, compassionate portrayal of Earle above. Dewayne's description seems to repeat the voice of Isshee's description below in tone, language, and conventionalized form by emphasizing compassionate kissing and touching that lead to love.

Dorothy held his hand, then kissed his tears. Earle smiled weakly and kissed her back. Their lips now pressed together, still neither one had yet realized why such a simple, innocent touch had so fired their souls.

Silently they kissed on, smoothing hands over sensitive swells that swelled still more under every soft touch. Now naked before the surf's mighty shout, they made love, not knowing how "technically" yet succeeding so triumphantly, so very gloriously, because it finally allowed them to release their raging adolescent emotions. Yes, their lovemaking was what all good lovemaking always is—a wordless "I love you." (176)

The thematized black male writer's liberation from the conventions of narrative mimesis in the terms of (white) postmodernism highlights and contrasts the unconscious restriction of voice; Calibanic discourse's restriction of voice and character stands out in the underlying narrative. Reprobate sexuality, questionable character, and failed liberating voice are qualities unconsciously embedded in the text.[5] The text's final image of Dewayne with an erection preparing to have sex with Ishee has ambiguous meaning that coalesces with his and Earle's ambiguous but crude and dubious characterization throughout, and this along with Dewayne's tentative, derivative voice of liberation enables the (re)inscription of Calibanic qualities instead of a liberating story. Is he deserving of Ishee and consequently sexually empowered after she has humanized him? Has he been humanized beyond his and Earle's negative sexual portrayals and questionable character throughout the text, to the point that his erection does not take on and reflect Dewayne's and Earle's earlier prurience?[6] Does the last brief episode portrayed by Dewayne, which culminates in the one brief sentence describing his erection and preparation, change things significantly? The answers may largely be "no."

A Different Drummer: Caliban's "Blood," Silenced Voice, and Destruction

A Different Drummer specifies the naming of Tucker Caliban's forefather, First Caliban, a slave, in the tradition of Caliban in *The Tempest;* focuses its plot primarily on the process that Tucker goes through in the present to free himself from the legacy of his naming; and clearly implies the rewriting of the play's oppressive legacy in a brief scene near the end (178). The text's surface theme and structure definitely point to Tucker's liberation, but clearly ambiguity and paradox in the underlying theme and structure that encompass the physical destruction of black males, potentially negative character portrayal, and the silencing of black male voice turn the narrative toward the symbolic (re)inscription of Calibanic discourse and (re)inscription through characterization.

The naming of *The Tempest's* Calibanic legacy is conscious, but the (re)inscription of Calibanic discourse is unconscious. Mister Harper, a leader among the imaginary Southern town's poor white men, controls the conversation that specifies the tradition of Calibanic naming. He concludes the story of the African ancestor of the Calibans as follows.

"Well, that's the story and you all know as well as me how that baby [the African's son] got named Caliban by . . . General [Dewey Willson], when the General was twelve years old."

"That's right. After the General read that there book by Shakespeare," Loomis added, sighing.

"Not a book, a play, *The Tempest*. Shakespeare didn't write no books; nobody wrote books then, just poems and plays. No books. You must not-a learned nothing your three weeks up at the university." Mister Harper stared Loomis down. . . .

"And Caliban, whose Christian name got to be First after he got a family and there was more than just one Caliban, was John Caliban's father, and John Caliban's grandson is Tucker Caliban and the African's blood is running in Tucker Caliban's veins." Mister Harper sat back, satisfied. (31–32)

The underlying substance of Mister Harper's story of the African has an ironic viewpoint that reveals a legendary heroism greater than the awe-inspiring mystery of the physically gigantic, revolutionary pagan that Mister Harper understands and relishes.[7] However, the substance of the story also reveals an ambiguous portrayal of the African in which Mister Harper's racist bias and the story's more substantive viewpoint are not clearly separable. This level of the story emphasizes the African's potential pagan voicelessness and evil, and it juxtaposes his physical destruction in this context. At the time of his capture, the African stood in front of a "pile of stones, which he seemed to be a-mumbling at" (29). He was "glistening in the fire, almost naked, his eyes just hollows of black." Besides his revolutionary actions, the African's one intelligible sign is a bow of "agreement" before Dewitt Willson (General Willson's father) "raised his rifle, sighted [his] upturned face, and shot him cleanly just above the bridge of his wide nose" (30–31). As the African tries to kill his child with a stone before he dies himself, Dewitt "shattered the back of his head before he could smash it down [on the child]. And so the African died" (31).

The African's potential voicelessness and evil and associated destruction gain substance from the overall ambiguous theme, structure, and character portrayal of the text. In this context, who is the African, and what is his characterization? Is his lack of voice a result of the fact that he does not know the English language, or does it represent an inability to use language to define his humanity that is innate and greater than his lack of knowledge of English? (The latter question is particularly interesting in light of his seemingly intelligible "agreement" to his murder.) Are his revolutionary actions, which include killing white people and freeing slaves, and "glistening" blackness signs of his evil? Should one read his murder after his revolutionary acts as punishment for the acts and for his evil? (In *The Tempest* and in *Philadelphia Fire*, Caliban tries the revolutionary action of having sex with Miranda to create an "isle [full of] Calibans" [I.ii.421]. For this and for everything else he does, Miranda concludes essentially that he is evil and should be punished: He is an "Abhorrèd slave, / Which any print of goodness wilt not take, / Being capable of all ill! . . . Who . . . deserved more than a prison" [I.ii.422–36; *Philadelphia Fire* 139].)

These are relevant questions because *Different Drummer's* overall development does not clearly oppose the portrayal of Calibanic voicelessness, evil, and consequent destruction. Throughout the text, the other Calibans have ambiguous qualities that are connected with the characterization of the African, and that affirm negative Calibanic traits as much as, and perhaps more than, they counter them. Though they supposedly carry the dormant heroic revolutionary "blood" that awakens in Tucker, none of them, including Tucker, has the voice to tell his own story, and given their lack of voice, they never clearly redefine themselves in terms that counter the African's potentially negative portrayal.

Racism inspires the white men to call Tucker "evil" (38), but at the same time, Tucker does not define himself and even fails to say that he is not evil when asked if he is. Harold "Mister" Leland, the eight-year-old white boy who likes the diminutive Tucker, hears the white men calling him "evil and crazy" (55) as Tucker defiantly burns his house and begins to leave the community. He wants to say that Tucker "'is not [evil and crazy]. He did it because . . .'" He catches up to Tucker to question him.

> "Go on back, Mister Leland. Do like I say."
> "Why you going?" . . . "You ain't really evil—is you, Tucker?"
> Tucker stopped and put his hand on the boy's head. The boy stiffened.
> "That what they saying, Mister Leland?"
> "Yes, sir."
> "Does you think I is?"
> Mister Leland stared into Tucker's eyes. They were large and too bright. "I .
> . . But why'd you do all them evil, crazy things?"
> "You young, ain't you, Mister Leland."
> "Yes, sir."
> "And you ain't lost nothing, has you."
> The boy did not understand and said nothing.
> "Go on back."

Although Tucker's actions are enigmatic and not clearly evil, he does not answer the question about his potential evil and speaks very few words in his own voice throughout the text. A first-person white voice usually frames Tucker's statements, and the narrative always adumbrates his voice when he does speak. For example, he says the following about the National Society for Colored Affairs: "'They ain't working for my rights. Ain't nobody working for my rights; I wouldn't let them'" (111). In the context of his revolutionary "black" motivations, it is not clear what he means here. Also, Tucker briefly contests another character's testimony to his father John's characterization as a man who sacrificed at the latter's funeral. Dewey Willson reports the following: "Then I heard a male voice say in disbelief: 'Sacrifice? Is that all? Is that really all? Sacrifice be damned!'" (122) Tucker says no more, and leaves the church, "his eyes blank and hard" (123). Further, Camille Willson describes how she confided her story in Tucker, and how he succinctly finished her story for her (146–48). But her voice is the frame of reference.

By the end, the text purports to show the success of Tucker's liberation, which symbolizes the liberation of all black people in the imaginary southern state. However, almost the entire second part of the novel that develops his story moves from one first-person white perspective to another. In this context, the aristocratic white man David Willson (the great-grandson of General Dewey Willson) defines Tucker's liberation through the voice of his diary, and he makes Tucker's liberation inseparable from his own (David's). Early in his diary, David claims that Tucker has liberated both of them: "He has freed himself; this had been very important to him. But somehow, he has freed me too. He is only one man, and this, of course, does not make a reality all the things I had dreamed of doing twenty years ago. But it is something. And I contributed to it. . . " (151). In spite of what he says about Tucker's freedom, David is speaking in his own voice and defining and affirming his own freedom.

In the final analysis, David Willson's words and account in the diary give Tucker voice and interpret his revolutionary ritual, making it unclear who gets liberated in the end—David or Tucker. Two passages from the text show this. The first deals with Tucker's attempt to purchase the Willson land that his ancestors worked as slaves and servants, and it is a thinly veiled reference to David's role in rewriting the legacy of *The Tempest.* David "had the feeling [that he] was in a play; I had certain lines to speak, and [Tucker] too, and we had to say them so the play would proceed in a predestined order" (178). Shortly after this, he says that "I found I was very much taken up in this mock drama, found myself caring a great deal." David sells Tucker the land, thus symbolically reversing Caliban's disenfranchisement of his island. However, the reference to the play's "predestined order" also invokes *The Tempest's* oppressive "predestined order." The lynching of the black man at the very end of the text that "Mister" Leland, in his white male voice, conflates with Tucker's return in his reconstruction of Tucker's story supports the idea that the "predestined order" is oppressive.

The last two sections of the text, David's narrative and the lynching episode, respectively, foreground David's liberation and make the text's conclusions about black male liberation ambiguous. I take the second passage from the end of David's narrative, which immediately precedes the beginning of the section that ends the book with the lynching; David concludes his section of the narrative with an account of Tucker's words.

[Tucker] looked at me. "You only get one chance. That's when you can and when you feels like it. When one of them is missing, ain't no use trying. If you can do it, but don't feel like it, why do it? And when you feels like it, and ain't no opportunity, you just knocking your head against the front of a car going a hundred miles an hour. There ain't no use in thinking about it if you ain't got both. And if you had both and missed out, you might as well forget about it; your chance is gone for good."
I nodded; I know all about that. (182)

Since Tucker's character and motivation remain a mystery because he seldom speaks in his own voice, and he never speaks without a white narrative to frame his voice, we do not "know all about" what Tucker means (as we do not know what the African means). We do, however, understand how

David might have liberated himself from an oppressive legacy, because he tells his story in detail in his own voice.

The end of the text is a paradox to Tucker's supposed liberation and decidedly turns the narrative toward (re)inscribing Calibanic discourse through thematic and structural symbolism. White men lynch Bennett Bradshaw, a black man with a nationalist ideology, and "Mister" Leland imagines that the screams he hears come from a party Tucker is having upon his return. The whites do not lynch Tucker, but they lynch Bradshaw for what Tucker does, as Dewey Willson III (the son of David) unsuccessfully tries to defend him: "'It was Tucker Caliban! It was Tucker Caliban!'" (193). The men insist on lynching Bradshaw because he is "'Our last nigger! That's good. He weren't really ours when he come down [from the North] in his big car, but he is now, and we can have him do anything we want him to do'" (195). Part of what they "want him to do" is "sing one of the old songs for us" (194), which emphasizes that Tucker's revolutionary act has changed the situation where whites make blacks sing.

However, the underlying effect of the ending section is to counter rather than affirm Tucker's revolutionary act; it does this through its conflated reference to Bradshaw and Tucker and through the symbolism of the lynching. In the last six paragraphs of the novel, Mister Leland imagines the lynching as a party celebrating Tucker's return.

And then he heard it again: a scream.
It came from the direction of the Highway, maybe near Tucker's, came through the muffling trees separating their two farms. Maybe Tucker was back and having a party. But where? Tucker did not have a house. But he could be having it outside, it was warm enough, and besides, no one else would be at Tucker's farm. . . .
Mister Leland lay on his back, listening to the faint laughter and to someone who had started to sing and thought about the party. . . . It would be a good party, with people happy to see each other like the reunions his people had at his grandfather's house. . . .
He lay on his back and thought about that, and then he knew what he would do when morning came. . . . He would take [his little brother] Walter by the hand and they would go back through the woods and come out on Tucker's field. Tucker would see them and wave. . . . He would say hello, and would be glad to see them. . . .
Then Mister Leland would ask Tucker why he came back. Tucker would say he had found what he had lost, and he would smile and tell them he had something for them. He would bring out large bowls of the leftover candy and popcorn and cracker-jack and chocolate drops. And they would eat until they were full. And all the while, they would be laughing. (198–200)

The ending is the third-person description given by an eight-year-old, and, like so much of the text, it is ambiguous. But from the overall perspective that I have defined, it does restrict the theme of liberation and affirm the pattern of black male voicelessness, evil, and punishment that is an underlying aspect of the text.

Overall, ambiguity and paradox clearly turn the narrative toward a symbolic (re)inscription of the terms of the Calibanic legacy.[8] In part at least, the African's "blood" that Mister Harper mentions represents the Calibanic traits that the text attempts to oppose with its story of liberation. *Different Drummer* cannot revise the Calibanic discourse implicit in the legacy of Caliban that it specifies because, in *Philadelphia Fire's* words, Calibanic discourse is "buried" and "unmentionable," but "nevertheless signified in the small-print forever-after clause" (141) of the story's language.

Finding the Voice and Story That Humanize: Liberation from the Calibanic Legacy in *The Chaneysville Incident*

In *The Chaneysville Incident,* John Washington opposes the white patriarchy through actions that are sometimes in essence misogynistic, and conversely tries to humanize himself and liberate himself through his narrative. He avenges himself on the white world by raping a white woman because she is white (75). John feels some guilt for the rape but justifies it: "'Things have happened and it's somebody's fault, and it sure as hell wasn't ours'" (75–76). John also takes revenge by possessing his white girlfriend Judith— that is, by taking her from her white father and from her white lover and potential white husband (290–91). John's practice as a historian allows him to attempt to take control of the story of slavery and racism and use history as another tool of revenge. He tries to create accounts of American history and, even more importantly, his family history that tell the facts, expose the atrocities, and indict the white patriarchy. But John's historical narrative also progresses toward the construction of an empowering voice that will express human sympathy and liberate him from the nightmare generated by his lack of sympathetic human imagination: "Something had shackled me in the dreaming state, and I could not open my eyes. . . . [It was n]ot even a dream; just an all-encompassing sensation of coldness, and a visual image of total white. . . . I could not free myself. I could not wake up" (149).

On a superficial level, *The Chaneysville Incident* concludes with a "good" ending through which John achieves the voice that liberates; however, the underlying substance of the narrative throughout the text—especially the last five paragraphs—casts doubt on the "good" ending. Judith's sympathy and physical touch warm John near the end as he seemingly tells the story that frees him (413–31), but the relationship he creates by telling the story at the end could only superficially change the course of John's entire life, which is an integral part of events that go back to 1787 (291). The last five paragraphs of the book, which critics often ignore, confirm this point.[9] This portion of the text implies that John may kill himself and follow his father and great-grandfather, whose history begins in 1787. If this is true, the loving, human(e) commitment that he makes to Judith just before these last paragraphs will not save and liberate him: His freedom, like his father's and great-grandfather's, may only be possible in death. The text leaves it very much unclear how John and other black men can attain liberating voice and freedom; their attainment seems doubtful as long as they are alive. John's and the text's liberation quests symbolically restrict or negate the black male voice of liberation in the underlying narrative and create an overall thematic and structural ambiguity and paradox that turn the narrative toward a (re)inscription of Calibanic discourse's signification of black male voice and freedom.

The story John tells Judith leading to the ending starts around the middle of this long text, but from the beginning the larger narrative starts to develop the ambiguous and paradoxical portrayal that (re)inscribes Calibanic discourse by the end. This early part of the narrative produces an underlying story that casts doubt on the efficacy of black male community; black male community does not seem to be a source of liberating voice, truth, and knowledge or of saving, supportive fraternity.

Old Jack Crawley tells a series of stories and connects John to the community of black men by relating the most important aspect of his longest story, which is about Uncle Josh White and his relationship with a white woman, to John's relationship to Judith. Also, John implies his connection to Jack and the community because, contradictorily, a major part of his relationship with Judith is his distrust of her because she is white, which is how Old Jack says John should feel and how he says Old Josh should have felt. Further, John's own story and its potential failure to liberate him connect him and his fate to his father's and great-grandfather's fate, which unfolds fully later in the text with the aid of the folio book that the great-grandfather left.

Jack tells stories portraying a seemingly fraternal community of black men who have legendary "adventures" together, but the fraternity of men, like the "good" ending, may be superficial. John always liked to hear his father's friend Jack tell stories about the legendary father and the "adventures" he took Jack and Josh on: "I always wanted to hear about Moses Washington . . . about the adventures that had taken him, and Old Jack Crawley, and Uncle Josh White, tearing across the mountains pursued by lawmen and irate fathers and angry farmers" (45). At first glance, the "adventures" would seem to forge a close relationship, but as Jack's stories reveal beneath their surface, the "adventures" are high-sounding, romantic, and ultimately superficial deeds that make exciting stories but do not relate to the more important substance of human interaction. The men engage in "adventures" together, but they fail to deal adequately with each other and the world.

Many aspects of Jack's story strongly point to the inadequacy of the relationship among men. Jack always believes that there is some substantive, hidden meaning behind what Moses does, but he never comes close to understanding what it is or what is going on among the men generally speaking. Jack says on numerous occasions that he does not understand Moses, and the two main stories that he tells—the story about meeting Moses (51–62) and the one about the attempted lynching of Josh (78–112)—reveal Jack's overall failure of perception as well as a failure of communication and connection in the group.

Jack's story about the attempted lynching of Josh perhaps provides the best example of this failure of communication and knowledge. Jack understands the racism that motivates the white men to try to lynch Josh, but he never understands what is much more important in human terms. He never sees the complex possibilities and dynamics of the relationship between Josh and the white woman—that is, that they could really love each other (108–9). Moses is primarily a larger-than-life, legendary figure whose human life and feeling we cannot know through Jack's stories (or later through John's either). Jack's story does not show that Moses understands, or more importantly, that he cares enough to try to understand. Josh remains characteristically mute, unable to express whatever he knows and feels.

It is, at most, unclear how men bound together by "adventures" in this way could have a significantly close relationship grounded in the knowledge of each other and of life. Reflecting on Jack's imminent death, John thinks that when a man dies, "his story is lost" (48), and later when Jack dies, John hears the "stories . . . breaking up inside" him (112). The loss, the breakup, and the failure of the stories suggest a lot about the community of men and its relationships.

The breakup of Jack's stories is in keeping with the fact that John learns nothing substantive about his father from Jack, although he does acquire superficial details. From approximately the middle of the novel to the end, John tries to use the writings of his father Moses and his great-grandfather C.K. to tell the story of Moses, first, and then C.K. In telling this story, John attempts to draw upon facts to discover and imagine what happened to them, and in so doing, he reveals his similarity to them and shows how his fate is related to their fate. Liberation is the central theme in his story, which focuses on slavery and goes back to 1787. Through his story, John tries to liberate himself as well as his father and great-grandfather.

John's story about Moses shows that Moses took the risk that death meant freedom; it also shows that Moses's freedom is problematized. John has difficulty learning the truth about Moses's life and death from the extensive written record that he left; he does, however, find out that Moses obsessively studied C.K.'s writings and life. Moses spent years testing the foundation of the theory that C.K. could find freedom in death, and he apparently killed himself to follow C.K. after developing faith in the theory. While he was alive, pursuing C.K.'s legacy and testing the theory of his death and freedom consumed Moses and made him an isolated, cold, callous man. In light of John's quest throughout the novel, one can say that Moses never attained the sympathetic human imagination or the voice that would liberate him in life. Moses seemingly convinces himself that death will free him, but in the context of a portrayal that reveals his narrow, distorted life, this is questionable.

Moses's story differs from John's in many specific details, but its substance implies and suggests much of what John's story does about freedom. In the process of undertaking a pursuit of C.K.'s legacy that is parallel to Moses's, John ironically reveals that he is very much like Moses and that he has the potential to do what his father did. In general terms, John describes himself when he describes Moses: His mother "lived with a man who was so crazy that one day he was going to walk twenty-two miles just to find a nice spot in which to blow his brains out, and [who was] so preoccupied as not only to do it, but not to care enough about the effect of it on his wife—and his children—to try to make it look like an accident; a man who showed her no mercy" (307). Moses seemingly cannot, or will not, develop human sympathy and be free while he is alive, and the text's ambiguity and paradox problematize the freedom he achieves through his death. John apparently does attempt to humanize himself through his narrative, but at the end, his efforts do not seem to be enough to free him from the dehumanizing coldness that could cause death. He, too, appears ready to kill himself.

C.K. was an abolitionist who lived during the eighteenth and nineteenth centuries, and John is a twentieth-century historian. But substantively their lives are synonymous. John makes this possible because he can only start to imagine C.K.'s human(e) qualities through a story that interweaves C.K.'s life with his own and syncretizes C.K.'s character with his own.

An analysis of key sections of the text that pertain to John creating their synonymous lives as men who try to attain humanity, who attempt to liberate themselves by attaining a similar human(e) feeling, shows a broader pattern of parallels and similarities. Early in the text, John says that Judith had "slept with her hand on [him], to feel the first shivering" (149), to awaken him and provide the warmth to shake his cold, icy, "white" nightmare. As John moves toward the end of his narrative, he stops resisting and tries to allow Judith to give him the human warmth that symbolizes human(e) feeling and initiates the voice to tell the story that will free him from the nightmare: "I became aware of her hand, warm, resting on mine. Not resting. Squeezing. I imagined the rest of [C.K.'s story] then" (425). At the same time that he describes his own human(e) feeling for Judith and the accompanying ability to imagine C.K.'s story, he makes C.K.'s life synonymous with his. The initial recognition of coldness in the quotation that follows is C.K.'s, but C.K. "is" John, because his devoted black lover Harriet Brewer is changing him at the same time and in the same way that Judith is changing John.

[H]e had not known about . . . the cold inside, the glacier in his guts that had been growing and moving, inch by inch, year by year, grinding at him, freezing him. He had not known that. But he knew it now. Because he could feel it melting. The heat that melted it did not come from the fire; it came from her, from the warmth of her body that pressed against his back, the warmth of her arms around him, the warmth of her hands that cupped the base of his belly. He lay there, feeling the warmth filling him, feeling the fatigue draining from him, feeling the aching in his ribs easing, becoming almost pleasant, and wishing that he would never have to move. (413)

This account of John/C.K. also obviously makes C.K. an integral part of John's imprisoned, terrorized state (149), and details in John's larger narrative about C.K. reveal the callousness, selfishness, and sexual proclivities that relate him to John. Like John, C.K. tries to take revenge on the white world for slavery and racism. He murdered logically according to the dictates of his plan against slavery (348), and in letters fabricated "adventures" (357) (which suggest the "adventures" of Moses, Jack, and Josh), perhaps to build his own ego (357). Later, he definitely got carried away with his own egotistical need and focused on sexual release and contesting white men for the possession of women, black prostitutes in New Orleans.

"I think he began to see the whole thing [his plan against slavery] as something of an ego boost. . . . And I know he got arrogant and careless. . . . And the plan itself was just plain crazy. He started it in the journal, wrote down that he was in need of the physical release that could only be provided by a female, and that in order to ease his discomfort and accomplish his higher aims at the same time, he was going to avail himself of the services of a nunnery."

[Judith] just looked at me.

"C.K. had read Shakespeare. . . . He was going to liberate a whorehouse." (358)

John/C.K. needs to find the voice successfully to tell the story that emancipates John before it becomes clear whether black males can break the pattern of imprisoned existence or, its apparent alternative, freedom in death; otherwise, the overall narrative of black male freedom symbolically restricts voice and freedom. In the following, C.K. leads Harriet Brewer and the other slaves to death and apparent freedom.

"He knew, then, that they were watching him, all of them. Waiting for him to lead them. It came to him that there was always escape, always, so long as one did not think too much . . . then so long as one believed. And so he stepped away from Harriet Brewer and stood alone, and he took the pistol from his belt and held it high, so they could all see. For a moment he was not sure that he could lead them, was not sure that they would follow, but then he saw Harriet Brewer take her knife from beneath her shawl and hold it high, and then he heard her, heard her singing softly, then louder, heard the others join in . . . . 'And before I'll be a slave I'll be buried in my grave, and go home to my God and be free.' For a chorus or two, or three, the song was loud and strong. And then the song grew weaker, the voices that had raised it falling silent one by one, until at last there was only one voice, a strong soprano voice, carrying the song.[10] And then that voice, too, fell silent. But the song went on. Because the wind had shifted again, and was blowing from the west; because now the wind sang." (430)

After this, John seems to indicate that he can speak in a liberating, human(e) voice, one that implies his empathy for Judith and white people. He ends the story by asserting that a white man took the time to bury C.K. and the others in his own cemetery (430–31).

One could draw positive conclusions about John's quest from this. Through the influence of Judith and the narrative voice that this produces, he attains sympathetic human(e) imagination and learns that as a human being he has a commitment to others. He has a greater responsibility than to oppose and punish white men by exposing a "long string of [historical] atrocities" (186) perpetrated by them. Once he approaches the past through imagination and with his own human investment in mind, he sees the world from a positive, human(e) perspective that allows him to imagine the past (the white man carefully burying C.K. and the others) in a way that coincides with forging the relationship with Judith in the present. This will make a better world. Through his story that demonstrates positive human(e) feeling, John frees himself from isolation, callousness, and hate, and thus frees himself to live.

The last five paragraphs make this conclusion doubtful by revealing that John may kill himself, thus perhaps affirming that the alternatives are imprisoned existence, as John has described it, or death. John sounds angst-ridden after he sends Judith away against her wishes (431), makes a "pyre" of all the "tools of [the historical] trade," leaves the "cabin for the last time" (432), and lights the "pyre." The last three paragraphs clearly end the novel with the possibility that John will kill himself.

When [Judith] was gone I took the folio down and put the books and pamphlets and diaries and maps back where they belonged, ready for the next man who would need them. I sealed the folio with candle wax, as my father had done for me. Then I gathered up the tools of my trade, the pens and inks and pencils, the pads and cards, and carried them out into the clearing. I kicked a clear space in the snow and set them down, and over them I built a small edifice of kindling, and then a frame of wood. I went back inside the cabin and got the kerosene and brought it back and poured it freely over the pyre, making sure to soak the cards thoroughly. I was a bit careless, and got some of it on my boots, but that would make no difference.

. . . And then I left the cabin for the last time and went and stood before the pyre and stood looking at the cards and the papers, and thinking about all of it, one last time.

As I struck the match it came to me how strange it would all look to someone else, someone from far away. And as I dropped the match to the wood and watched the flames go twisting, I wondered if that someone would understand. Not just someone; Judith. I wondered if she would understand when she saw the smoke go rising from the far side of the hill. (431–32)

The five concluding paragraphs do not necessarily negate John's feeling for Judith, but they would seem to imply that the relationship with her and the concomitant humanizing imaginative voice are superficial, because they cannot overcome the legacy that he shares with his father, great-grandfather, and other black males. As long as John voices the oppositional narrative, he remains confined, isolated, separated, and dehumanized, like C.K. and Moses. When he achieves the seemingly humanizing, liberating imaginative voice under the influence of Judith, he briefly frees himself before he apparently gets ready to kill himself, like C.K. and Moses.

The paradoxical and ambiguous conclusion is part of the pattern that (re)inscribes Calibanic discourse by turning the narrative back toward a (re)statement of its legacy. The "books and pamphlets and diaries and maps" will be there "ready for the next man who will need them," but the text does not show how the "next man" can break the black male legacy of C.K., Moses, and John. Everything considered, this pattern contributes to the doubt that John and other black men can free themselves and live, too. And John's angst heightens the inherent contradiction in the idea that death frees black males. John does not appear to have the same "enthusiasm" for death that C.K. and Moses had, and this may imply that death means uncertainty or oblivion more than freedom. Instead of being affirmative, the text unconsciously coincides with *Philadelphia Fire's* appropriation and critique of the Caliban trope and Calibanic discourse, respectively. Black maleness and black male opposition to the patriarchy are justifications for imprisonment (both symbolically and literally in this novel) and/or death, but male voice can never humanize or liberate. As is the case in *Philadelphia Fire,* intelligence and education are not tantamount to voice. In the final analysis, the story of liberation shows that black men may not be able to attain freedom.

Calibanic Discourse and Problematized Black Male Voice and Identity in *Tragic Magic*

Tragic Magic purports to achieve a voice symbolizing liberating human identity that makes real Melvin Ellington's ability to act safely and securely. However, in the process of telling his own story, Melvin tells a general story of black men that virtually negates black male voice. Black men almost uniformly do not make symbolic form and style, largely of voice, the substance of an empowering human identity, and do not make form and style the reality of safe, secure actions in the world. While the portrayals of black women almost essentialize security, freedom, substantive character, and effective, liberating voice, black men are ultimately signifiers of failed voice and proscribed freedom and character. The main theme of *Tragic Magic* is Melvin's achievement of voice in an unsafe existential world, but the novel's underlying narrative counters the theme of successful liberation. Paradox and ambiguity in the underlying narrative about black men turn it toward (re)inscribing the theme of failed black male voice and the proscription of black male character.

For Wesley Brown, jazz musicians and jazz symbolize freedom and revolutionary voice unachieved by black men in any other facet of black life.[11] In the beginning section, "A Few Words Before the Get Go," the text thematizes jazz as an alternative critical voice that signifies on the dominant power structure: "Scatology is a branch of science dealing with the diagnosis of dung and other excremental matters of state. Talking shit is a renegade form of scatology developed by people who were fed up with do-do dialogues and created a kind of vocal doodling that suggested other possibilities within the human voice beyond the same old shit" (5). The speaker here is talking about skatting, a form of vocal jazz that, he seems to imply, counters the dominant discourse through its black signification. Brown symbolizes jazz's improvisational style through the language, form, and style of the text as he portrays Melvin's quest for self-identity, relevance, and freedom. Knowledge about the history of jazz musicians and the jazz life is a counterpoint to Melvin's confused, blundering daily existence; jazz gives Melvin intellectual material for his imagination and improvisational style for his speech as he moves toward making symbolic style the substance of human(e) character, identity, and action.

The portrayals of all the black men except Melvin directly oppose the achievement of voice and freedom. In an interview, Brown implies the essentialized portrayal of black men that counters Melvin's achievement of voice and freedom. Brown says that in *Tragic Magic* he approaches masculinity "with a sense of humor and irony. Many . . . situations are dealt with in a humorous way precisely because the poses of masculinity are in large part rigid and dogmatic. Humor always overturns such postures and shows them for what they are—camouflages against fear, confusion, and just plain not knowing" (Lynch 48).

Several of the black men whom Melvin meets in prison present superficial self-identities that only appear to give them security and control of life in spite of their physical incarceration. These men speak in jazzy, improvisational voices similar to Melvin's but live according to the rigid style coded in their names. "Chilly" is always cool, calm, and aware. "Cadillac" makes a big deal of everything he does. "Shoobee Doobee" not only speaks in a jazzy voice; he lives his entire life through music by "shaking his head, tapping his feet. . . .wearing a sun visor, a string of reed mouthpieces around his neck, and a drumstick strapped to his waist" (37). "Hardknocks" accepts everything that life offers and preaches a philosophy of self-acceptance to Melvin. "Hardknocks" seems to have the most substance because of the advice that he gives Melvin about always accepting and being true to the self, but he later contradicts his own advice when he tells Melvin that "'[you] too self-reliant'" (34). Melvin reaches the conclusion that "'there ain't nothing I can be sure of'" (40). Melvin makes this statement to "Hardknocks," and it is relevant for him, because the rigidity coded in his name and philosophy fails to map a direction for secure, liberated actions in his life and in Melvin's. Chilly's rumored assassination after the prison authorities move him to another prison graphically shows the danger and insecurity of the lives of these men who attempt to develop rigid codes to deny their insecurity.

The life and death of Melvin's friend Otis shows that the lives of "free" black men outside prison are just as dangerously insecure as the lives of those inside prison. Otis lives symbolically through the brave style and persona which he projects in his language, but he lacks the substance to act accordingly. The text makes clear the difference between Otis and Pauline, a black woman who talks very much like Otis but who shows knowledge of her true self and genuine self-security that Otis lacks. The following repartee takes place between Otis and Pauline after a physical confrontation between Otis and another man that is more "fierce clinching," "teeth gritting," and "wrestling" than it is a real fight (116).

"That dude was lucky he came at me in-between moves. I didn't have a chance to get my breathin together."

"Nigger," Pauline said, "if you was as bad as your breath, you would a been able to deal no matter how he came at you."

"Yeah, that's easy to say when you on the sidelines."

"And I ain't never claimed to be nowhere else. You the one grandstandin, not me. And if you talk shit on front street, your ass should be ready to make a public appearance!"

"You keep runnin off at the mouth and my foot's gonna make a public appearance in your ass."

"Oh, yeah? Try it. And I bet I'll kick you in your balls so hard you'll think it's the World Series!" (116–17)

Pauline has the last word because she is right—Otis is all talk and no substance. If he "was as bad as [his] breath [or his words], [he] would a been able to deal no matter how [the man] came at [him]."

Later, Otis openly displays his own confusion about the difference between the style and persona of his talk and the genuine character that manifests itself in action. In the confrontation with the man who kills him, Otis asks, "'[D]o you believe that style is character?'" (144). After the man slaps Otis, before finally stabbing him to death, he reminds Otis that "'[y]ou said style was character. . . . Well, let's see some'" (145). Otis has style but not the character to produce effective action. He is in some ways like the men in prison. He tries to create his persona and prescribe his actions through a jazzy, improvisational voice, but this voice generates a rigid, superficial code that is only a façade, which fails to substantiate genuine character and action. None of the black men in the text has substantive, genuine character, and therefore none is secure and free.

The portrayals of black women are part of the narrative that emphasizes the point about black men; their portrayals diametrically oppose the men's. For the black women, voice/style/persona do substantiate genuine character and effective action that put them in control and make them secure. Pauline knows that she is "on the sidelines," and she "ain't never claimed to be nowhere else." She never "make[s] a public appearance," but her kibitzing gives substance to her character and to effective action in a way that Otis's style and façade do not. Her words cut and silence Otis much more effectively than the mock actions of the man in the "fight" (116–17). Pauline knows how to make her words take action and fight, and she creates her place in the world by doing so. As Alice tells Melvin, "'That's why I like Pauline. She fights all the time'" (127).

Alice also fights "[e]very chance I get." Her voice is not jazzy and improvisational, but she projects a more conservative style and persona that substantiate her control and security in the world. Her talk with Melvin reveals her superiority, just as Pauline's exchange with Otis does.

> "I don't know about you, Melvin. Why can't you accept the fact that I see something in you I like? I don't know which is worse—a man who assumes I want him or someone like you who can't believe I would be interested in him at all. What I'd like from you, Melvin, is a little less opposition. Don't worry. I know what I'm doing."
>
> "I bow to your superior knowledge. . . ." (129)

Melvin responds to Alice ironically and sarcastically, but she really does "know what [she's] doing." For the black women, "style is character."

Both the general portrayal of superficial black male voice and identity that counters Melvin's achievement of voice and Melvin's similarly insecure identity before and after he achieves voice relates his characterization to the other black men's. After the conversation with Alice, Melvin moves toward actualizing the voice that will translate improvisational style into human(e) character capable of substantive, effective action. When he takes action that concretizes character, he reveals his insecurity and existential danger. He tells an improvised, creative story to the police that saves him and Otis from going to jail and that juxtaposes his voice and story to Otis's unsuccessful ones. (140–42). However, Melvin's central, defining spontaneous act that shortly follows the scene with the policemen relates him to Otis and other black men. He spontaneously tries to take a broken bottle from a boy fighting another boy in the aftermath of Otis's murder, and he gets stabbed and almost suffers the same fate as Otis. Later, at the hospital in conversation with the doctor (159–65), Melvin justifies his action. He has the following exchange with the doctor.

"But I didn't do what I did for those kids. I did it for myself. And you know, that was the first time I can remember doing something where I wasn't trying to prove something to somebody else?"
"And you damn near got yourself killed for your trouble."
"Well, at least it was my doing and not anyone else's."
"You're a fool.
"So what!"
"Touche!" (164)

Melvin firmly states his case, but the implications here are ambiguous in the context of the overall black male portrayal. Melvin says that he achieves self-affirmation in this instance, but the next instance of such spontaneous self-affirmation may kill him. Is he a fool in constant danger as the doctor clearly implies? The doctor's "[t]ouche" concession confirms Melvin's wit in being able to apply their common interpretation of a musical statement in a Miles Davis song (162–63)—"So what"—to Melvin's spontaneous, impulsive act. But this existential-sounding assertion has nothing to do with making Melvin secure or, even more basically, keeping him alive from the general black male perspective.

Melvin's spontaneity could easily have had the same results as Otis's rigid adherence to a style and façade, and any of the black men in prison who live through superficial style could have done the same thing. He ends this episode with the doctor by questioning himself and by trying to affirm his philosophy at the same time. He says, "Was Doctor Blue right about me being a fool? I walked out [of the hospital] into all of that and all the rest, hoping I'd be able to play the chord changes between what I did mind and what didn't matter" (165). In the last sentence, he uses his explicit reference to improvisational jazz style and the improvisational style of his own language as symbols of his ability to act spontaneously. Perhaps he is not a fool, but little more than luck separates Melvin from Otis and the fate of other black men.

The portrayal of Melvin's sexuality is another aspect of the text that fits its overall pattern that is shaded toward ambiguous and negative implications of black maleness. Melvin plays "[o]ne last riff before we hit it and quit" (166) to affirm his self-identity, security, and freedom. This "riff" is a four-page romantic/sexual episode with Alice (166–69). Alice gets Melvin to admit that he does not feel compassion for Otis. Compassion for Otis is "'what you're supposed to feel, and not what you do feel. You want to be on everybody's side but your own'" (166–67). She then rubs his wound, perhaps showing that she is on his "side" because she is his potential healer (167). They have sex, and near the end Alice warns Melvin that he must fight: "'I like you, Melvin, but we won't get along if you don't fight or try to stop me from fighting'" (169).

The text never represents the independent sexual acts of black men, individually and collectively, clearly as the expression of human(e) feeling and motivation. Throughout the text, Melvin is a sexually inept man with no substantive voice. After his wounding by another black male and potential healing by Alice, he has the first good sexual encounter of his life under the guidance of Alice. In a sense, Alice frees and authenticates him sexually, and she tells him how he should feel about himself and express himself. In effect, Alice defines significant aspects of his identity. But Melvin does nothing independently and in his own right; his inability to feel secure about his sexuality raises questions about the substance of his human(e) character. Nothing in the text shows that other black men are radically or significantly different.

Although Brown does not acknowledge it, *Tragic Magic* resonates with thematic echoes of *Invisible Man* throughout its entirety.[12] An example is a scene simultaneously reminiscent of *Invisible Man's* prologue, Battle Royal scene, and castration scene (*Tragic Magic* 148–58). This section of *Tragic Magic* seems to conflate thematic references and nuances of setting from various parts of *Invisible Man*. It recalls the prologue of *Invisible Man* when Melvin moves among multiple layers of reality as he considers the overall context of his life, his incarceration, and his freedom. The Invisible Man moves among multiple layers of reality when he tries to define his freedom in the novel's prologue, and on one level, he asks the old ex-slave, "'*Old woman, what is . . . freedom . . . ?*'" (*Invisible Man* 11) Also, the interaction among the boys trying to play the game, Melvin's inability to get the game right, and the boys' threatening language toward Melvin (*Tragic Magic* 149–50) recalls the Battle Royal scene from *Invisible Man,* where the Invisible Man does not understand that the other boys are playing a game during the fight scene (*Invisible Man* 22–26). After the fight in *Invisible Man,* the Invisible Man gives a speech and gets a briefcase for his efforts; Melvin gets a "'token of . . . appreciation [a hammer] for what he has done'" (*Tragic Magic* 154–55). Further, in chapter 25 of *Invisible Man*, several characters he has interacted with during the novel stand above him and threaten him before they castrate him (*Invisible Man* 569–70). In *Tragic Magic,* Melvin gets threatened—"Is his ass grass?" (*Tragic Magic* 154)—and various characters with whom he has interacted during the novel observe him (154) before he gets stabbed (155–56).

The "last riff" ends the novel with a passage recalling the ending of the epilogue of *Invisible Man:*

Everything that had happened over the last week had taken a lot out of me, and listening to Alice gave me the jitters. She was definitely up to something more than a little light sport. But I figured I had done enough fighting for a while and didn't know if I had the energy to get conjugated with her. A part of me wanted to renege and just lay dead. Hadn't I earned that right? I had paid my dues. Yet what I would trade off by basking in the non-use of myself could be even worse, since a thing never meant a thing until it moved.

I pulled Alice's full spoon-shape closer to me. (169)

Melvin decides to "come out" and take action very much like the Invisible Man, who at the end of the epilogue of Ellison's novel decides to come out from underground and take a "socially responsible role" (*Invisible Man* 581).

Reminiscent of *Invisible Man's* epilogue, which makes the narrator's empowerment to act uncertain, the "last riff" provides a "good" ending but does not displace the uncertainty about Melvin's ability to move from empty symbolism of voice to secure, liberated, human(e) actions in his life from the perspective of the general black male portrayal. (Brown's unconscious thematic and structural repetition of Ellison also repeats *Invisible Man's* restriction of the black male voice of liberation. My next chapter shows that the general literary influence of Ellison conflates with Calibanic discourse in the contemporary black male postmodern novel. *Tragic Magic* is a modernist black male novel in which both the effect of Calibanic discourse and the influence of Ellison are clear.)[13] Besides constructing and supporting Melvin's self-identity as much as, and perhaps more than, he does in his own right, Alice affirms his rejection of Otis's fraternity and implicitly the fraternity of all the other black men whose "side" he has taken. It is very much doubtful that Melvin can find the basis for constructing self-identity and support among black men and questionable whether he can do it individually without, somehow, learning how to "fight" on the terms of Alice and other black women. He claims that he has already been "fighting" and has already "paid dues," but the evidence in the text shows that his "fighting" has been sporadic, brief, and ineffectual overall. Nothing makes it clear that Melvin will be able to synthesize voice and action and "fight" the way that women "fight," the way that Alice demands that he "fight."

In spite of Brown's intention to portray Melvin's achievement of freedom in terms of a racist, existential reality, the text also unconsciously (re)inscribes Calibanic discourse through its overall structure and theme. The improvisational jazz voice symbolizes Melvin's freedom to express the self and live beyond the restraints imposed by society and by individuals. Melvin speaks in the voice throughout the novel, and at the end he discovers the improvisational action that actualizes his freedom. When he does act, he almost gets killed. This is the text's lesson about the precariousness of life and the tenuous quality of freedom. But there is also another story being told in which black women do have the voice to define a safe, secure, and liberated existence and human(e) qualities. Black men lack this voice, or at best they can define Melvin's very precarious freedom. What does the restriction of black male voice and freedom mean? In the process of telling Melvin's story of liberation, the text tells an ambiguous, paradoxical one that leaves the potential of black male liberating voice unclear and portrays black male insecurity and inferiority. The text works back toward (re)stating the Calibanic legacy of black men.

6

Ralph Ellison and the Literary Background of Contemporary Black Male Postmodern Writers

This chapter traces the literary tradition of Calibanic discourse as manifested in the contemporary black male postmodernist fictions of John Edgar Wideman, Clarence Major, and Charles Johnson. This tradition goes back to 1940 when Richard Wright published *Native Son,* which is when the black male voice first tried to express fully freedom in the context of realist/modernist/ postmodernist fiction. To serve his protest agenda, Wright consciously sets out to create a story of liberation that fails in order to show graphically the effects of white racism on Bigger Thomas. Within this context, *Native Son* portrays Bigger's failure of voice and general bestiality. Initially, this kind of restriction of voice and portrayal might seem necessary only as part of Wright's protest. However, Wright's restriction of voice in the terms of Calibanic discourse becomes clearer if one compares Bigger to Lutie Johnson in Ann Petry's *The Street* (1946). Lutie's story of liberation fails, but she is still not effectively voiceless, and certainly not bestial, like Bigger. During the 1940's, Chester Himes was a black male writer highly influenced by Wright, and he generally restricts the black male voice as Wright does.

The main emphasis of this chapter is the connection of Ralph Ellison to the postmodernist fictions and to the related critical voices of Wideman, Major, and Johnson. Ellison helped to set a new direction for black fiction by writing *Invisible Man* (1952) and defining his aesthetic in opposition to Wright in his critical discourse; he broke with Wright's social realism and opened the way for other narrative approaches in black fiction. It would be going too far to say that Ellison has had a significant influence on every black male writer since the publication of *Invisible Man,* but as a critic and fiction writer, Ellison has been the greatest influence on a large number of black male writers since the 1950s. This must be true, if for no other reason than the fact that black male writers who resisted Ellison's influence had to write themselves from beneath the shadow of *Invisible Man,* just as Ellison had to do with *Native Son.* Although Ellison opposed Wright, the story of liberation in *Invisible Man* is still challenged (contested) and compromised (restricted) in the terms that I have defined, and thus Ellison is generally one of the literary influences that contributes to the challenge and compromise of the black male story of liberation since the 1950s.

More specifically, Ellison is the most distinguishable figure whose work is a literary precursor to Calibanic discourse in the contemporary black male postmodernist novel; I focus on *Invisible Man* and use the critical discourse of both Ellison and the three writers to establish the background to the writers' work. Ellison's novel manifests the influence of Calibanic discourse and resonates with the (white) postmodernism of Wideman, Major, and Johnson, and the writers' critical discourse sometimes echoes Ellison's. (White) postmodernism can be appropriated, transformed, and voiced in black terms that thematize liberation or portray the clear potential for liberation; however, black male writers use it in an overall process that highlights Calibanic discourse's restriction of voice. As the explicit naming and account of writing in the epilogue shows, *Invisible Man* is concerned with the different versions of reality that it writes. In this context established by the epilogue, the text consists of multiple stories—multiple fictions—that it must manipulate to make the Invisible Man visible. Most importantly in the epilogue, the text must reconstruct the fiction of democracy against an unfathomable chaos. In the final analysis, however, the Invisible Man can only go so far, because he cannot de-center the dominant white fictions that render him invisible. In portraying dominant fictions that the narrator cannot deconstruct or de-center, *Invisible Man* prefigures the contemporary black male postmodernist novel in which the liberating potential of (white) postmodernism highlights the oppressive power of Calibanic discourse.

From Ellison's influence in the past, the writers get a resonance of (white) postmodernism and also the influence of Calibanic discourse. As Wideman's *Philadelphia Fire* (1990) shows, Calibanic discourse is the major cultural/semiotic influence that contests and restricts voice in the contemporary black male postmodernist novel. However, the cultural/semiotic is not separate from a secondary literary influence. Past and present coalesce; Ellison's fiction and critical discourse both respond to Calibanic discourse and conflate with it as part of a continuum of influences in the black male postmodernist novel as well as in Wideman's, Major's, and Johnson's critical discourse.

Unconscious Compromise of the Story of Liberation in *Invisible Man* and Unconscious Analogy in *Shadow and Act* and *Going to the Territory*

Johnson, Wideman, and Major have each created a body of nonfictional critical discourse, and the writers' critical discourse supports what they are doing in their fictions. That is, explicitly and implicitly, the writers often define black freedom and freedom for themselves as writers in the critical discourse. In this context, the critical discourse also responds to Calibanic discourse, particularly to its signification of black male voicelessness, and Calibanic discourse compromises the critical discourse's voice of liberation. In some instances, the critical discourse consciously responds to black male cultural proscription [as Johnson does when he talks about responding to "Caliban's dilemma" in *Being and Race* (40)], but more substantively, the critical discourse responds unconsciously, as do the fictions.

Bringing the critical discourse into my discussion, I use the term unconscious analogy, which refers to the manifestation of Calibanic discourse's influence in nonfictional critical discourse. Unconscious analogy is a traceable pattern and resonance of the voice in the fictions that is manifested or spoken disparately in the nonfictional critical discourse as paradoxical and ambiguous portrayal or de-formation of self, writer, or writing. From a different perspective, paradoxical and ambiguous portrayal or de-formation in the critical discourse are symbols of the restriction of the black male voice of liberation in the fictions. In the context of this study, unconscious analogy takes different forms among the different writers. An examination of Ellison's *Invisible Man* and his nonfictions will show a similar process leading to restriction and unconscious analogy, respectively, to that evident in the work of Wideman, Major, and Johnson, and it will illustrate how the novelistic past influences the discursive contours of contemporary works.

In *Invisible Man,* a partly implicit, partly explicit discursive process contests and restricts the story of liberation; the story duplicates some specifics of the patriarchal imposition on Caliban. Generally, the text restricts the black male story of liberation because it shows that in its quest to portray black humanity and civilization, it cannot escape the white patriarchy's imposition of bestiality and chaos, which white patriarchs such as Mr. Norton unconsciously fear are also "white" male and universal. Implied in this also is the signification of the texts of great white masters such as William Faulkner that produced similar black realities, which "distorted Negro humanity [and] seldom conceive[d] Negro characters possessing the full, complex ambiguity of the human" (*Shadow* 25). These constructed realities of blackness render all other black realities invisible.

The white patriarchy clearly and specifically signifies black men such as Trueblood (and sometimes the narrator) in the terms of Calibanic discourse; black men use various cultural forums or settings of counter-signifying and the black mask of invisibility as a form of counter-signifying to oppose the patriarchy by projecting alternative versions of reality.[1] The counter-signifying of black men only gives them, and ultimately the narrator, the text itself by the end, and Ellison implicitly, a liminal space of freedom: They cannot counter-signify or constitute their humanity and visibility against the hegemony of the white patriarchy.

The epilogue specifies that the Invisible Man is a writer (579) and poses a linguistic pattern (580–81), a fiction, that opposes the fictions of white patriarchal culture. The text analyzes both the illusory quality and dangerous power of language throughout its chapters; early in chapter 5, for example, the narrator realizes the emptiness of his own "words hurled to the trees of the wilderness, or into a well of slate-gray water; more sound than sense" (113). In the epilogue, the narrator says: "the mind that has conceived a plan of living must never lose sight of the chaos against which that pattern was conceived. That goes for societies as well as for individuals. Thus, having tried to give pattern to the chaos which lives within the pattern of your certainties, I must come out, I must emerge" (580–81). Chaos is the reality that the white patriarchy tries to impose a pattern on with the fiction of white American civilization; further, it is the disorder, intractability, and bestiality in human nature that white men deny in themselves and impose on the black humanity that they have also denied and made invisible. The fiction that the text poses attempts to signify against, to give pattern to and bring light to, this white patriarchal fiction.

The counter-signifying pattern of the text brings reality—both his own and the world's—to light for the narrator, producing a restricted space of freedom: It cannot free him from the confines of invisibility hegemonically imposed by the patterns of white culture. The counter-signifying pattern of the text reveals to the narrator that he can find freedom within the confines of invisibility. The narrator says: "Step outside the narrow borders of what men call reality and you step into chaos—ask Rinehart, he's a master of it— or imagination" (576). Stepping outside the definitions of reality as defined by white culture does not mean abandoning a pattern of reality and truth, which is to give oneself up to any and all patterns, a Rinehartian approach that concedes to the formlessness, disorder, and chaos beneath everything.

He can use his imagination to constitute a world that rejects the binary pattern of white civilization and black disorder and intractability. He can impose a pattern of universal humanity on the world that is liberating.

In his imagination, the narrator reduces the textual problematics by giving a different pattern to the world that allows him to liberate himself and emerge from underground. However, this is only a pattern of *his* imagination: His imagination and the counter-signifying pattern of the text cannot free him from the signification of black bestiality and primitiveness imposed over the invisibility of blackness by the white patriarchy. When the narrator emerges, he will be visible to himself and the world will be visible to him, but he will not be free of the signification of a white patriarchy that imposes its own patterns on him. *Invisible Man* places a tentative, restricted fiction of freedom in the foreground.[2]

Shadow and Act (1964) and *Going to the Territory* (1986) unconsciously analogize Calibanic discourse and its restriction of voice. The texts clearly counter-signify the shortcomings of the white tradition and its masters and of American culture. However, a white cultural voice, which articulates the aesthetic and literary superiority of the white tradition and writers over the Negro tradition and writers, and which articulates a preference for the "American" over the Negro, speaks louder than the black counter-signifying voice. *Shadow* and *Territory* are both forms of counter-signifying in the public forum of print; along with signifying against the white tradition, the texts subtly place Ellison among the supposedly untouchable white male masters. However, the texts' black counter-signifying is an integral part of a concession to the greater importance of white Western literature and tradition and American culture.

Two quotations, the first from *Shadow* and the second from *Territory,* show the texts' view of the importance of the white literary tradition and writers as compared to the Negro tradition and writers, and show the importance of their American experience for Negro writers as compared to their Negro experience. In "The World and the Jug," in a now-famous passionate denial of Irving Howe's claim that Richard Wright influenced him, Ellison responds to Howe: "[P]erhaps you will understand when I say that [Wright] did not influence me if I point out that while one can do nothing about choosing one's relatives, one can, as artist, choose one's 'ancestors.' Wright was, in this sense, a 'relative'; Hemingway an 'ancestor.' Langston Hughes, whose work I knew in grade school and whom I knew before I knew Wright, was a 'relative'; Eliot, whom I was to meet only many years later, and Malraux and Dostoievsky and Faulkner, were 'ancestors'—if you please or don't please!" (140).

The second quotation, from "A Very Stern Discipline," names two of the same writers and talks about the importance of the "American-ness of [the Negro writer's] experience."

The Jewish American writers have, [as opposed to Negro writers], identified with Eliot, Pound, Hemingway, and Joyce *as writers* while questioning and even rejecting their various attitudes toward the Jews, toward religion, politics, and many other matters. They have taken possession of that which they could use from such writers and converted it . . . to express their own definitions of the American experience. But we Negro writers seem seldom to have grasped this process of acculturation. Too often we've been in such haste to express our anger and our pain as to allow the single tree of race to obscure our view of the magic forest of art.

. . . What the Jewish American writer had to learn before he could find his place was the American-ness of his experience. He had to see himself as American and project his Jewish experience as an experience unfolding within this pluralistic society. When this was done, it was possible to project this variant of the American experience as a metaphor for the whole. (278–79)

These are the prevailing views in *Shadow* and *Territory* of the superiority of white Western literature, tradition, and writers and of the importance of the American experience above the Negro experience for the Negro writer. Ellison's description of literary and cultural integration unconsciously analogizes Calibanic discourse's restriction of voice in black male fiction. The influence of Negro literature and writers should be insignificant by comparison to white literature and writers, and the pluralistic "American" should speak louder than the provincial "Negro."

In the introduction to *Shadow,* Ellison talks about finding his voice as a Negro writer in American and European literature, contributing to that literature, and changing its view of reality at the same time: "More important and inseparable from this particular effort, was the necessity of determining my true relationship to that body of American literature to which I was most attracted and through which, aided by what I could learn from the literatures of Europe, I would find my *own voice,* and to which I was challenged, by way of achieving myself, to make some small contribution, and to whose composite picture of reality I was obligated to offer some necessary modifications" (xix; italics mine).

Here, Ellison's subtle counter-signifying is an integral part of a concession to the greater importance of white Western literature, tradition, and culture. Ellison places himself among the great masters by making "some small contribution" to the great Western tradition, and also signifies against it—subtly criticizes it—by stating his obligation "to offer some necessary modifications." However, the highly predominant idea is that Ellison's *"own voice"* is one that speaks through a powerful white tradition, not a black one.[3]

On a symbolic level, the last two essays in *Shadow* and *Territory*, "An American Dilemma: A Review" and "Perspective on Literature," respectively, more explicitly analogize the discursive process initiated by Calibanic discourse and its restriction of the story of liberation. The essays explicitly respond to a negative signification of blackness by American culture, which parallels Calibanic discourse's signification of black men, but they also concede to the greater significance of American culture, which parallels Calibanic discourse's challenge and compromise of the story of liberation.

In "*An American Dilemma,*" Ellison talks about the process that whites and Negroes must undergo to realize an American humanity. He discusses a white American cultural/psychological signification of blackness: A white "'conflict [of] . . . moral valuations [exists] on various levels of consciousness'" (304). Indeed, it seems very unconscious: "*An American Dilemma . . .* [shows] how [a] mechanism of prejudice operates to disguise the moral conflict [to make it unconscious] in the minds of whites." At the end, the essay stresses that the races must overcome their pathologies, and Negroes, especially, must make themselves "more human American[s]" (317). Ellison does not conclude that Negroes should develop a voice that articulates that which is "much of great value" (316) in Negro culture or that articulates Negro humanity free of "the white American mind" (304). In light of the racism analyzed early in the essay, the voicing of Negro humanity and freedom would seem logical, but there is no black male voice that speaks in terms that are black and that frees, humanizes, and empowers.

In "Perspective on Literature," Ellison focuses on an American individualism that implies an individual will, consciousness, and ability to act beyond the unconscious symbolization/signification of Negroes that he names a few pages earlier. He first talks about the symbolization/signification "Negro" that has become "firmly embedded in the operation of the American language" (336) and thus embeds an unconscious cultural signification, apart from the conscious will of the individual. In this context, "Negro Americans were all unwittingly endowed with the vast powers of the linguistic negative, and would now be intricately involved in the use and misuse of a specific American form of symbolic action, the terminology of democracy." Negroes are also unwitting, or unconscious, of the power of their unconscious constitution through language in the "symbolic action . . . of democracy." At the end, Ellison says that this must be "raised to consciousness," and then the individual will have the ability, implied in the concept of democracy, to act consciously out of the resources of the self beyond the unconscious forces of culture manifested in linguistic symbolization/signification (338).

Ellison collapses a category of semiotics, where the unconscious subject is the product of unconscious cultural constitution through language, into the category of liberal humanism, where the individual acts freely and consciously in democracy. The "collectivity of [democratic] individuals" (338) can take away the negative symbolization "Negro" by making Negroes "American." However, one cannot collapse these incompatible, contradictory categories and achieve this so easily. The hegemonic language of the patriarchy will not signify black freedom, humanity, and empowerment; the true reality is the negative "Negro" symbolization/signification (335–36). Ellison's categorical jump to claim the individual Negro "American" hides the negative "Negro" symbolization/signification at the same time that it concedes to its power. The "American" subsumes the "Negro"; there may be at least a restricted space of freedom in the former.

Calibanic Discourse, Unconscious Analogy, and the Influence of Ralph Ellison in John Edgar Wideman's Fictions and Critical Discourse

Unconscious analogy takes a different form in Wideman's critical statements, some of which he makes in interviews, than it takes in the work of Major and Johnson, who have published critical books that talk about writing. Wideman's comments show that undoubtedly many writers have influenced him, but Ellison is a very important and distinguishable one among them. At various places in his critical statements, Wideman clearly implies the influence of Ellison's nonfictional critical discourse and references *Invisible Man* as a central influence on him.[4] Ellison's fiction and critical discourse are important secondary literary influences on voice in Wideman's postmodernist fictions and critical discourse that are inseparable from Calibanic discourse's cultural/semiotic influence.

Sometimes in his critical discourse, Wideman speaks in a voice of unconscious analogy very much like Ellison's. Wideman has said that in his early career he tried to appropriate white literary masters, mostly white male ones, to authenticate his work. This appropriation parallels Ellison's emulous, counter-signifying behavior toward white male writers as he describes it in *Shadow* and *Territory*. In interviews over the years, Wideman clearly articulates different phases of his career that are unique to him and that make him distinct from Ellison, but the description of the early career echoes Ellison's description of his own. In a 1989 interview, Wideman says: "I was trying to hook that world [of the 'Great Tradition'] into what I thought would give those [black] situations and people a kind of literary resonance, legitimize that [black] world by infusing echoes of T.S. Eliot, Henry James, Faulkner, English and Continental masters"[5] (Rowell 54–55).

Wideman and Ellison name, emulate, and implicitly rival the most prominent white male writers; in doing so, they place themselves among these writers and signify against a tradition and group of writers that consider black literature and black writers inferior. However, black literature, tradition, and culture only attain "resonance" and legitimacy by an infusion of the "echoes" of the "Great [White] Tradition." The white voice establishes a hegemony over the black voice in Wideman's description of his early work.

The critical statements sometimes reference Ellison and imply the liberating postmodern potential of *Invisible Man,* but Wideman's fictions restrict voice in a context of liberating postmodernist potential, just as *Invisible Man* does. In interviews and more recent statements, Wideman ties himself to Ellison and links both himself and Ellison to a fluid, multiple-voiced, de-centered (white) version of postmodernism. Wideman sometimes says that he finds personal freedom when writing his fictions and implies the potential for liberating voice in these fictions similar to *Invisible Man*'s. In contrast to the interviews and statements, his recent fictions highlight the incompatibility of black voice and liberation with the fluid, de-centered freedom defined in the terms of (white) postmodernism.

In a 1989 interview, Wideman implies the postmodernist influence on recent works such as "Fever" (1989) and *Philadelphia Fire,* both of which he talks about in the interview. He discusses a "play" in his writing that positions his recent work outside the modernist seriousness of purpose and theme of Eliot, Faulkner, and Hemingway and of his early work. Wideman says that his written narrative is a "multiple, fluid," de-centered, postmodernist narrative that liberates him through its "play" instead of limiting him to a serious job; writing liberates him because it allows "personal expression" that is "arbitrary.... [and even] silly . . . [and] profane." Wideman is "talking to you in the writing," but he is also "trying to take something away from you. Multiple consciousness and energy, the fluid situation of freedom that multiple consciousness creates, that's what I mean by play" (Rowell 56–57).

Philadelphia Fire and other recent fictions shift Wideman's comments to a black context that makes it clear how different the achievement of black male voice and black liberation is from the achievement of fluid, multiple, de-centered freedom described through Wideman's paradigm of (white) postmodernism. In *Philadelphia Fire,* because of the conscious and unconscious effects of Calibanic discourse, Wideman cannot "play" with the words "father" and "son" to make them tell the liberating story (103). No playful consciousness mediates the angst about the narrative's potential failure to do the serious job of black liberation. Also, in *Philadelphia Fire,* Wideman specifically talks about "[i]magin[ing] our fictions imagining us" (97–98), which suggests the postmodernist "[m]ultiple consciousness and energy, the fluid situation of freedom that multiple consciousnes creates," he talks about in the interview. However, in the novel, "[m]ultiple" voices that constitute reality, particularly the voice of Calibanic discourse, threaten black freedom and contest and restrict the black voice that constitutes a liberating black male fiction. In the novel, Wideman sounds doubtful that he can create the fiction that will liberate. In the interview, the black male liberating voice speaks in terms of liberating postmodernist potential, the same terms that highlight the restriction of voice in the fictions.

Wideman has specifically linked Ellison and *Invisible Man* to this potentially liberating postmodernist context. He talks about Ellison in one instance of his more recent critical statements when he says that liberating, "alternative versions of reality" represent an influence by Ellison at the same time that they represent, in essence, a postmodernist influence.

[A]s the assumptions of the mono-culture are challenged, overrun, defrock themselves daily in full view of the shameless media, more and more of the best fiction gravitates toward the category of "minority." The truth that each of us starts out alone, a minority of one, each in a slightly different place (no place), resides somewhere in the lower frequencies of our communal consciousness. New worlds, alternative versions of reality are burgeoning. In spite of enormous, overwhelming societal pressures to conform, to standardize the shape and meaning of individual lives, voices like Ralph Ellison's reach us, impelling us to attend to the *chaos which lives within the pattern* of our certainties.

Good stories transport us. . . . inside another's skin. Mysteriously, the dissolution of ego also sharpens the sense of self, reinforces independence and relativity of point of view. People's lives resist a simple telling, cannot be understood safely, reductively from some static still point, some universally acknowledged center around which all other lives orbit. . . . When a culture hardens into heliocentricity . . . when otherness is imagined as a great darkness except for what the star illuminates, it's only a matter of time until the center collapses in upon itself, imploding with sigh and whimper. (*Breaking Ice* vi)

Wideman seems to suggest that finding voice among multiple, de-centered realities in *Invisible Man* and in his own work creates freedom. However, *Invisible Man, Philadelphia Fire,* and other recent fictions by Wideman try and potentially fail to center liberating black realities to counter and close out harmful white ones. These fictions do not voice black male freedom within or through the potential of (white) postmodernism. The fact that "the most powerful voices are always steeped in unutterable silences" (*Breaking Ice* x) does not mean that the black male voice can be a powerful one that articulates freedom. In the fictions, Calibanic discourse contests and restricts black male voice, which "silences" it to an extent. Calibanic discourse is a "powerful" voice because of its unconscious hegemony.[6]

To a very limited point, black male freedom in Wideman's and Ellison's fictions may be the unrestricted freedom that Wideman talks about in his critical statements, a freedom that is consistent with the potential of (white) postmodernism. However, much more substantively, it is a restricted black male freedom that anticipates, in Ellison's case, and constitutes, in Wideman's, a black context where the potential of (white) postmodernism to liberate does not materialize. Wideman's thematized black male writers in *Philadelphia Fire* do not seem to define "[their] sense of self" (*Breaking Ice* vi) in a fashion that liberates. And they can by no means be sure that their fictions mediate the "otherness" created by the "mono-culture" and give voice and definition to the "others." Similarly, the Invisible Man has a compromised, liminal freedom created by the possibility of his linguistic construction. This is a freedom compromised "betwixt-and-between" invisibility and visibility.[7] Invisibility means having the self dissolved in "otherness" by white fictions; visibility means having the self realized through the Invisible Man's linguistic construction. The Invisible Man is doubtful that his fiction will make him, and others like him, visible.

Generally, Wideman's nonfictional comments about his writing reveal his influence by and relationship to Ellison in both his fictions and criticism. Ellison's critical discourse influences the voice of Wideman's early critical statements, and the later critical statements that evoke *Invisible Man* and its postmodernist potential call attention to a paradoxical restriction of voice in the fictions of both writers. In the critical statements, Wideman sometimes speaks in a voice of unconscious analogy that is similar to Ellison's but also speaks an unambiguous, unrestricted liberating voice of postmodernist potential opposing the contested and restricted voice of liberation in his and Ellison's fictions. In this latter critical context, the writers' fictions are a crucible that brings to bear cultural dynamics that restrict voice in a way that it is not restricted in Wideman's critical statements.

The Connection of Anti-Realistic De-formation in Major's and Ellison's Discourse

Past and present coalesce in a continuum of secondary literary and primary cultural/semiotic influences. Ellison's fiction and critical discourse are both influenced by Calibanic discourse and conflate with it as an influence in the fictions and critical discourse of later black male writers. This is true for Wideman, and the same is true in different ways and from different perspectives for Major and Johnson.

For Major, the obvious literary influence is the mostly white writers who write postmodernist, highly self-referential narratives. However, Ellison's work is also a very substantive influence that builds the foundation of Major's work. Looking at Major's novels, one would not initially think that this is true, but Major's nonfiction book *The Dark and Feeling* (1974) reveals that it is. *Dark* articulates an anti-realistic de-formation of self, writer, and writing consistent with Ellison's fiction and philosophy and central to Major's, and speaks in terms that implicitly connect de-formation to the postmodernist modes of Major's more recent fictions.

Structural and thematic de-formation—that is, "shifting" and destabilization that converge with chaos—is the key: It starts with Ellison's fiction and critical discourse, provides essential material for the foundation of Major's fiction and critical discourse, and inseminates Major's more recent postmodern fictions. From this perspective, the various aspects of the writers' fictional and critical voices relate; the literary influence of Ellison is inseparable from the primary cultural/semiotic influence of Calibanic discourse in Major's texts. On one hand, de-formation means that the black writer is free to explore the mystery and complexity of the individual self through the postmodernist potential of language to suggest the universal chaos the self encounters and the taboos the self encounters in society. On the other, de-formation restricts the definition of black male voice and the black male quest in the underlying black male story of liberation as Calibanic discourse does. The freedom to explore that it gives the writer in the first instance contrasts the restriction of voice and definition in the second.

A common story of the writer in both the fictions and critical discourse emerges as the two writers critique their own writing. The writers define a similar universal humanity in their story of the quest for freedom in the critical discourse. In *Shadow and Act* and *Going to the Territory*, Ellison talks about portraying a complex, mysterious, and paradoxical universal humanity in its societal interaction, and about showing the nature of reality, which is chaos. In this context, the ultimate goal of the writer is to enhance the importance of the individual in the process of pursuing a truly human democracy. This pursuit does not impose order and eliminate chaos. However, the novel allows the writer somehow to survive the confrontation with "the nature of the soul and the nature of society. . . . to survive the consequences of encountering the chaos he must reckon with when he attempts to deal with the basic truths of human existence" (*Territory* 310–11). Ellison goes beyond social realism to uncover a basic "democracy" of human life that is a necessary constituent part of true democracy. Unlike Ellison, Major does not specify the novel's role in achieving a true democracy; however, he does have ideas about the novel and art embodying the universal traits of human existence that are consistent with Ellison's portrayal of universal humanity. In *Dark*, Major associates Ellison's anti-realistic approach with his own portrayal of a universal "inner life," a "'hidden system of organization' [that is]. . . .present in all life and therefore should be in all art" (19).

One of the most obvious indications of Ellison's influence on Major is his general reference to Ellison's fiction and ideas as the basis for the aesthetic standards of black fiction. For example, *Invisible Man* is the first among the novels that Major holds in "high esteem" in "Formula or Freedom" (26–27), and Ellison's anti-sociological, anti-realistic approach that strives for what Major calls the "wholly human novel" (25) is also Major's approach and goal in his writing. Further, Major finds a "mystery of being [that is] . . . beneath our urge to communicate" (22). The self, the individual manifestation of being, is difficult to express; in his first novel, *All-Night Visitors* (1969), Major "finally through . . . hard work . . . came (in Ralph Ellison's words) 'to possess and express' the spirit and to understand *with feeling* the footnotes on who and what I was" (15). The "so-called self" is a "shifting" entity that he tried to portray in his second novel, *No* (1973), by giving the main character, Moses, multiple names, roles, and identities (141–42). Major says that he uses Moses's character to exploit "a range of taboos, fears, cultural limitations, and social traits, springing from attitudes concerning a wide range of human experience, sexual, racial, bi-racial, national and personal" (17). Major relates this to an anti-realism: "I think most of the trouble [in black writing] stems from a fear of or disrespect for one's inner life, the unconscious experience, and its interplay with one's conscious life. The social realist can never suggest that 'hidden system of organization' because he has never touched it." (19). Talking about the "interplay" between the conscious and unconscious is another way of expressing the mysterious, "shifting" self. This self lacks clear definition and is either lost within its own "shifting," chaotic conditions or is limited by society, or both.

Juxtaposing *Invisible Man* and other texts by Ellison and Major reveals similar themes and expressions of the self that exemplify this. Major's comments in *Dark* about coming to understand "who and what I was" echo Ellison's words in "A Very Stern Discipline" (1967), an interview from *Territory*. Ellison said that during his Harlem experience, "I wanted room . . . to discover who I was" (290). Also, the Invisible Man during his Harlem experience says, "When I discover who I am, I'll be free" (243). Further, knowing the self and expressing the self, with all of its complexities and oppositions, its ultimate chaos, is a central quest in *Invisible Man*. Not only does this relate to the Invisible Man and his self-discovery. It also relates to Rinehart as the dominant symbol of the chaos of human personality, the chaos of self. Rinehart is change and metamorphosis personified, and he is both enlightening and challenging for the Invisible Man in his quest for self. Rinehart realizes his existence by using the formless chaos of self to exploit society's taboos, fears, limitations, and general blindness. (Ellison says, "Rinehart is my name for the personification of chaos" [*Shadow* 181]. The "P" [in B.P. Rinehart] is for 'Proteus'" [56]). The Invisible Man, realizing the need of a socially responsible role in democracy, understands Rinehart's reality but cannot exploit society as he does. Moses Westby in *No* is a lot like the Invisible Man, but even more like Rinehart. Society for Moses is a "penal colony" that he opposes through the proteanlike reality of the self. Whether it is the proteanlike Moses or another one of Major's main characters, the self in the discursive process and development of Major's fictions is mysterious and "shifting" and close to chaos.

A critical description of the postmodern in Major's work relates the postmodern to the mysterious, de-formed self and art as portrayed by both writers, and further connects various aspects of the writers' voices. Major's fictions "thematize a self-reflexive process of the creation of a dynamic, multi-faceted self and art. Each novel is [progressively] . . . more fragmented and discontinuous in structure . . . and each engages in self-conscious linguistic play that blurs the line between the worlds of fantasy and social reality" (Bell, "Major's Double Consciousness" 8). This is consistent with Major's description of the mysterious, "shifting," "so-called" self and anti-realistic fiction that he talks about in *Dark* (141–42). It is also consistent with Ellison's description of the novel as a dynamic form that enables the writer to deal with the ultimate mystery of chaos (*Territory* 310–11). Furthermore, various acts of linguistic play in *Invisible Man*, sometimes clearly thematized and self-conscious, blur the lines between fantasy and reality and make parts of the text's structure fragmented and discontinuous in ways that are congruent with this analysis of the postmodern in Major. Fragmentation and discontinuity are also representations of *Invisible Man*'s de-formation and mystery.

As far as the fictions are concerned, Major takes his voice from Ellison, whose voice is a precursor of (white) postmodernism in the black male text, extending and taking the voice further than any other black writer. For both writers, the liberating postmodernist potential of "self-conscious linguistic play" highlights the restricting power of Calibanic discourse in the underlying narrative of their fictions. Although *All-Night Visitors* and *No* may seem to have little in common with *Invisible Man,* the self and the art of these texts more clearly relate to the art and character portrayal of *Invisible Man* in light of the writers' critical discourse. *Reflex and Bone Structure* (1973), *Emergency Exit* (1979), and *My Amputations* (1986) seem to have even less in common with *Invisible Man.* (And indeed, these two latter texts also seem to be outside the black fictional tradition.) However, again in the context of the writers' critical discourse, these texts also relate to *Invisible Man* because they portray art and self in terms of the de-formed, "shifting," and mysterious.

The Phenomenology of Formless Being and the Influence of Ellison in Johnson's Fictions and Critical Discourse

The relationship between Ellison and Johnson is unique, but there are parallels and general similarities philosophically between this relationship and Ellison's and Major's. As is the case in looking at Major's work, one may initially find that Johnson is radical and significantly outside the black tradition, which is his intention. Much of Johnson's radical approach develops from his phenomenology, which seems to be influenced solely by "white" ideas and philosophy, just as mostly white writers seem to influence Major's self-referential metafiction. However, just as the foundational concept of deformation in Major's fiction and critical discourse has its origin in Ellison's influence, Johnson's central phenomenological concept of "formless being" originates with Ellison at the same time that it is the product of "white" philosophy.

In conceptual terms broadly similar to those of the relationship between Major and Ellison, Ellison's fiction and critical discourse are both influenced by Calibanic discourse and conflate with it as an influence in Johnson's fiction and critical discourse. Johnson makes clear his connections to Ellison while simultaneously defining his intersubjective/phenomenological paradigm, which he makes an explicit thematization that is the basis of his writing. In *Being and Race* (1988), Johnson names *Invisible Man* as "one of those rare books that cannot be ignored [and which] provided an artistic direction for black writing in the 1970s" (17); "its central idea [is] that meaning cannot be fixed, that Being is formless, a field of imagination and possibility that defies intellectual systemization" (16). In both his fictions and critical discourse, Johnson's main theme is a phenomenological formless being similar to Major's "mystery of being" (*Dark* 22). Formless being is a basic concept in *Invisible Man,* in Ellison's critical discourse, and in Johnson's fictions and critical discourse. In the writers' fictions, achieving formless being entails deforming black maleness and the black male quest for freedom; at the same time that they de-form black maleness and the black male quest, the fictions (re)inscribe Calibanic discourse symbolically through thematic development and (re)inscribe its qualities specifically through character portrayal. The writers' critical discourse deals with this same theme of formless being, and the voice there is a symbol or unconscious analogy of the voice in the fictions. (In Johnson's case, the voice of the critical discourse sometimes straightforwardly restates the same idea instead of symbolically restating it.) In addition, Johnson announces his "own quirky variations on phenomenology" (*Being* ix), but his paradigm generally is postmodern. Its de-centered, formless postmodernist subject coincides with the resonance of (white) postmodernism in *Invisible Man.*

Johnson's and Ellison's fictions and critical discourse constitute a broad discursive setting in which the black male voice of liberation is similarly contested and restricted/negated in the general context of the symbolic and specific development of the concept of formless being. Both writers establish a relationship of the white over the black in which the white voice is dominant or the black voice is negated. Johnson criticizes the white Western tradition at the same time that he makes himself part of it (*Being* 39). Johnson places his textual portrayals among those in the white Western tradition. Johnson's bracketing of the white tradition to present his own fresh perceptions is not a way of signifying on the tradition's moral vision to modify it as Ellison does, but it is a linguistic play within the tradition to broaden its vision and change it at the same time. However, Ellison and Johnson both concede the greater importance of the white tradition and perspective, and Ellison and Johnson, respectively, advocate submerging the black voice in the white and giving it up to the white. Ellison submerges the black voice of protest into the "magic forest of art" (*Territory* 278) and the "Negro" into the "American." Johnson finds freedom in giving up the "all too easy [black] interpretations of our being in the world" ("Philosophy" 60). Ultimately the black writer/subject must lose its black voice in this tradition before it can free itself.

Johnson reverses, extends, elides, and modifies Ellison's formulations in the process of inventing his phenomenological paradigm: "Ellison gets the point wrong, or backward: it is not reality or the world that is formless and fluid but human perception—consciousness itself that allows us infinitely to perceive meaning as a phenomenon of change, transformation, and process; it is Mind (the subject pole of experience), not Matter (the object pole), that gives the perceived world a polymorphous character" (*Being* 16). Johnson de-centers and destabilizes the subject, makes it formless and fluid. The subject merges into the polymorphous world that it perceives. Concomitantly, it creates a space of freedom that is open-ended and without borders. A process of constant change and transformation, in which it is ever in polymorphic combination with everything else, constitutes the subject, and this is its open-ended, borderless freedom.

Johnson's emphasizes open-ended textuality and written literature in constituting his phenomenological paradigm, and Ellison also emphasizes open-ended textuality and the written tradition. In the following quotation, Johnson grounds his phenomenology in the process of intertextual debate and revision that he thinks produces all art, including fiction, and in the written tradition:

Malraux tells us that "artists do not stem from their childhood, but from their conflicts with the achievements of their predecessors; not from their formless world, but from their struggle with the forms which others have imposed on life." Some of this curious idea can be seen in, for example, figure-drawing classes, where you stand with the canvas to your side and with brush poised as you study the model at the front of the room, and then, miraculously, something happens in the flickerish moment between shifting your gaze from the model, with all his concrete, specific, individual features, to the canvas. You have drawn, you discover, not *his* hand but instead your *idea* of how a hand should look, an idea built up doubtlessly from viewing, not hundreds of individual models, but rather other artists' renditions of the hand. It is precisely this heavily conditioned seeing, this calcification of perception, that figure-drawing classes seek to liberate—we might well call this retraining of the eye the artist's equivalent to the phenomenological *epoché*, or "bracketing" of all presuppositions in order to seize a fresh, original vision.
    Malraux's point is that often the apprentice artist, thinking about the world of experience transfigured in the text—a novel, painting, poem, or film—says, "That's not so." Or, "He didn't get it quite right." He might also say, "How perfectly done. Let *me* reply with a composition of my own." Whatever the case, fiction—indeed, all art—points to others with whom the writer argues about what *is*. He cannot begin *ex nihilo*. He must have models with which to agree, partly agree, or outright oppose, and these can come only from the tradition of literature itself, for Nature seems to remain silent, providing no final text or court of judgment. If any of these ruminations sound reasonable, does it seem possible that the "black experience" in literature truly exists only there—*in* literature—and therefore must vary from one author's viewpoint to the next, with nothing invariant in the "experience" that we can agree on as final? (4–5)

Johnson's and Ellison's ideas about textuality are only slightly different. For Ellison, the text is open-ended because its linguistic patterns cannot impose order and closure on the unfathomable chaos that is reality, and cannot always subvert other patterns that those in power pose as reality. For Johnson, the text is open-ended because each author phenomenologically brackets the written textual portrayals of other authors and poses his own fresh, new portrayal as part of an intertextual process. Further, in *Shadow and Act*, Ellison names a body of American and European written literature and a group of white writers as his influences. Johnson says in the preceding quotation that the black experience exists only "in [written] literature." (Johnson largely leaves out the effect of oral discourse and oral culture on the writer.) Also, he implies above what he states more specifically in *Oxherding Tale* (118–19): that it is all the various Western written traditions that influence his work.[8]

Johnson uses the ideas of phenomenologist Maurice Merleau-Ponty to create a layered Lifeworld of words, books, and traditions in which meaning is synchronously generated by writers in all the past and in the present: "[W]hat we have, from the standpoint of phenomenology, are not different worlds but instead innumerable perspectives on *one* world; and we know that, when it comes to the crunch, we share, all of us [according to Merleau-Ponty], the same cultural Lifeworld—a world layered with ancestors, predecessors, and contemporaries. To think of this world properly is to find that all perspectives take us directly to a common situation, a common history in which all meanings evolve"(44).

Interaction in this Lifeworld—readers with writers and writers with writers—is a surrender of perception, a surrender of self: "To read is to inhabit the role and real place of others;[9] to write is a stranger experience yet, for it involves a corresponding act of self-surrender such that my perceptions and experiences are allowed to coincide with those who came before me and despoiled words, shaped their sense and use, who impose the 'accumulation' of sense . . . upon us until my life and the life of others 'intersect and engage each other like gears,' according to Merleau-Ponty" (39).

This is Johnson's borderless, open-ended space of the black writer/black subject. In its surrender, the subject simultaneously asserts its perceptions against all the previous others and becomes an additional part of those perceptions. The subject gets transformed from its own perceptions into the other perceptions in an endless process. To free itself, the subject loses itself. In the final analysis, Johnson uses his own terms, and invents his own unique paradigm. However, both Ellison and Johnson claim that there is a body of written literature—a large part of it white literature—to which he, the subject/writer, responds. Ellison says that he makes "some small contribution [and] . . . offers some necessary modifications" to the "composite picture of reality" (*Shadow* XIX). Johnson says much the same thing and tries to do this also.

As the writers' critical discourse makes clear, the influence of Ellison is central to Johnson's work, and it is inseparable from the constitution of voice in his fictions and critical discourse. From the specific perspective of Johnson's and Ellison's literary relationship, the portrayal of formless being unconsciously (re)inscribes Calibanic discourse in the fictions, and the conceptualization in the critical discourse is a symbolic negation/restriction that unconsciously analogizes the voice in the fictions.

Conclusion

The "Special Edge" Tension Between the Conscious and Unconscious in the Contemporary Black Male Postmodern Novel

I begin the conclusion by emphasizing the accomplishment of contemporary black male writers, especially Wideman, Major, and Johnson, in spite of the impact of Calibanic discourse. Wideman has made comments in a recent interview that help me to move toward summing up the success and importance of black male writers in the context of the foregoing chapters.

When I'm really going well, afterwards, I can sit down with [the writing] just as a critic might and say, "oh yeah, this book embodies great time, because characters move without any kind of barriers between past and present and future. The dead can talk to the living, the living can talk to the dead." So when the writing really works, it means I'm speaking from inside the culture, African-American culture, representing the depths and the complexity that I have taught myself by residing consciously and unconsciously within it. (Berben-Masi 577)

[T]here is a rhythm, a musical tension between the conscious me—what I know, what I've learned, what I think about—and the person that I am at a level of unconscious being. I want those two to integrate without losing their separate identities. . . . it is the tension between the [conscious and unconscious], the sort of mysterious way that the two can dialogue, that might give the writing its special edge, when it has that edge. (577–78)

Our everyday sense of reality is oppressive in the sense that it works unconsciously and stifles choice or is directive without your knowing it. I think that's the worst kind of oppression because it's invisible. (582)

The language is subversive, its oppositional and subversive and not just for show but for go. If you're fighting for space, if you're fighting for voice, who knows what the final result will be. Because that space, once it's achieved, has a way of expanding, of incorporating, and you can't exactly make a distinction between the disciplined space and the larger space. They begin to bleed into one another. (584)

The "space" of the postmodern in which the black male writer seizes language to tell his story is where Wideman works, and where black male writers "fight for voice." The result of the quest, which Wideman says is uncertain, is unconsciously restricted liberating voice that is often an aspect of very powerful and good writing with a "special edge."

Wideman always speaks "from inside the culture . . . representing the depths and complexity that [he has] taught himself by residing consciously and unconsciously within it." *The Cattle Killing,* which I analyze along with *Reuben,* is an example of this remarkable depth and complexity. It symbolically restricts voice and (re)inscribes Calibanic discourse in its overall discursive process, which concludes ambiguously and paradoxically with the conversation between Wideman and his son Dan, who are both writers. In *Fatheralong* (1994), Wideman could be talking about the ending of *Cattle Killing* when he explains how the "paradigm of race works to create distance between sons and fathers" (71).

One of the worst aspects of this distance is the unwitting complicity of the victims perpetuating it. Because we don't talk or can't talk father to son . . . each generation approaches the task of becoming men as if no work has been accomplished before. . . . Imagine how different we might be if we really listened to our fathers' stories. If we preserved them, learned to make them part of our lives. Wouldn't the stories, if known and performed over generations, be infused with the power of our music. . . . Power to link us as our music links power to plant seeds, nurture them, celebrate their growth.

Our fathers' stories, like their songs, their bodies, can be stolen, silenced, alienated from them, sold, corrupted. We must learn to resist those who come between us, those who destroy the messages we must pass on. (71–72)

In the context of this study's analysis, it is the unconscious signification of the language itself that causes distance and prevents the stories from giving liberating connection. However, in spite of the potential distance between father and son at the very end of *Cattle Killing* that contests and restricts the liberating voice it might otherwise more clearly achieve, "the writing really works." The "dead can talk to the living, the living can talk to the dead" about "past and present and future" in the ongoing *quest* for liberating voice. In this quest, the text depicts the African American struggle from extremely rich perspectives that are new in African American fiction. Ultimately, Wideman is a marvelous writer and critic, who specifies the "different languages . . . different levels . . . [and] different registers" (Berben-Masi 584) of his own writing, and provides keys to what happens in other black male texts as well.

Black male texts do not always try to tell liberating stories about fathers and sons, but most often they do talk about some aspect of black male liberation. Clarence Major initially seems to be the most atypical black writer, and would seem to have very little connection to Wideman the writer and critic, and to other black male writers who write about liberation. After the first, his novels apparently deviate from all traditional black concerns, but in their overall context, they are good examples of discourse in which black male stories and writing are unconsciously contested and restricted in potentially liberating postmodern "space" where the writer "fight[s] for voice." Major's novels portray thematized writers who attempt to construct narratives that at first appear to achieve voice but become increasingly oppressive and attempt to construct a specific black male story of liberation in this context. Major talks about finding the form that will create voice in his first novel: "I discovered early that what I was trying to do in *All-Night Visitors* could not be done in a smooth symphonic fashion. I needed short broken chapters, little twisted episodes. Omitting traditional plot and other kinds of traditional devices was dictated by the same need to capture all the elements of this 'unreal world' into a form specifically designed for it" (O'Brien 133).

The form that the thematized writers try to create in the first two novels purportedly liberates, but in the final analysis self-referential narrative clearly imprisons the writers in the ongoing quest for liberating voice and narrative. Throughout the texts of this ostensibly most unconventional black writer, there is evidence of this quest, but in their very esoteric fashion, the texts undercut and restrict the quest thematically and symbolically.

In essence, none of the thematized writers fully escapes *All-Night Visitors'* main character's vulgarity and portrayal as the "*nigger raping a white girl!*" (*All-Night* 28), but Major's texts still definitely have a "special edge." It is the yearning for liberating voice and definition in a context in which liberation becomes increasingly limited and restricted that gives Major's writing the "special edge" in the terms of this study. From the portrayal of Eli in *All-Night Visitors* (1969) to Mason, the thematized writer in *My Amputations* (1986), no writer struggles harder than Major for a black male voice of liberation. Eli tries to express black male sexuality unambiguously and unabashedly by using language that draws attention to his body's sexuality, but he ends up portraying himself as sexual reprobate. The later texts try to do much the same through thematized black male writers who increasingly lose voice, and also increasingly have their black male liberating story contested and restricted in the postmodernist "space" that would liberate. It is ironic that the quest for voice, which starts with the potentially liberating postmodernist form that Major talks about creating in *All Night Visitors,* concludes with the virtually silenced voice of self-referential narrative.

In Johnson's texts, a radical assertion of African American freedom achieved in postmodernist "space" and the paradoxical restriction of black male voice and freedom in the underlying narratives is definitely part of excellent writing with a "special edge." On the conscious level, Johnson's paradigm of freedom is fresh and ingenious. It challenges the African American literary tradition's portrayal of the quest for freedom, because in Johnson's estimation it is narrow and limiting. At the same time, it implicitly and explicitly shows black liberation through white Western philosophical/religious perspectives that are also African American. By doing so, Johnson's texts open up endless possibilities for new interpretations of African American freedom.

For example, Johnson's paradigm broadly fits a more universal pattern of religious/philosophical paradox and mystery that would include the Old Testament, a philosophical/religious source of liberation, as well as a source of the representation of the physical struggle to overcome bondage, in the African American cultural tradition. Johnson's characters must learn to fall in line with "Being" by accepting its process of evolution, which consumes people along with everything else and does not discriminate between good and evil. "Being" will ultimately conserve everything, and this is more important than what seems to be the worldly reward of good or the triumph of evil in human eyes. In general, this is the same paradox and mystery of the story told throughout the Old Testament, in which human beings have the lawful obligation to do good, but good is "vanity" that leads to death, while evil is "vanity" that may prolong life. ("All *things* have I seen in the days of my vanity: there is a just *man* that perisheth in his righteousness, and there is a wicked *man* that prolongeth *his life* in his wickedness" [King James Bible, Eccles. 7:15].) Nevertheless, good and evil somehow work together to achieve the will of God.

Ultimately, Johnson's novels innovate because they depict liberating African American philosophical/religious traditions from perspectives that go beyond the literary tradition's representation of the quest for freedom. In Johnson's texts, achieving freedom by giving up the individual self and will to the process of "Being," which is unpredictable and ongoing, coincides with the traditional African American belief in deliverance and freedom through acquiescence to the Old Testament God, who is mysterious and inscrutable. One could argue that this belief has allowed black people to transcend physical bondage and has been the staple of survival in African American culture over the centuries. This representation of African American freedom certainly would not be new in the literary tradition in and of itself, but again, Johnson's approach and presentation through his paradigm make it fresh and new.

Johnson's *Oxherding Tale* (1982) presents all of this. Explicitly, the text is a rewriting of African American literary tradition as a palimpsest of all literary and philosophical traditions, particularly "white" and European ones. Implicitly, it is much more: It is a palimpsest that includes the white Western philosophy of Johnson's paradigm and the Old Testament as it relates to African American cultural tradition. For instance, in *Oxherding Tale,* in a bizarre connection that one would not suspect, the misfortune-ravaged character named Karl Marx says to Andrew's angst-ridden tutor Ezekiel what the Book of Ecclesiastes would say: "Rejoice" (*Oxherding Tale* 87; King James Bible, Eccles. 2:10, 3:22, 11:9) because all else is "vanity." Further, the novel's conclusion shows that everything, including both good and evil, works together in a salvific process that also gives his father's love back to Andrew Hawkins, the main character: "[T]he profound mystery of the One and the Many gave me back my father again and again, his love, in every being from grubworms to giant sumacs, for these too were my father, and in the final face I saw . . . which shook tears from me—my own face . . . I was my father's father and he my child" (175–76). *Oxherding Tale* expresses a white Western philosophical/religious worldview that is congruent with the concept of Old Testament saving faith in the African American cultural tradition, and it is the new angle of vision on African American liberation generated through Johnson's paradigm that is important.

In this context, in which African American liberation is shown from new angles in postmodernist "space," it is striking how *Oxherding Tale* also portrays the continuing slavery and victimization of black male slaves and thus (re)inscribes Calibanic discourse. The key is the threat and doom that are uniquely represented by black men and that are unconscious in the underlying discourse. Perhaps the best indication of this is what happens to all the characters along the lines of race and gender. Black men partly share the reality of all men with white men, and partly share the experience of all slaves with black women. But black men remain slaves with no liberating voice as long as they retain their identities as black men. This portrayal is an aspect of the paradigmatic process of "Being," but it is also clearly a representation of the restriction of black male voice and freedom that is unique. Slavery decimates black women. However, black women do have liberating voice—particularly a communal one—and the text envisions the freedom of at least one black woman slave, Minty, before she dies (167). On the other hand, the character George struggles against slavery, is brutally executed, and apparently suffers a deserved eternal bondage in hell after death because he was "determinant for his life" and "*chose* misery"(142). He "fell into West Hell to precisely the reward all black revolutionaries feared: an eternity of waiting tables" (175). George's punishment is part of the larger context in which his fellow slave and friend Nate McKay also demonstrates bestial behavior that deserves punishment. Overall, what is different is the way the text denies black males voice and shows that they deserve what they get.

From the perspective of my analysis of black male texts, the unconscious signification of the story in Johnson's novels is part of the depth and complexity of being an African American male and "speaking from inside the culture." Wideman says: "The language is subversive, it's oppositional and subversive. . . . If you're fighting for space, if you're fighting for voice, who knows what the result will be. . . . you can't exactly make a distinction between disciplined space and larger space. They begin to bleed into one another." This is true of the "disciplined space" of the conscious and the "larger space" of the unconscious in the work of other black male writers as well, which includes that of Ralph Ellison, the most important literary influence on contemporary black male writers. Ellison's fiction and critical discourse is influenced by Calibanic discourse and conflates with it as an influence that restricts voice in contemporary black male fictions.

Invisible Man is obviously one of the great American novels of the twentieth century and definitely has the "special edge." A cursory comparison of the novel and the novels of Wideman, Major, and Johnson does not reveal the influence of Ellison, but a reading of Ellison's and the contemporary writers' critical discourse along with their fictions clearly does. An analysis of the fictions and critical discourse of these writers uncovers a commonly contested and restricted voice in the overall discourse that relates to *Invisible Man* and to Ellison's critical writing. The theme of anti-realism in Ellison's critical discourse and *Invisible Man* and the thematization of writing in *Invisible Man* are the foundation of postmodernist thinking in the critical discourse and postmodernist practice in the fictions of contemporary black male writers. *Invisible Man* is the precursor to the contemporary black male novel that fights for voice in postmodernist "space."

My students sometime say, "I don't see somebody's race; I just see a human being." "But this is not true," I'll exclaim; "the effects of race and racism are still very powerful and even more insidious than they have ever been." Somehow though, the notion that racism is "gone," or at least that race is no longer a serious factor and "things are so much better," seems to prevail. It is fashionable these days to critique and criticize black men as though they have traditionally shared the same oppressive power positions as white men, and the outcry becomes vociferous if I try to talk about the special way that the concepts of race and racism impact black men in contemporary times. So I usually do not say anything about it. If all that I say is true, especially about black men, what is the evidence of it? How does it manifest itself in everything that we can see around us?

I do not intend to answer these questions in the context of their broad societal implications, but I do want to make some comments that relate the questions to the analysis of the foregoing chapters, in which I have tried to demonstrate that the contemporary black male postmodernist novel shows best an unconscious restriction of liberating voice unique for black male writers. In some ways, the manifestation of Calibanic discourse in black male fiction is subtle and hard to see, because there is no one *specific* pattern that reveals itself across the range of texts that I have analyzed. There is, however, a very telling general pattern constituted through the identifiable characteristics of Calibanic discourse and its responsive story of liberation. For reasons not apparent on the surface, the narratives all implicitly and/or explicitly restrict or compromise the story of liberation that they tell about black men. It comes down to many black male writers contesting their own freedom stories about black men; a similar pattern of the broad, general terms of black male writing emerges. My argument is that Calibanic discourse is pervasive in the culture—constituted in the cultural unconscious through language and non-linguistic signs. It therefore saturates everything and its generic story takes over and comes out—sometimes in subtle, symbolic ways, but nevertheless comes out—very often in black male fiction. Bearing the burden of the Calibanic legacy can, ironically, make it more likely that black male writers will (re)write it.

I turn again to Wideman's *Philadelphia Fire* (1990), as I have done several times for this specific reference and for the foundation of much that I have said: the story of black men is "buried" and "unmentionable" but "nonetheless signified in the small-print forever-after clause" (141). *Philadelphia Fire* tries to critique and deconstruct this story, but ends up (re)writing it both consciously and unconsciously precisely because of the reason that the text itself gives—it is written "forever" in the language that the text uses and the physical signs of black maleness encoded in that language. Take the signs and symbols of black maleness and the story told through them and shape, twist, and revise the story however you want. But given the hegemonic proscription of black men, the story will likely reveal in some form what is already signified in it. It is particularly ironic that this is true in postmodernist fictions that make clear the liberating potential of a fiction, and in fictions that thematize the power of what is already signified in language.

The only way to change all of this is somehow to change what is already signified in the words and other signs that construct societal consciousness—and even more deeply and importantly unconsciousness. I have not analyzed Calibanic discourse in black male fiction to make the point that it detracts from the substance of the fiction; I only want to make sense of an important factor in the writing. Very clearly, black male writing will continue to thrive, as it has done so far, whether or not the change occurs that would deconstruct Calibanic discourse at the fundamental level of language and semiotics. However, the Calibanic legacy that reveals itself in black male writing does imply the truth that racism is still pervasive, insidious, and harmful, and we do need to think seriously about how basic it is to the society's deepest reality and how hard it will be to change.

Notes

Introduction

1. Wideman goes on to talk about his "impulse to give voice to the dead, the unborn, to outlaws and outcasts whose voices have been stolen or muted by violence. . . . Alternate forms of speech, in my fiction, which celebrate the body's ingenuity, how it compensates the loss of one expressive sense with eloquence in another. My ongoing attempt to define African-American culture, explicate its heavy debt, its intimacy with silence. . . . My struggle to emulate the achievement of African-American artists in song, dance, sport; invent a language that doesn't feel secondhand, borrowed, a language rich with time and silence that animate the written word" (549). Wideman succeeds brilliantly in "invent[ing] a language that doesn't feel secondhand." However, I will attempt to show that "silence" still affects the story of liberation his texts tell in the language of the patriarchy.

2. In "Discourse in the Novel," Mikhail Bakhtin says the following:

As a living, socio-ideological concrete thing, as heteroglot opinion, language, for the individual consciousness, lies on the borderline between oneself and the other. The word in language is half someone else's. It becomes "one's own" only when the speaker populates it with his own intention, his own accent, when he appropriates the word, adapting it to his own semantic and expressive intention. Prior to this moment of appropriation, the word does not exist in a neutral and impersonal language . . . but rather it exists in other people's mouths, in other people's contexts, serving other people's intentions: it is from there that one must take the word, and make it one's own. And not all words for just anyone submit equally easily to this appropriation, to this seizure and transformation into private property: many words stubbornly resist, others remain alien, sound foreign in the mouth of the one who appropriated them . . . they cannot be assimilated into his context and fall out of it; it is as if they put themselves in quotation marks against the will of the speaker. Language is not a neutral medium that passes freely and easily into the private property of the speaker's intentions; it is populated—overpopulated—with the intentions of others. Expropriating it, forcing it to submit to one's intentions and accents, is a difficult and complicated process. (293–94)

The quotation from Bakhtin helps to establish a context for my argument. Bakhtin suggests that the speaker, after a struggle, can make language serve his intentions. In the context of my study, the hegemony of Calibanic discourse makes a difference. It compromises—limits, restricts, and diminishes—the black male speaker's intentions and constantly and consistently signifies negative black male subjectivity in the mouths of speakers. "Expropriating" Calibanic discourse from language is very difficult.

3. In "Caliban: Notes Toward a Discussion of Culture in Our America," for example, Roberto Fernandez Retamar focuses on Latin America and traces Calibanic signification and its counter-signification in texts, including Shakespeare's *The Tempest,* from the fifteenth to the twentieth century. Another example is the previously mentioned reference from Houston Baker's *Blues, Ideology, and Afro-American Literature* (1984). Further, in *Black Skin, White Masks* (1967), Frantz Fanon talks about the relationship of Prospero and Miranda to Caliban in both colonialist and American racial terms. In the latter context, "Prospero assumes an attitude [toward Caliban] that is well known to Americans in the southern United States. Are they not forever saying that the niggers are just waiting for the chance to jump on white women?" (107).

4. I fully realize that the black male quest to achieve voice and freedom in these terms fully places black men in a position where they try to define themselves in some of the same ways that the oppressive, hegemonic patriarchy defines itself; although this should not be true, I am saying that the dynamics of the culture make it true. The culture's semiotics produce Calibanic signification that most severely proscribes black men and sets them in opposition to white men and to phallocentric white male privilege; in this context, the Calibanic "black man" cannot be a true man and also cannot have what "the [white] man" has. Black men's response to Calibanic proscription is, to a significant extent, an attempt to define a "true" black manhood that is not proscribed and to define black manhood in the terms of the phallocentric power, prestige, and entitlement that they lack and which white men have. Powerful dynamics make this true in the culture, and these dynamics also manifest themselves in black male texts.

5. My main focus will be to deal with this in texts. However, when applied to the extra-textual world, this statement does not sound at all extreme when one considers that lynching rituals are a defining part of American history and that brutality towards black men has been allowed by the law. (Examples of this are the license to brutalize given to white policemen and the proclivity to "burn" black men in death chambers even when the evidence against them does not exist.) This is not something of the past, either, as shown by the June 7, 1998, "lynching" of James Byrd Jr. in Jasper, Texas.

6. I will use the terms challenge/contest and restrict/compromise interchangeably throughout my analysis.

7. Michel Foucault provides a definition of unconscious discourse that I can "shift" to support and explain my definition of Calibanic discourse. (The concept of "shift" is one that I take from Karla F.C. Holloway's *Moorings and Metaphors* (1992). For Holloway, "shift" means taking critical paradigms developed

by white theorists for non–African American contexts and "bending" them so that they become relevant in African American contexts. (See p. 62 of Holloway's text.) Throughout this study I will use "shift" more flexibly than Holloway: I will use "shift" to change or alter theoretical concepts that I take from any theorist or critic to explain or support my analysis of Calibanic discourse.) In *The Order of Things* (1970), Foucault says that society operates through "*a system of cultural unconsciousness the totality of formal structures which render mythical discourse significant,* give their coherence and necessity to the rules that regulate needs, and provide the norms of life with a foundation other than that to be found in nature, or in pure biological functions" (380; italics mine). For me, Calibanic discourse is "embedded in the culture's semiotic signs," which suggests that it is part of a discursive "system" like Foucault's, but I still "shift" Foucault's emphasis on "a system of cultural unconsciousness." I then use his terms to support and explain my point: Calibanic discourse is a major unconscious discourse in American and Western culture (represented through language and nonlinguistic signs) that allows society to mythify itself—to make sense of, give necessity to, and justify itself—and to provide a basis of normalcy for life. Calibanic discourse is a *story* that society fabricates to serve itself; it is set aside from any natural, positivistic knowledge.

In *Psychoanalysis and Black Novels: Desire and the Protocols of Race* (1998), Claudia Tate draws heavily upon the theories of Sigmund Freud and Jacques Lacan to develop a psychoanalytical model to analyze black novels; her model consists of conscious, preconscious, and unconscious discourses. Tate says that unconscious discourse is "those longings that are inscribed in the novel's most deeply encoded rhetorical elements. Like the cryptic elements of dreams, the unconscious elements of a text must be deciphered within the dynamics of its representational design" (13). Conscious discourse is that which is "explicit social content," and preconscious discourse is a text's "stylistic features." Tate's definition of unconscious discourse shares with mine an emphasis on "deeply encoded rhetorical elements" and on "elements of a text [that] must be deciphered within the dynamics of representational design." My definition differs from hers in that I define unconscious discourse as a story that gets told on a culturewide basis without the tellers having to be conscious of telling it, because it is deeply embedded in the culture's linguistic and semiotic signs; the story is therefore an unconscious linguistic/semiotic structure of the culture, or the product of an unconscious cultural system that constructs meaning. Calibanic discourse is *the* dominant, hegemonic unconscious story or discourse of black men in America and Western culture.

Although her model is also psychoanalytical, Kaja Silverman states a definition of unconscious discourse that is more compatible with my definition, which emphasizes reality constructed unconsciously in a semiotic system and structure of the culture. In *The Subject of Semiotics* (1983), using Foucault, Sigmund Freud, and Jacques Lacan, Silverman makes the point that "human reality [is] a construction . . . the product of signifying activities which are both culturally specific and generally unconscious" (130). Silverman uses her psychoanalytical model to talk about the construction of the subjectivity of women that oppresses and the construction of men that privileges, and she emphasizes that these constructions are generated by an unconscious discursive process embedded in the culture's semiotics. In the context of my analysis, the culture's semiotics do not construct black men in a way that privileges them; the culture's semiotics produce unconscious significations of black men that place them in negative opposition to white men, thus making this opposition their bane and making black men the bane of the entire culture.

8. There are, of course, several major theorists who deal with postmodernism from different perspectives. Some of these are Jean Baudrillard, Jean-Francois Lyotard, Frederick Jameson, and Terry Eagleton. The latter two theorists, for example, critique postmodernism (and the positions of the former two theorists) from a Marxist perspective that decries postmodernism's lack of political utility.

9. In their fictions, black women writers voice (white) postmodernism in black terms by creating versions of history and truth that position themselves against racist versions. Black women's fictions imply an appropriated and critiqued (white) postmodernism that serves their needs by giving them liberating voice. Black women writers such as Toni Morrison and Sherley Ann Williams, in *Beloved* and *Dessa Rose,* respectively, for example, create narratives that are very much postmodernist. However, the narratives present black versions of history in politicized voices that are positioned against racist white versions, and because of the power of their voices, they do not have to reference explicitly or to thematize (white) postmodernism to abrogate it. There is a difference between their black voicing of postmodernism and black male foregrounding and thematizing of (white) postmodernism in a context that limits black male voice and highlights that limitation.

I include poststructuralism under the rubric of postmodernism. Postmodernism de-centers accepted systems of thought that normalize and standardize. Within the broad contours of postmodernism, poststructuralism totally de-centers and destabilizes the meaning of words and the meaning of texts. *Philadelphia Fire's* thematization ranges along the common border of poststructuralism and structuralism, its precursor, because Wideman, seemingly unsuccessfully, looks for order, meaning, and liberating narrative in a closed, arbitrary, self-referential system, a structuralist system (pp. 103–4, for example).

10. Black male counter-signifying, which occurs most clearly and definitively among black men, means taking control of Calibanic discourse, appropriating the power, prestige, and voice that the white patriarch Prospero has forbidden, and taking back the sexual function of the penis that has been cut off or mutilated in Calibanic phobic rituals. Counter-signifying black male discourse tells the story that black males were castrated and actual black male penises, the "anatomical appendages" (Silverman 139), were cut off during lynching rituals and other Calibanic phobic rituals. Thus, black male discourse focuses heavily on restoring the penis and its sexual function as well as changing the larger Calibanic symbolism. This discursive quest to restore the penis cannot be separated from the quest to change the Calibanic symbol. However, in its sexual

signification of the penis, black male discourse only inadvertently (re)inscribes Calibanic phallicism and the broader symbolism of Calibanic discourse.

1. The Conscious and Unconscious Dimensions of Calibanic Discourse Thematized in *Philadelphia Fire*

1. The linguistic challenge and compromise of the story of liberation also applies to Wideman's earlier works. *Hiding Place* (1981), which I analyze in the introduction, is an example. In "Beyond Discourse: The Unspoken Versus Words in the Fiction of John Edgar Wideman," Jacqueline Berben says, "If language [in *Hiding Place*] is not to be trusted and even dreams cradle falsehoods, what terms are there to use, what values are agreed upon, in order to come to necessary understanding? —Sense. Good sense, the five senses of seeing, smelling, hearing, touching, tasting, and the sixth sense or intuition. Kinship. And names. . ." (532). I would emphasize that the text restricts voice through its discourse.

2. See the introduction for a definition of Calibanic discourse (an unconscious discourse) and (white) postmodernism and for a discussion of the relationship between them.

3. Many times in contemporary critical and theoretical analyses, commentators refer to "the gaze" as the look of men imposed upon women from the standpoint of patriarchal power. Obviously, I am not using the concept of a black male "gaze" the same way in this instance. The text makes it very ambiguous whether Cudjoe's "gaze" has any real power. What is clear is that he internalizes the debilitating guilt and angst that the white patriarchy indirectly imposes on him.

4. Interestingly, the text leaves Sam's race ambiguous. Cudjoe is black, and from one perspective, the fact that Sam is an older writer who is a mentor to him might suggest that Sam is black as well. But nowhere does the text make this specific and clear. The ambiguity of Sam's race fits with the ambiguity and doubt about the ability of black men to "own" the rights to a secure place (Sam's island) and to atone for wrong (Sam's atonement to his wife). However, even if one does assume that Sam is black, the text questions the underlying substance of Sam's possession and atonement through its reference to Sam's adulterous sexual escapades, drinking, and death; through the account of the tragic and untimely death of Sam's daughter Cassy, whom he tries to lavish with love to make up for what he did to her mother; through the account of the later death of Rachel, the wife and mother; and through the portrayal of Cudjoe's uneasy relationship with him.

5. Silverman's phrase "symbolic order" references Jacques Lacan in the context of the psychoanalytical grounding of her study in the work of Sigmund Freud and Lacan. Silverman uses Lacan to show that the psychological construction of the human subject is inseparable from its cultural linguistic/semiotic construction. In my definition of unconscious discourse, I use Silverman's model but "shift" my analysis more toward Michel Foucault's paradigm emphasizing the "structures" of the culture more than the psychoanalytical. Foucault grounds

the construction of reality in a "system of cultural unconsciousness the totality of formal structures which render mythical discourse significant" (Foucault 380). See the introduction for a definition and discussion of unconscious discourse and pp. 157-59n7 for a definition of "shift." Also see pp. 157-59n7 for a discussion of how my definition of unconscious discourse differs from Claudia Tate's in *Psychoanalysis and Black Novels: Desire and the Protocols of Race.*

6. Significantly, in *Philadelphia Fire,* the character John Wideman makes clear (117–19) that the black women in his family have a connecting bond that he does not have with males and for which he has no words. At this specific point in *Philadelphia Fire,* the differences between black men and women seem almost essentialized: Black women have a power that is equivalent to voice, and black men lack voice. The bond can potentially support the women against legacies of horror such as the one that imprisons Wideman in the text. Other texts that I analyze clearly show that black women have a liberating bond or voice that black men lack: Wideman's *Reuben* (1987); Charles Johnson's *Oxherding Tale* (1982); and Wesley Brown's *Tragic Magic* (1978).

In *Moorings and Metaphors,* Karla Holloway explains, perhaps, the bond of connection among black women implied here. Holloway talks about physiological and cultural resources of black women. She says that black women have a sense of self grounded in motherhood (26–31) and their own mythologies, generated from black women's collective oral, communal voice, that gives them the potential to revise their histories and define themselves anew (34). Holloway uses the term recursion in her analysis of this process of revision and redefinition (13–14, 102).

Holloway talks about a much fuller restorative process in the texts of contemporary black women writers than the process of response, challenge, and compromise that this study shows in black male texts and in black male culture. Holloway's process is by no means an easy, simple one, and in texts such as Toni Morrison's *Beloved,* for example, it is not clearly a successful one. However, my point is that according to Holloway, the potential for restoration does exist in the black female character—the black female self—because of physiological and cultural resources.

7. Michel Foucault says that society functions through "a system of cultural unconsciousness . . . [that] provide[s] the norms of life with a foundation other than that to be found in nature, or in pure biological functions" (380). What sounds "natural" in Calibanic discourse is that which society constructs. It is no more real, true, or "natural" than any other construction. Nevertheless, this fact by no means diminishes the power of Calibanic discourse.

8. *Philadelphia Fire* quotes Miranda's "Abhorrèd slave" speech (139; *The Tempest* I.ii.422–36) that inscribes Caliban's uncivilized nature and bestiality. The text describes how Prospero's language, which Miranda teaches Caliban, establishes the hegemony that Cudjoe cannot break—a hegemony "buried" and "unmentionable" in the language, but one that is "nonetheless signified in the small-print forever-after clause" (141). The text describes a discourse that is most substantively unconscious and effectively indelible.

9. Silverman says the following.

To begin with, the subject's discourse is constrained by the rules of language; it can only speak by means of a pre-existing linguistic system. Moreover, "language" must here be understood in the broadest possible sense, as encompassing not only the operations of denotation, but those of connotation. In other words, every utterance must be conceived as having various levels of signification, and issuing from multiple voices. It is spoken not only by the palpable voice of a concrete speaker, writer, or cluster of mechanical apparatuses, but the anonymous voices of cultural codes which invade it in the form of connotation. As [Roland] Barthes remarks in *S/Z*, "Alongside each utterance, one might say that off-stage voices can be heard: they are the codes: in their interweaving, these voices (whose origin is 'lost' in the vast perspective of the *already-written*) de-originate the utterance . . . (21). These "off-stage" voices belong to earlier discourses; they repeat what has already been said, written, or filmed, and to a very large degree determine what can now be said, written, or filmed.

Silverman's analysis presents a perspective in which discourse determines subjectivity instead of the reverse. This parallels the effect of Calibanic discourse in *Philadelphia Fire*. However, postmodernist black male texts such as *Philadelphia Fire* also foreground (white) postmodernism from a perspective that is potentially liberating because the writer can create fictions that deconstruct oppressive ones. This potential of (white) postmodernism is never realized, though, and thus highlights the power of Calibanic discourse to limit voice.

In the full context of her analysis, Silverman quotes Emile Benveniste's essay "Language in Freudian Theory" and gives her critique a psychoanalytical emphasis. My emphasis is on cultural linguistic/semiotic construction, following the paradigm of Michel Foucault to a significant extent. I would also relate what Silverman says here about the speaker's words being, in essence, contested by the culture to what Mikhail Bakhtin says about the culture contesting the speaker's words (Bakhtin 293–94).

10. In interviews Wideman talks about the liberating potential of (white) postmodernism's fictions, but this liberation does not occur in his novels. In a 1989 interview, Wideman implies the influence of (white) postmodernism on recent works such as "Fever" (from the 1989 volume *Fever*) and *Philadelphia Fire,* both of which he talks about in the interview. He discusses a "play" in his writing that positions his recent work outside the modernist seriousness of purpose and theme of Eliot, Faulkner, and Hemingway and of his early work. Wideman says that his written narrative is a "multiple, fluid," de-centered, postmodernist narrative that liberates him through its "play" instead of restricting him to a serious job; writing liberates him because it allows "personal expression" that is "arbitrary. . . . [and even] silly . . . [and] profane." Wideman is "talk[ing] to you in the writing," but he is also "trying to take something away from you. Multiple consciousness and energy, the fluid situation of freedom that multiple consciousness creates, that's what I mean by play" (Rowell 56–57).

Philadelphia Fire and other recent fictions shift (white) postmodernism to a black context that makes it clear how much different the achievement of black voice and black liberation is from the achievement of fluid, multiple, de-centered freedom described through Wideman's paradigm of (white) postmodernism. (White) postmodernism highlights the power of Calibanic discourse to compromise black voice in the black context. In *Philadelphia Fire,* because of the conscious and unconscious effects of Calibanic discourse, Wideman cannot "play" with the words "father" and "son" to make them tell the liberating story (103). No playful consciousness mediates the angst about the narrative's potential failure to do the serious job of black liberation. Also, in *Philadelphia Fire,* Wideman specifically talks about "[i]magin[ing] our fictions imagining us" (97–98), which suggests (white) postmodernism's "[m]ultiple consciousness and energy, the fluid situation of freedom that multiple consciousness creates," which he talks about in the interview. However, in the novel, "[m]ultiple" voices that constitute reality, specifically the voice of Calibanic discourse, threaten black freedom and challenge and compromise the black voice that constitutes a liberating black male fiction. In *Philadelphia Fire,* Calibanic discourse challenges and compromises freedom in the contested black setting and compromises the black male voice of liberation; therefore, Wideman sounds doubtful that he can create the fiction that will liberate. In the interview, the black male liberating voice speaks in terms of (white) postmodernism that are the same ones complicit with Calibanic discourse. The challenged and compromised voice of the fiction contests the voice of the critical statements.

11. Richard Cory is also the seemingly enviable, exemplary figure in the E.A. Robinson poem entitled "Richard Cory." Ironically, "Richard Cory, one calm night, / Went home and put a bullet through his head."

12. Michel Fabre talks about the closing scene in terms consistent with my point about the potential failure of liberation. He says: "The closing scene recalls the 1805 Fourth of July celebration in Independence Square from which African Americans were excluded even before the festivities began: memories of the past (history repeats itself) interwoven with a recent protest rally commemorating the massacre on Osage Avenue" (589).

13. The text describes the character Caliban as he enters the stage: "Enter Caliban, heavy, heavy dreadlocks resembling chains drag nearly to the floor. A cloak of natty wool. His natural cape, suggesting, repudiating Prospero's dashing midnight-blue silk one with all its devices. . . . Caliban is naked under his dreads, but they cover him without hiding him, his proper, modest fur. . ." (120).

14. See note number 6 above.

15. Jean-Pierre Richard says in "*Philadelphia Fire,* or The Shape of the City": "So to Cudjoe's double question 'Who's zooming who? Is someone in charge?' we may safely answer: yes, with Wideman we are all in charge. And his readers would like to believe that they are his tricksters—not the creator, not makers, but shapers—that his Philadelphia as a city of words needs them as readers, indeed, as brothers" (611). However, in light of the effect of Calibanic discourse as the text itself analyzes it, an affirmative interpretation of the reader's potential is not clear.

2. The Thematized Black Voice in John Edgar Wideman's *The Cattle Killing* and *Reuben*

1. *Reuben's* main emphasis is articulating freedom in a black male liberating voice through its primary focus on the relationship between the characters Reuben and Wally, but a secondary emphasis is defining black male character through an exploration of sexuality and the feelings and human relationships associated with it. The portrayal of Wally's attitude toward sex and sexual acts shows inadequate human sympathy and compassion. The following account of one of Wally's relationships is an example.

Felisha couldn't stand silence. She needed to be talking or needed Wally talking to her. Riding that perfect body was the only way to shut her up. Then she was quiet as church on Monday. Not a peep out of her. No heavy breathing, no sighs or moans or groans. Stillness perfect as that lean-hipped, pillow-bosomed, every-pubic-hair-in-place body like none he'd ever seen before or since. Quietest, stillest bitch he'd laid. . . . Quiet like that. I wanted to hurt the bitch sometimes. . . . See if she'd holler if I pinched her behind or pulled a hair out her pussy. Scared sometimes the bitch was dead. I'm doing my best. Pounding away. . . . I'm pile driving and sky diving and bitch's dead to the world down there under me. No sooner I unplug, though, there go her mouth. Yakedy-yak. Yakedy-yak. Asking me a question. Bothering me with some off-the-wall mess I ain't hardly in no mood to be hearing. . . . That's just the way the chick was. Why don't you ever talk to me, Wally? Only way to shut Felisha up stick your dick in her. (103)

Wally lacks the voice to communicate with both men and women, and in his relationship to women, he is restricted to a silent, inhumane sexual expression that is negative. Wally's other sexual relationships in the text are portrayed in similar terms. Although the text may show that Wally is a victim in ways, ambiguity plays less of a role as a device that moves his portrayal toward (re)inscription than it does in the text's overall treatment of voice thematically and structurally. Wally's portrayal more directly (re)inscribes Calibanic discourse.

Reuben expresses love in his relationship with Flora, and his sexual relationship with her does not reveal proscribed black male sexuality. But neither does it provide a clear positive definition. In the section entitled "Flora," Reuben, a physical dwarf, has a bizarre sexual encounter with Flora, a beautiful prostitute. Reuben "buries his face in titty. He thinks he knows what she's talking about and nods and grunts as he roots in her softness. She's saying yes to him and as he digs and pushes deeper into her, all fingers and nose and blind eyes, he replies yes to whatever it is she's asking, begging" (84–85). Before Reuben can actually get his clothes off to have sex, the white fraternity boys, for whom he is a factotum, burst in from the door where they have been surreptitiously watching to punish Reuben and Flora for plotting against them. As a result of the melee, the house of prostitution gets burned down and Flora gets burned up.

2. This is a reference to *The Cattle Killing*. Although it comes later, *Cattle Killing* provides a vantage point from which to gain a more substantive critical

perspective on *Reuben,* because it helps to make sense of what happens in the earlier text. Furthermore, although *Philadelphia Fire* is the main paradigmatic text that relates to and encompasses other texts in the past and future, *Cattle Killing* also embroiders and augments *Philadelphia Fire's* paradigm. As my analysis will show, *Cattle Killing* complements *Philadelphia Fire's* paradigm by naming an open-ended process of "[n]ext and next. Always unknown. Always free." *Cattle Killing* makes the content and outcome of the liberating story important, as *Philadelphia Fire* implies it is, but unlike *Philadelphia Fire,* it projects above the content and outcome an open-ended process that keeps the story alive and therefore liberates. The "very power of storytelling lies in its capacity to embrace the endless movement of language itself, 'writing,' if not necessarily 'righting,' the wrongs of an 'upside-down' world" (Birat 641).Generally, my analysis uses an approach that allows Wideman's three novels to be "[m]any places at once" in the past and future and therefore to practice part of what they thematize.

3. See the introduction for a definition and discussion of Calibanic discourse and (white) postmodernism.

4. For instances in the text, Wally sounds sympathetic. Here, one can understand what Wally means because he is only responding to the racism that has victimized him. However, given Wally's negative sexual portrayal, his meanness, and his threatening persona, one sees that he is clearly a Calibanic figure who never defines himself beyond his negative qualities, the fact that everything about him is "abstract" notwithstanding.

5. Kwansa's words here are reminiscent of the words of Jesus Christ in the New Testament and words from the books of major prophets in the Old Testament. From this perspective, her words reinforce the idea that black women's words have defining, liberating power for those capable of listening and understanding. The text suggests that Kwansa and Toodles can listen and understand and that black men cannot.

In Luke 8:8, Christ concludes his narration of the parable of the sower and the seed to the uncomprehending multitude by saying, "He that hath ears to hear, let him hear" (KJV). After these words, Luke 8 continues with Christ's further explanation of the parable to his disciples, who want deeper understanding. For other examples in the New Testament, see Matthew 11:15 and 13:9 and 43 and Mark 4: 9 and 23. In the Old Testament, see Jeremiah 5:21 and Ezekiel 3:27 and 12:1.

6. Also, Karla Holloway talks about black women's bonding in *Moorings and Metaphors* (13–14, 26–31, 34, and 102). Holloway, in essence, makes the point that there is an essentialized difference between black women and black men because of black women's ability and black men's inability to use the "word." See my broader references to Holloway in chapter 1.

7. *Philadelphia Fire* again provides a very helpful gloss here. *Philadelphia Fire* urges that we "[p]retend" that the fire never existed and that we can "imagine events into existence or out of existence" (97): "Imagine our fictions imagining us" (97–98). The text sounds doubtful about its own imaginative power even as it urges imagination. It cannot imagine a story that will free black people

of the oppressive legacy of the fire, just as the black male writers in *Philadelphia Fire* and the men in *Reuben* cannot imagine liberating stories.

Also, in "Brother Figures: The Rift and Riff in John E. Wideman's Fiction," Yves-Charles Grandjeat makes the following statements about recovering the African home in *Reuben*. The "mythic kingdom of Egypt . . . 'has already lost all trace of you in the well of its memory' ([*Reuben*] 205). It can only be recovered as lost, lost and found, in the kingdom of poetic imagination where Wideman, Reuben, and Brother Tate [from *Sent For You Yesterday*] must be trading stories somewhere" (621). For me, the idea of "trading stories somewhere" suggests the tentativeness of "great distance" that *Reuben* (207–8) associates with the black male voice. This relates to my point about the doubtfulness of black male stories in *Reuben*.

The "great distance" of the voice suggests its eventual silence, but in Wideman's work, "silence" is a "riff" on speaking that "animate[s] the written word" (Wideman, "In Praise of Silence" 549). (With regard to silences that "speak," see also Wideman's fictional piece "The Silence of Thelonious Monk," in *Callaloo*, 22. 3, 550–57, and Yves-Charles Grandjeat's "'These Strange Dizzy Pauses': Silence as Common Ground in J.E. Wideman's Texts.") The "word" is indeed ingeniously "animated" in Wideman's texts, but the thematic and structural elements of the texts still challenge and compromise the liberating fictions created through words in the terms of *Philadelphia Fire's* analysis of Calibanic discourse.

8. The following explains the significance of the title and that Wideman juxtaposed important events in South African history and American history in the novel. The novel's title "refers to an episode in South African history still vehemently debated among scholars: the Xhosa cattle-killing movement of 1856 and 1857 which resulted in the proud nation losing its independence and its people becoming an oppressed class within the South African colony. The great importance the author attributes to this event and especially to the prophecy that seems to have sparked it shows in the fact that he moved the incident back in time and made it the kernel of a novel related to the Philadelphia yellow fever epidemic in 1793" (Gysin 623).

9. In "Opening of the Symposium in Tours," *Callaloo*, 22. 3, 587–93, Michel Fabre comments on Wideman's use of the postmodern. He thinks that "Wideman's craft in [*Cattle Killing* is] superior even to the achievements in *Philadelphia Fire* because the later novel manages an exquisitely subtle and convincing use of postmodernist stances, yet keeps us really involved in historical calamities and in present-day issues" (589). Later in the essay, he says, "Most American postmodernist novelists have gotten caught at playing with language for the sake of itself and have found it impossible to transcend the artificiality of that kind of writing. The gap between creating new modes of expression, and writing in a way that is relevant to our daily lives and contemporary situation is hard to bridge. John Wideman is one of the few who can manage it, and in *The Cattle Killing* does it even more daringly than Toni Morrison in *Jazz*" (593).

I strongly agree with the general tenor of what Fabre says about the quality of Wideman's writing and the seriousness and integrity of his use of the postmodern. In the context of my analysis, I would not agree that *Cattle Killing* is better than *Philadelphia Fire because* it represents a more "convincing use of postmodernist stances." Also, the novel has "transcend[ed] . . . artificiality" in its use of the postmodern, but it does not realize its postmodernist potential to tell a liberating fiction.

10. These words sound very much like the words from *Reuben:* "Who was Reuben, what was he?" (132).

11. Liam's storytelling in the first person is never completely separate from the storytelling of others and always "many places at once," thus implicating the intersubjective process.

12. The text conflates the portrayal of George Stubbs with the historical figure of eighteenth- and early nineteenth-century English painter George Stubbs.

13. Kathie Birat has the following assessment of the narrator's stutter: "Although Wideman's narrator admits failure, 'the language coming apart in my hands,' his narrative generates its own double, creating life out of death. Just as his own fate cannot be seen as the result of a linear process, but must be considered as intertwined in the stories of all black people, the doubles or alternative stories he brings to life are the underside, or shadow, of the act of storytelling" (637–38). As my analysis of the storytelling process shows, I largely agree with what Birat says about the narrator; however, my analysis of the novel overall will reveal that it still symbolically undercuts its achievement of voice through its theme and structure.

14. Dr. Thrush is a "fictional version of the famous surgeon Benjamin Rush"; he played an important role during the Philadelphia fever epidemic. Rush's attendant during the epidemic was Bishop Richard Allen, also a fictional character in the novel (Gysin 628, note 18).

3. Clarence Major's Quest to Define and Liberate the Self and the Black Male Writer

1. The "unexpurgated" version of *All-Night Visitors* was published in 1998. The 1998 version includes many chapters left out of the 1969 version and is almost double the length of the first. It alters the plot by adding a lot more facts, background, and details about the main character's life and by changing the order of the story's events. However, it is still substantively the same story, with almost exactly the same beginning and ending.

In Bernard Bell's "Foreword to the 1998 Edition," he quotes Major as saying that the original publishers left out half the book as he wrote it, and the "'true book the way I wrote it should be published'" (ix). In one important instance, Major has changed the supposedly "unexpurgated" version. He has deleted a long section from the original: most of a section entitled "Cathy" on pages 16–23 and all of the same section on pages 23–30. It deals with the main character's "rape" of Cathy, his white girlfriend, his threat to kill her because of love, and the consequent racial stereotyping by a white man who sees the "rape." This section that Major expurgated from the 1998 edition is part of the "true book" because, as he says, it is what he wrote originally. It is still there in the 1998 edition, implied by what he wrote in the 1969 text, just as what he expurgated from the 1969 edition is still there, implied by his (re)writing of the 1998 text. The "true book" is a composite, implied text, the substance of which both the 1969 and 1998 texts represent. I use the 1969 edition, and in my notes I make the connections between the texts to show that both versions conform to my analysis.

2. As my analysis will show, the failed quest for sexual freedom that lies below the surface opposes the text's pretensions of sexual definition and liberation. This underlying level of unconscious signification creates paradox and reveals an ambiguous, liminal freedom. I take the term "liminal" from Victor Turner's *The Forest of Symbols* (1967). For Turner, the liminal period is one of "fruitful darkness" tantamount to a form of unity in the culture (110). I "shift" Turner's concept and give it a different meaning in the black American male context. See my definition of "shift," pp. 157-59n7.

3. The preoccupation with Cathy, the white woman, is reminiscent of Caliban's relationship to Miranda, whom, according to the language that Prospero imposes on him, he tries to "violate."

4. This quotation is part of the section dealing with Eli and Cathy that Major deletes from the 1998 version. Besides deleting most of the section, the later edition adds two sections entitled "Eunice"—another white woman with whom Eli has a sexual relationship—and adds other scenes with Cathy. In the foreword to the 1998 edition Bernard Bell says that changes in the new version make Eli more "sympathetic than in the first" (xvii). However, the same emphasis on black male sexuality is there in the recent version, and in the context of my analysis of Calibanic discourse, there is no clear, significant difference in Eli's portrayal. This is especially true when one reads the "true book" that Major originally intended, which includes the "rape" and threatened murder of Cathy.

5. As is true in Wideman's works, the black male writer who is trying to find his voice to tell a story of liberation is either an explicit theme or an implied reality in Major's fictions. Major is similar to Wideman because his writers try to find the voice that will define and empower them as human beings and define their sexuality and legitimate sexual expression. Nevertheless, Major's thematized writers and writing are also very different in many ways.

6. This language is also part of the original section deleted from the recent version that has been mentioned in notes 1 and 4 above. This is a good example of the way that the two versions of the text relate and that one substantively implies the other. The language and portrayal of Eli as a rapist is a part of both texts because of the way that Major conceives of the "true book" as what he first wrote. They are also part of both because the even more protracted emphasis on sex with white women in the recent version, especially given its overall similarity to the first in the way that Eli uses language, makes Eli the "nigger rapist."

7. This specific phrase was excluded from the recent version of *All-Night Visitors*, but most of the concluding sections of both versions are the same or very similar. The phrase "vibrantly alive," which the recent version retains, has

essentially the same meaning as "firmly a man." In this instance and throughout the recent version, there were small incidental changes that relate to editing as well as the deletions and additions that I have emphasized.

8. In *The Forest of Symbols* (1967), Victor Turner uses the phrase "betwixt-and-between" to describe a positive liminal period. In saying that Eli's position is liminal, I also mean that it is "betwixt-and-between," but I mean that it is a hard and perhaps dangerous place because it is not clearly a place of freedom and may not represent a stage before freedom. Also, the text sounds confident of what it says on a conscious level, but the underlying level of its unconscious development supports the (re)inscription of Calibanic discourse because the ending is paradoxical.

9. Arguably, Major foregrounds and thematizes narrative more than any other black male writer, and in this context, the challenge and compromise of the black male voice of liberation take form in ways that are unique to Major. However, he has in common with the other black male writers in this study the concern with telling a story that defines black male freedom as well as black male humanity and sexuality.

10. I conclude the discussion of *No* because *Reflex and Bone Structure* takes up and develops a similar concern with discourse. I will, however, give another example of the text's discourse to show the variety of its shape and structure. The following quotation shows this, but generally, it represents the challenge and compromise of Moses's freedom and self-definition in the same ways as the discourse throughout the text. Moses tries to describe how he wants to "love" a "Puerto Rican girl" (160), and thus, apparently, to define a positive, liberated sexual self. However, the discourse makes freedom and self-definition ambiguous, leaving open the possibility that it may (re)inscribe his negative sexual signification.

How can I run and hide from something that's in me? The hallway, as always, smells of fresh piss—both dog and human. Warm waves slapping inside my intentions. Is it possible to pull the stem of this new thing? Inner streams of my own pity feeding the poverty of my present moment, this ache—the danger of it!
Suddenly   her mother   a woman as hard and
    as big   as a washtub   rushes up   to
me and   plunges   a 95¢ butcher knife   into
    an area   of my   throat   :I
stab this fear   and   stack it   under
    the flower bed   rocks
of some safety   valve

I shiver to fornicate (though I don't like that word) with this precious angel, this Hispanic nymphet! To fuck her in the lotus posture, to rock her till her rectal axis and spinal cord break with love! (161)

11. More than any other black male writer, Major thematizes the poststructuralist theoretical system encompassed in the larger context of postmodernism. In *Reflex* and the later texts, the words are only symbols on a

page that deny the author the access to the reality of his characters that he wants. As the passage that I quote in my analysis shows, words deconstruct instead of construct meaning.

12. In *The Dark and Feeling,* Major has talked about the Freudian influence on *No* (137). In *Reflex,* the Freudian influence conflates with the author's larger emphasis on self-definition and sexual definition and on his attempt to control his discourse: "Cora was not afraid of her own unconscious life. She believed in the interplay between it and what she saw and felt everyday. Like Canada's dick. Or his face. Or the pots and pans" (33). Though the author is talking about his characters here, he is first and foremost defining his self and sexuality through his attempt to deal with the characters. In *Reflex,* various elements of the narrative become complicit in the author's oppression and failure of self-definition and of voice.

13. Lisa C. Roney links the paintings in *Emergency Exit* to the "heightening of the power of racial themes" (Roney 68).

14. Throughout the text, Mason refers to Ellison and other writers, perhaps referring to Jean Toomer more often than anyone else. The quotation is reminiscent of Toomer's *Cane,* in which the old man has a central role in "Kabnis" at the end. In "Kabnis," however, the character Kabnis is the one wearing the robe. As far as *Invisible Man* is concerned, the quotation evokes the setting of the epilogue, and it superimposes the grandfather and his character on this setting.

I also want to emphasize that there is a connection between *Invisible Man* and *My Amputations,* two texts that would seem to be unconnected. I will show this later in chapter 6 in my discussion of the broad tradition of Calibanic discourse's influence and Major's, Wideman's, and Johnson's literary relationship to Ellison in this context.

15. Analyzing *My Amputations* from the perspective of the paintings that are in the text, Lisa C. Roney also sees a quest for "sexual identity" in the first part (Roney 70) and a search for a "unified self" throughout the text (72).

16. Major's seventh novel, *Painted Turtle: Woman with Guitar* (1988), is the attempt of the narrator, a male who is part Navajo and part Hopi, to tell the story of a Zuni Indian woman, a musician, named Painted Turtle. The novel does not deal with African American characters or culture.

4. Charles Johnson's Response to "Caliban's Dilemma"

1. Rushdy says that the answer to "Caliban's dilemma" concerns Johnson in his "four narratives of slavery [*Oxherding Tale,* 'The Education of Mingo,' 'The Sorcerer's Apprentice,' and *Middle Passage*]" (375), which constitute a significant part of his fictional writing. Johnson names "Caliban's dilemma" as the condition of "black and feminist writers" (*Being* 39–40), but clearly in these narratives "Caliban's dilemma" refers to Johnson's condition as a black male writer mainly concerned with a world of men and primarily with the oppression of black men in this world. The "black and feminist writers" phrase is largely spurious.

Rushdy states that "throughout [his] narratives of slavery Johnson's American characters discover in the Allmuseri [Johnson's mythical African tribe] an ideal of intersubjective relations—that condition of resolving Caliban's dilemma by inhabiting what Johnson calls the 'transcendence of relativism'" (376). In his fictions, his black male main characters grow to understand the importance of "intersubjective relations," and concomitantly, they free themselves by giving up their black male voice and their black male identity to intersubjectivity. This is their escape and Johnson's escape from "Caliban's dilemma." The Allmuseri, Johnson's phenomenology, and "intersubjective relations" that resolve "Caliban's dilemma" are all synonymous, and their realization and acceptance entail giving up a black male voice of liberation and a black male identity.

2. Johnson applies his theory both to living beings and to inanimate things. The central concept in Johnson's various applications of intersubjectivity/phenomenology is that everything is part of a convoluting, constantly moving, constantly changing process of polymorphic wholeness that equally accepts all states, viewpoints, and perceptions of reality because of the very nature of its constant process.

In the act of theorizing the slave narrative in *Oxherding Tale,* Johnson demonstrates how his theory encompasses literary texts, living (human) being, and polymorphic states.

The Self, this perceiving Subject who puffs on and on, is, for all purposes, a palimpsest, interwoven with everything—literally everything—that can be thought or felt. We can go further: The Subject of the Slave Narrative, like all subjects, is forever *outside* itself in others, objects; he is parasitic, if you like, drawing his life from everything he is not, and at precisely the instant he makes possible their appearance. . . . to think the Slave Narrative properly is to see nowhere a narrator who falteringly interprets the world, but a narrator who *is* that world: who is less a reporter than an opening through which the world is delivered: first-person (if you wish) universal. (152–53)

The Self of the slave narrative is palimpsestic because it is a part of all literary traditions—such as the tradition of the "nineteenth century picaresque novel and story of manners" (119)—and all other living being and polymorphic states in the universe. It is "forever outside itself" because it is a part of everything else, and it draws its life from and gives life to this reality because it is a part of it. This quotation implies what Johnson goes further to state about reality elsewhere in *Oxherding Tale* and *Middle Passage.*

I would add to this that Eastern philosophy is a very important part of Johnson's palimpsest. Besides being grounded in Western philosophy, Johnson's fictions have parallel grounding in Eastern religion and philosophy, particularly in Zen Buddhism. See William Gleason's essay, "The Liberation of Perception: Charles Johnson's *Oxherding Tale," Black American Literature Forum,* volume 25, 705–28.

3. I take the phrase "liberating perception" from William Gleason's essay, "The Liberation of Perception: Charles Johnson's *Oxherding Tale," Black American Literature Forum,* volume 25, 705–28.

4. As my analysis of *Oxherding Tale* will show, black women have superior individual spiritual power and collective, communal spiritual power that sometimes control and always mitigate the actions of black men. A humorous episode in the text describes Mattie forcing George to pray with the proper sentiment and feeling. Andrew remembers that "Some nights . . . [George] prayed 'Oh Lord, kill all the whitefolks and leave all the nigguhs,' and Mattie, miffed, slapped him from behind, which made George yelp, 'Lord! Don't you know a white man from a nigguh?'" (142). Earlier, fear of Mattie influenced his decision to go to bed with the master's wife instead of going home to Mattie drunk: "She made him bend his knees beside her each night, their heads tipped and thighs brushing, praying that neither jealousy nor evil temper, boredom nor temptation, poverty nor padderolls, would destroy their devotion to each other. 'You have me, I have you,' Mattie whispered, 'and we both have Jesus.' It made George shudder. Why were black women so mystical? . . . 'No,' he said, shaking his head, glancing left at Jonathan, 'I'd best not go home tonight'" (5). Mattie's power over George is indicative of the power of black women generally.

5. Andrew narrates the story of his own conception and birth, which is reminiscent of both a black folktale and Laurence Sterne's *Tristam Shandy*. *Oxherding Tale's* address of the reader as "sir" also references *Tristam Shandy's* address of the reader as "Sir." Incorporating Sterne's text into his own is an example of Johnson's palimpsestic intersubjectivity/phenomenology.

6. In a recent interview, Johnson reads from another critic's soon-to-be published book about Johnson's work: "'His art and criticism now imply the preeminence of the intangible spiritual realm as a foundation for ethical, political, and social strategies in ways that are more liberal humanist than postmodern'" (Boccia 618). However, this notwithstanding, "Johnson is," as William Gleason says, "in practice (if not in theory) a self-consciously postmodern writer" (707). The multilayered, malleable form of his work is a large part of the foundation of this assertion. Gleason lists the postmodernist features of Johnson's work: "I cite its self-conscious dissolution of generic boundaries (including those that would distinguish non-fiction, autobiography, the eighteenth-century English novel, the slave narrative, and the Zen parable); the delight it takes in playing with these forms; its juxtaposition of stances (straight, ironic) and moods (comic, violent); its almost bewildering intertextuality (the tissue of references to literary, philosophical, and scientific works); its deliberate anachronisms; its humor; and its rampant ambiguity."

7. In his essay "*Oxherding Tale* and *Siddhartha*: Philosophy, Fiction, and the Emergence of a Hidden Tradition," Rudolph Byrd talks about various Eastern and Western philosophical/religious and literary influences on *Oxherding Tale*; his primary focus is Herman Hesse's *Siddhartha* and its influence on *Oxherding Tale*. Hesse's main character quests to attain "*moksha,* or release from *samsara*," "the cyclical nature of existence" (Byrd 551). Overall, Johnson both repeats and varies Hesse's thematic pattern, but both texts show the main character gaining knowledge of moksha, which is an enlightenment or liberation. Byrd's essay very well shows the palimpsestic layering that constitutes

Johnson's text. As I have said, palimpsestic textuality is an aspect of Johnson's intersubjective/phenomenological paradigm.

8. The plantation in *Oxherding Tale* named Leviathan is a self-contained commonwealth that in many ways subverts the narrow, restricted principles of Thomas Hobbes's *Leviathan* (1651). The intertextual relationship of Hobbes's text to Johnson's is another example of the palimpsestic layering in the latter text.

9. The Allmuseri is Johnson's mythical African tribe that symbolizes the process of polymorphic wholeness that is the intersubjective/phenomenological paradigm.

10. Wideman appropriates the Caliban trope and shows how the discourse that is concomitant to the trope influences the story told by black men, which incorporates the symbol of the mutilated, disfigured black male body. *The Tempest* would seem to imply that this symbol is incorporated in the trope through Miranda's accusation that Caliban "deserved more than prison" (*The Tempest* 436; *Philadelphia Fire* 139). In *Philadelphia Fire,* a primary depiction of the mutilated, disfigured black male body is the anonymous boy—"his neck broken and drawers droopy and caked with shit and piss" (93–94)—lynched publicly on the basketball court in the first-person black male narrator's waking nightmare. In *Philadelphia Fire,* the lynched boy is the narrator "and every black boy I've ever seen running up and down playing ball and I'm screaming for help and frozen in my tracks and can't believe it" (93).

This symbol of Calibanic discourse manifests itself in different black male texts, such as *Philadelphia Fire* and *Oxherding Tale,* and in the language and rituals of American culture. A historical tradition of lynching shows the latter, and contemporary events such as the dismembering of James Byrd Jr. in Jasper, Texas, on June 7, 1998, show this also.

11. Jonathan Little concludes that George "suffer[s] a comic fate. . . . George experiences 'the reward all black revolutionaries feared: an eternity of waiting tables'" (Little 145). However, George's fate hardly seems comic when one adds to Little's quotation from the text that the Soulcatcher also placed a gun to George's head and brutally shot him before he fell into hell to his revolutionary future.

12. Like Ellison who came before him, Johnson deals with black life and uses black experience and cultural reference in his work, but does not make black literature and black perspective central. Ellison's ideas influence Johnson, and a major way that they do is in terms of his borrowing from white, Western tradition and privileging of that tradition and in terms of his refusal to accept a fixed black perspective. In *Being and Race* (16–17), Johnson names *Invisible Man* as an important influence and emphasizes that "its central idea [is] that meaning cannot be fixed" (16). For Johnson, the black writer particularly should not assume a "fixed" black perspective that tries to control the black image (17–18). Further, throughout his critical discourse and fictions, he names various white, Western texts and traditions as influences that have a palimpsestic relationship to his work. This is similar to Ellison's naming of white writers as his "ancestors." So, Ellison, another black writer, is important to Johnson, but it is

Ellison's refusal to center blackness that influences him. I will talk further about the literary relationship between Johnson and Ellison in chapter 6.

13. The portrayal of Rutherford's brother Jackson does not fit the discursive pattern. However, like Reb in *Oxherding Tale,* whose portrayal also does not fit the pattern, Jackson is more an embodiment of the intersubjective/phenomenological paradigm than he is a character who is part of the more general black male reality.

14. Ashraf Rushdy makes the point that "*Middle Passage* is about [Rutherford's] middle passage to identity—and the ways theft, love, and writing help one ex-slave achieve a semblance of identity" ("Properties of Desire" 105). He does not, however, talk about the secondary black male characters who are slaves in *Middle Passage* and *Oxherding Tale,* who fail to achieve voice or identity.

15. In "Interrogating Identity: Appropriation and Transformation in *Middle Passage,*" Daniel Scott says that "Rutherford's sex and race and life are not inconsequential in the end, but they have been reconfigured according to more complex, less oppositional strategies of identification and—once identity has been considered—living" (648). In the context of my analysis, the "reconfiguring" of sex and race *do* make them inconsequential.

16. By the end of the text, Rutherford fits freed "colored men" (179) in the "country called America" into the thematic context of the intersubjective/phenomenological paradigm. The Allmuseri males from the ship, who already represent the paradigm, will fit into the "cauldron of mongrels" that is America, which is another representation of the paradigm, and this "cauldron" produces and accommodates black rascals like Papa Zeringue. Also, Santos remembers that his "granddaddy use to call hisself" Allmuseri (201).

5. Calibanic Discourse in Postmodern and Non-Postmodern Black Male Texts

1. Ellis defines a New Black Aesthetic ("The New Black Aesthetic," *Callaloo,* 12. 1, 233–43). According to Eric Lott, the foundation of Ellis's New Black Aesthetic, which underlies *Platitudes,* is the potential of a liberating "black postmodernism" (Lott 244) constructed through the "disparate work" of pastiche: "hip hop and the Black filmmaker foundation, George Wolfe and Alva Rogers, Terry McMillan and Lorna Simpson. . . ." I use the term "(white)" to describe the postmodern in *Platitudes* (and other black male texts) because the postmodern is a "(white)" theoretical configuration if its potential is not appropriated and voiced in terms of black liberation, and *Platitudes* does not achieve this black voicing. Lott does not talk about *Platitudes* but sounds skeptical about the claims of Ellis's New Black Aesthetic.

See my definition and discussion of Calibanic discourse as an unconscious discourse and of (white) postmodernism in the introduction.

2. The fact that the texts purport to achieve a voice of liberation that they do not achieve would seem to relate them directly to Clarence Major's *All-Night Visitors.* However, Major's text does thematize the writer and writing, and it is

the first in a series of closely connected texts by Major that become increasingly more postmodern over time. Major's later texts help to reveal *All-Night Visitors'* connection to them as well as the postmodernist characteristics that it has in common with them. In the context of my analysis in which I deal with these texts as a collective body, the external manifestation of liberation and/or achievement of voice becomes less clear as the texts go further toward the self-referential after *No* (1973).

3. In the introduction to *A Flann O'Brien Reader* (1978), Stephen Jones quotes Graham Greene's assessment of *At-Swim-Two Birds:* "It is in the line of *Tristam Shandy* and *Ulysses:* its amazing spirits do not disguise the seriousness of the attempt to present, simultaneously as it were, all the literary traditions of Ireland" (2).

4. The name, perhaps, ridicules Isshee's pretentiousness and the naïve, romanticized stories she tells, and at the same time suggests her security of self and ability to tell these stories. One reading of Isshee Ayam is "I She, I Am." This caricatures Isshee, but it also echoes a certainty and sufficiency akin to God's divinity in the Old Testament. In Exodus 3:14, God tells Moses "I AM THAT I AM . . . Thus shalt thou say unto the children of Israel, I AM hath sent me" (KJV).

5. In his essay about *Platitudes,* J. Martin Favor describes his project as, among other things, "locat[ing] those utterances which Ellis privileges as authentic and valuable in African American expression" (694). He concludes after analyzing the text: "Ellis spends a great deal of time undercutting voices which he feels are inauthentic, or at least non-representative of his [new black] aesthetic, but once he gives us a position which seems to be new (Earle as young, self-aware, urban, bourgeois black man) he subverts that, also. The real thing— in terms of 'true' African American voice—is a celebration of diverse blackness, not some sort of mediating voice, but even this formulation proves problematic." (703). For different reasons and from a much different critical perspective than mine, Favor reaches similar conclusions about the tentativeness of voice in *Platitudes.*

6. At the end of *Platitudes,* J. Martin Favor sees an apparent "turn toward the 'traditional' love plot," which is really a "turn toward a type of male sexual domination" (703), as represented by Dewayne's erection. Again, for different reasons and from a different critical perspective, Favor reaches a conclusion parallel to mine: The "turns of the plot" move the text toward a negative portrayal of Dewayne at the end.

7. In general terms, Mister Harper's story of the African is a "tall tale." It also has elements of African American folk stories of freedom that depict legendary Africans performing superhuman feats, such as escaping slavery by walking on the water or flying back to Africa. Mister Harper says that the men trying to capture the African "figured [he] must-a just tried to swim back home" (25). Later, he says "they thought they had him trapped with his back to the river and he just turned around, dove in and swam it underwater" (27).

8. See W. Lawrence Hogue's essay entitled "Disrupting the White/Black Binary: William Melvin Kelley's *A Different Drummer," CLA Journal*, volume 44,

no. 1. Hogue's essay follows in the line of most of the critical essays on *Different Drummer*, several of which he cites. In these essays, the black revolution in *Different Drummer* is successful. Hogue concludes that "Kelley produces an African-American male character who ceases to be a victim or a devalued Other. He produces an African-American male character who becomes a liberator" (40). This may be Kelley's intention, but my analysis very clearly shows that the text unconsciously challenges and compromises Tucker's voice and liberation quest.

9. An example is Matthew Wilson's "The African American Historian: David Bradley's *The Chaneysville Incident*," *African American Review*, volume 29, number 1, 97–107. Wilson stops short of considering the ending and concludes that John comes to understand himself and creates a "community legend." It is a "community legend that finds its source in Western conceptions of history and in the African American vernacular tradition, one that is made possible through the creation of a common discourse between John and Judith" (106).

10. Interestingly, the last voice in the story that John tells about C.K. is Harriet's voice.

11. Brown implies this through the novel's theme, and he implies it in statements that he has made. For example, in a 1977 interview, Charles Lynch asks Brown about Ellison's influence on his work, and Brown responds that jazz was the influence. Jazz musician Miles Davis is the symbol of expressive, liberating voice in the quotation from the interview that follows:

LYNCH: It struck me when reading your prologue that the "tragic magic in IF, MAYBE, SUPPOSE, and PERHAPS" touches upon that "invisible history" Ellison explores in *Invisible Man*. How would you relate the two phrases?

BROWN: There's something very unresolved or inconclusive about those words "if," "maybe," "suppose," and "perhaps," and that's what gives them their strength. Human behavior is neither absolute nor one-dimensional. For example, many have said that what is important about jazz is what is left out. Miles Davis can evoke by the innuendo of his muted sound far more possibilities than he can by hitting a note straight on. It is that illusive dimension in jazz and in life that is far more compelling than a kind of journalistic accounting of experience where more attention is paid to what happened than to what it felt like. (49)

12. In his interview with Brown, Charles Lynch asks, "Did Ellison or any other writer influence the writing of *Tragic Magic?*" (48–49). With regard to the specific influence of Ellison, Brown answers ambiguously: "Obviously I've been influenced by what I've read, but I don't believe books were a major influence on the structure of the novel. I would say I was more directly influenced by jazz, which influenced me in its reliance on improvisation."

13. Critics have lauded *Invisible Man* as the novel that broke the hold of social realism [as initiated by Richard Wright's *Native Son* (1940)] on the black fictional tradition and opened up the "universal" possibilities of modernism. Among other reasons, *Invisible Man* is a modernist novel because it tries to force a re-perception and reconstruction of the world based on the novel's vision that institutions and traditions have become corrupt, calcified, and stagnant. In part

at least, Ellison, like Brown, uses the mode of the surreal to expose the underlying modernist reality that he wants to portray. In the context of modernism, both novels use the surreal mode to force readers to new perceptions.

However, *Invisible Man* is also a novel that has qualities making it a precursor to black male texts that imply the need for a black voicing of (white) postmodernism. As the explicit naming of the act of writing the novel in the epilogue shows, *Invisible Man* is concerned with the *multiple* versions of reality that it writes. In the context of (white) postmodernism, the text writes multiple fictions, and it cannot construct a black fiction that opposes dominant racist fictions. I talk about the black voicing of (white) postmodernism by black male writers in chapters 2, 3, and 4.

6. Ralph Ellison and the Literary Background of Contemporary Black Male Postmodern Writers

1. In analyzing Trueblood in chapter 2 of *Invisible Man* in *Blues, Ideology, and Afro-American Literature*, Houston Baker says that the "black phallus is a dominant symbol in the novel's formal patterns of behavior. . . . [It] offers an instance of ritual in which the black phallus gathers an extraordinary burden of disparate connotations, both sensuous and ideological. . . . Ellison recognizes the black phallus as a dominant symbol of the sometimes bizarre social rituals of America and incorporates it into the text of the novel" (181). The black phallus is also a dominant symbol for this study in the context of the effects of the hegemony of Calibanic discourse, in which Calibanic phallicism is a major theme.

2. In *Invisible Man*, it is hard to separate the unconscious compromise of the story of liberation from what Ellison does on a conscious intellectual level. However, conscious intellectual perception, formulation, and practice do not change the point that Calibanic discourse is (un)conscious in the text. As is true in Wideman's *Philadelphia Fire* (1990), Calibanic discourse has virtually the same overall effect although it may be consciously thematized at times.

3. In the texts, Ellison stresses the influence of white male writers, whom he calls his literary "ancestors," and the literary voice of white, Western culture above the influence of black male writers, his literary "relatives," and the voice of black literature and black culture. However, as Henry Louis Gates Jr. points out, Ellison's "ancestors [also] provided model texts for revision" (121). Especially in *Shadow and Act*, Ellison's "revision" is a clearly stated criticism of the moral failures of the texts of the "ancestors" in the midst of effusive praise. This is an understated and subtle counter-signifying on white men and their fictions. (*Invisible Man* is a "revision" of the texts of the "ancestors" that makes this counter-signifying more apparent.) Yet, in the final analysis, the white male literary voice and tradition are still reference points that contest and restrict Ellison's counter-signifying black voice in the texts. The counter-signifying "revision" in Ellison's texts is strong, but the more powerful effect in the texts is still unconscious analogy.

4. In *Interviews With Black Writers* (1973), John O'Brien, ed., Wideman

says, "[T]he novels of Richard Wright and Ralph Ellison have been most important to me. And . . . are just beginning [around 1973] to become embodied in the
things that I write. [Jean] Toomer's *Cane* . . . was very important . . . because of
its experimentation and open form and also because of Toomer's vision" (216).
In an interview by Wilfred Samuels (*Callaloo*, 6.1, 40–59), Wideman says that
he is "eclectic," and that a range of black writers, not just Ellison, have "transformed" his fiction since the late 1960s (45). In this same interview, he also
repeats what he said in the O'Brien interview: Ralph Ellison and Richard Wright
were the first two black writers he read, sometime before 1967 or 1968 (44). As
I say at the beginning of this chapter, Wright's fiction broadly and generally
corresponds to Ellison's in the black male tradition of restricted liberating voice.

5. Wideman also specifies Eliot as an influence in the O'Brien interview
(216). In connection with comments about Toomer's influence as an experimen-
talist, he goes further to say, "I go back to the eighteenth century and the beginning of the novel when I talk about influences of experimentalists—to Defoe,
Fielding, and particularly Laurence Sterne. If there is any single book I learned a
lot from, its *Tristam Shandy*" (217).

6. One of Wideman's critical essays is entitled "Defining the Black Voice in
Fiction" (*Black American Literature Forum*, 11.3, 79–82). Wideman focuses on
the fiction of Charles W. Chesnutt, Zora Neale Hurston, and Gayl Jones. He
says that "black speech cannot escape entirely the frame of American literary
language," but he clearly implies that "the black voice in fiction [has] become a
distinct, independent index to reality" (82). This is true because "Chesnutt,
Hurston and Jones each attack the authority of the literary frame which mediates between black speech and reality." There is indeed an authentic black voice
in Wideman's own fictions, but this voice is also contested and restricted when it
tells a story of liberation.

7. The term "betwixt-and-between" references Victor Turner's concept of
liminality in *The Forest of Symbols* (1967). For Turner, the "betwixt-and-between period" is one of "fruitful darkness" (110). I "shift" Turner's concept and
give it a different meaning in the black American male context of restricted or
compromised voice and freedom.

8. In *Oxherding Tale*, Johnson says that the slave narrative (and therefore
the book he is writing) has "a long pedigree that makes philosophical play with
the form less outrageous than you might think" (118). In the slave narrative,
"meanings accumulate in layers of tissue as the form evolves" (119). Johnson
calls St Augustine the "first philosophical black writer," and names his *Confessions* as a seminal text for white Western traditions—the Puritan narrative,
picaresque novel, and novel of manners among them—that give the slave narrative its pedigree.

9. The Lifeworld is a representation of Johnson's paradigm. To create this
representation of the paradigm, Johnson draws on phenomenological theory that
accounts for the relationship between readers and writers and their texts as well
as the relationship between different writers and their texts. Mediation is a key

term. Generally, in the former relationship, the mediation among author, text, and reader is uncertain and ambiguous, but it is powerful in its potential to produce fresh perspectives. The reader's perspective is fresh and liberating, but it is not a replication of the author's intention.

Some phenomenologists whom Johnson cites in *Being and Race* besides Maurice Merleau-Ponty are Edmund Husserl, the "father" of phenomenology, Max Scheler, Martin Heidegger, Jean Paul Sartre, Mikel Dufrenne, and Roman Ingarden.

Works Cited

Baker, Houston A ., Jr. *Blues, Ideology, and Afro-American Literature: A Vernacular Theory.* Chicago: Univ. of Chicago Press, 1984.

Bakhtin, Mikhail. *The Dialogic Imagination: Four Essays.* Trans. Caryl Emerson and Michael Holquist. Austin: Univ. of Texas Press, 1981.

Bell, Bernard. "Clarence Major's Double Consciousness as a Black Postmodernist Artist." *African American Review* 28.1 (1994), 5–9.

———."Clarence Major's Homecoming Voice in *Such Was the Season.*" *African American Review* 28.1 (1994), 89–94.

Berben, Jacqueline. "Beyond Discourse: The Unspoken Versus Words in the Fiction of John Edgar Wideman." *Callaloo* 8 (fall 1985): 525–34.

Berben-Masi, Jacqueline. "From *Brothers and Keepers* to *Two Cities:* Social and Cultural Consciousness, Art and Imagination." *Callaloo* 22.3 (1999), 568–84.

Birat, Kathie. "'All Stories Are True': Prophesy, History and Story in *The Cattle Killing.*" *Callaloo* 22.3 (1999), 629–43.

Boccia, Michael. "An Interview With Charles Johnson." *African American Review* 30.4 (1996), 611–18.

Bradley, David. *The Chaneysville Incident.* New York: Harper Row, 1981.

Brown, Wesley. *Tragic Magic.* New York: Random House, 1978.

Byrd, Rudolph. "*Oxherding Tale* and *Siddhartha:* Philosophy, Fiction, and the Emergence of a Hidden Tradition." *African American Review* 30.4 (1996), 549–58.

de Sausurre, Ferdinand. *Course in General Linguistics.* Trans. Roy Harris. Lasalle, Ill.: Open Court, 1983.

Ellis, Trey. *Platitudes.* New York: Random House, 1988.

———. "The New Black Aesthetic." *Callaloo* 12.1 (1989), 233–43.

Ellison, Ralph. *Going to the Territory.* New York: Random House, 1986.

———. *Invisible Man.* New York: Random House, 1952.

————. *Shadow and Act*. New York: Random House, 1964.

Fabre, Michel. "Opening of the Symposium in Tours." *Callaloo* 22.3 (1999), 587–93.

Fagel, Brian. "Passages From the Middle: Coloniality and Postcoloniality in Charles Johnson's *Middle Passage*." *African American Review* 30.4 (1996), 625–34.

Fanon, Frantz. *Black Skins, White Masks*. New York: Grove Press, 1967.

Favor, J. Martin. "'Ain't Nothin' Like the Real Thing, Baby': Trey Ellis's Search for New Black Voices." *Callaloo* 16.3 (1993), 694–705.

Foucault, Michel. *The Order of Things: An Archaeology of the Human Sciences*. New York: Random House, 1970.

Gates, Henry Louis, Jr. *The Signifying Monkey: A Theory of African American Literary Criticism*. New York: Oxford, 1988.

Gleason, William. "The Liberation of Perception: Charles Johnson's *Oxherding Tale*." *Black American Literature Forum* 25.4 (1991), 705–28.

Grandjeat, Yves-Charles. "Brother Figures: The Rift and Riff in John E. Wideman's Fiction." *Callaloo* 22.3 (1999), 615–22.

————. "'These Strange Dizzying Pauses': Silence as Common Ground in J.E. Wideman's Texts." Callaloo 22.3 (1999), 685–94.

Gysin, Fritz. "'Do Not Fall Asleep in Your Enemy's Dreams': John Edgar Wideman and the Predicament of Prophecy." *Callaloo* 22.3 (1999), 623–28.

Henderson, Stephen, ed. *Understanding the New Black Poetry: Black Speech and Black Music as Poetic References*. New York: Penguin, 1973.

Hobbes, Thomas. *Leviathan*. 1651.

Hogue, W. Lawrence. "Disrupting the White/Black Binary: William Melvin Kelley's *A Different Drummer*." *CLA Journal* 44.1 (2000), 1–42.

Holloway, Karla F.C. *Moorings and Metaphors: Figures of Culture and Gender in Black Women's Literature*. New Brunswick, N.J.: Rutgers Univ. Press, 1992.

Hutcheon, Linda. *A Poetics of Postmodernism*. New York: Routledge, 1988.

————.*The Politics of Postmodernism*. New York: Routledge, 1989.

Johnson, Charles. *Being and Race: Black Writing Since 1970*. Bloomington: Indiana Univ. Press, 1988.

————. *Middle Passage*. New York: Penguin, 1990.

————. *Oxherding Tale*. New York: Grove Press, 1982.

————. "Philosophy and Black Fiction." *Obsidian* 6.1–2 (1980), 55–61.

Kelley, William Melvin. *A Different Drummer*. New York: Doubleday, 1962.

Klinkowitz, Jerome. "Clarence Major's Innovative Fiction." *African American Review* 28.1 (1994), 57–63.

Kutnik, Jerzy and McCaffery, Larry. "'I Follow My Eyes': An Interview With Clarence Major." *African American Review* 28.1 (1994), 121–38.

Little, Jonathan. "Charles Johnson's Revolutionary *Oxherding Tale*." *Studies in American Literature* 19 (1991), 141–51.

Lott, Eric. "Responses to Trey Ellis's 'The New Black Aesthetic.'" *Callaloo* 12.1 (1989), 244–46.

Lynch, Charles. "Wesley Brown's *Tragic Magic:* An Interview." *First World* 2.2 (1979), 47–49.

Major, Clarence. *All-Night Visitors.* New York: Olympia, 1969. Unexpurgated version with foreword by Bernard W. Bell. Boston: Northeastern Univ. Press, 1998.

———. *The Dark and Feeling.* New York: Third Press, 1974.

———. *Dirty Bird Blues.* San Francisco: Mercury House, 1996.

———. *Emergency Exit.* New York: Fiction Collective, 1979.

———. *My Amputations.* New York: Fiction Collective, 1986.

———. *No.* New York: Emerson Hall, 1973.

———. *Painted Turtle: Woman with Guitar.* Los Angeles: Sun and Moon, 1988.

———. *Reflex and Bone Structure.* New York: Fiction Collective, 1975.

———. *Such Was the Season.* San Francisco: Mercury House, 1987.

Morrison, Toni. *Beloved.* New York: Knopf, 1987.

O'Brien, John, ed. *Interviews With Black Writers.* New York: Liveright, 1973.

Petry, Ann. *The Street.* Boston: Houghton Mifflin, 1946.

Retamar, Roberto Fernandez. "Caliban: Notes Toward a Discussion of Culture in Our America." *Massachusetts Review* 15.1–2 (1974), 7–72.

Richard, Jean-Pierre. "*Philadelphia Fire,* or The Shape of a City." *Callaloo* 22.3 (1999), 603–13.

Robinson, E.A. "Richard Cory." 1897.

Roney, Lisa C. "The Double Vision of Clarence Major, Painter and Writer." *African American Review* 28.1 (1994), 65–75.

Rowell, Charles. "An Interview With John Edgar Wideman." *Callaloo* 13.1 (1990), 47–61.

Rushdy, Ashraf H.A. "The Phenomenology of the Allmuseri: Charles Johnson and the Subject of the Narrative of Slavery." *African American Review* 26.3 (1992), 373–94.

———. "The Properties of Desire: Forms of Slave Identity in Charles Johnson's *Middle Passage.*" *Arizona Quarterly* 50.2 (1994), 73–108.

Samuels, Wilfred. "Going Home: A Conversation with John Edgar Wideman." *Callaloo* 6.1 (1983), 40–59.

Scott, Daniel. "Interrogating Identity: Appropriation and Transformation in *Middle Passage.*" African American Review 29.4 (1995), 645–55.

Shakespeare, William. *The Tempest.* 1611.

Silverman, Kaja. *The Subject of Semiotics.* New York: Oxford, 1983.

Sterne, Laurence. *Tristam Shandy.* 1759–67.

Tate, Claudia. *Psychoanalysis and Black Novels: Desire and the Protocols of Race.* New York: Oxford, 1998.

Toomer, Jean. *Cane.* New York: Boni and Liveright, 1923.

Turner, Victor. *The Forest of Symbols: Aspects of Ndembu Ritual.* Ithaca, N.Y.: Cornell Univ. Press, 1967.

Wideman, John Edgar. "Preface." *Breaking Ice.* Ed. Terry McMillan. New York: Penguin, 1990.

———. *The Cattle Killing.* New York: Houghton Mifflin, 1996.

———. *Damballah*. New York: Avon, 1981.

———. "Defining the Black Voice in Fiction." *Black American Literature Forum* 11.3 (1977), 79–82.

———. *Fatheralong*. New York: Pantheon, 1994.

———. *Fever*. New York: Holt, 1989.

———. *Hiding Place*. New York: Avon, 1981.

———. "In Praise of Silence." *Callaloo* 22.3 (1999), 547–49.

———. *The Lynchers*. New York: Harcourt Brace, 1973.

———. *Philadelphia Fire*. New York: Holt, 1990.

———. *Reuben*. New York: Holt, 1987.

———. *Sent for You Yesterday*. New York: Avon, 1983

———. "The Silence of Thelonious Monk." *Callaloo* 22.3 (1999), 550–57.

———. *Two Cities*. New York: Houghton Mifflin, 1998.

Williams, Sherley Anne. *Dessa Rose*. New York: Morrow, 1986.

Wilson, Matthew. "The African American Historian: David Bradley's *The Chaneysville Incident*." *African American Review* 29.1 (1995), 97–107.

Wright, Richard. *Native Son*. New York: Harper and Brothers, 1940.

Index

All-Night Visitors (Major): attempt to subvert Calibanic discourse, by explicit opposition, 62; —, through compassionate expression, 63–65; —, through sexual language, 14, 60, 61–63; Calibanic discourse as unconscious discourse in, 61–65; Calibanic discourse's (re)inscription, by essentialized language, 61, 65, 168n. 6; —, through male cultural ritual, 63; Calibanic phallicism in, 61, 64; liminality in, 61, 65–66, 168n. 2, 169n. 8; main character and *Philadelphia Fire*'s critique of Caliban, 61, 65–66; male dominance by linguistic signs for body, 61–62, 65; male writers' quest to free himself by writing, 64, 168n. 5; superficially "good" ending of, 61, 65–66; thematic paradox and Calibanic discourse's (re)inscription, 65. *See also* Calibanic discourse

Allen, Bishop Richard, 167n. 14

Augustine, Saint: *Confessions*, 178n. 8

Baker, Houston A., Jr.: *Blues, Ideology, and Afro-American Literature*, 3, 157n. 3, 177n. 1

Bakhtin, Mikhail: "Discourse in the Novel," 156–57n. 2, 162n. 9

Barthes, Roland: *S/Z*, 162n. 9

Baudrillard, Jean, 159n. 8

Being and Race (Johnson): 81, 96, 131, 143, 144, 145, 173n. 12, 179n. 9

Benveniste, Emile: "Language in Freudian Theory," 162n. 9

Bell, Bernard: "Clarence Major's Double Consciousness as a Black Postmodernist artist," 142; "Clarence Major's Homecoming Voice in *Such Was the Season*," 79; "Foreword to the 1998 Edition [of *All-Night Visitors*]," 167n. 1, 168n. 4

Berben, Jacqueline: "Beyond Discourse," 160n. 1

Berben-Masi, Jacqueline, 148, 149–50

Birat, Kathie: "All Stories are True," 165n. 2, 167n. 13

black male and female writers, contemporary: generally compared 1–2, 159n. 9, 161n. 6

black male counter-signifying: and Calibanic discourse's compromise of black male subjectivity, 6–13; complementing symbolic and sexual terms of, 6–13; concept as derived from signifying, 6; and cooperative achievement of manhood, power, and status, 8–9; cultural dispersal through forms and forums, 6–13; examples of, 6–8; and history of black male oppression, 9; and intelligence, humanity, civilization, and virtuoso voice, 6–13; irony, hyperbole, improvisation, and subtlety in male competition, 8–9; the "man," "main man," and "bad man" in, 7–9; primary signs of, 9–11; words, acts, rituals, and forms of, 6. *See also* Calibanic discourse

black male postmodernist novels: (white) postmodernism's highlight of Calibanic discourse in, 5–6

black male postmodernist novels, overall influences in: Ellison, Calibanic discourse, and (white) postmodernism as, 16, 129–47 (*see also* (white) postmodernism). *See also* Calibanic discourse; postmodern

black male writers, comparisons of: de-formation in writing of Ellison and Major, 140–43; postmodern potential in writing of Ellison and Major, 140, 142–43 (*see also* postmodern); the similarities of Ellison, Johnson, and Major, 143–44; textuality and subjectivity in Ellison and Johnson, 145–47, 144; voice in writing of Ellison and Johnson, 140–41; writer's quest in writing of Ellison and Major, 140–41. *See also* Calibanic discourse

black male writers, contemporary: achievement of, 148–53, 155; Calibanic discourse's manifestation in critical writing of, 13 (*see also* unconscious analogy, defined); the connection among, 1–2, 13, 154–55; conscious and unconscious "space" in postmodernist novels of, 148–49, 153 (*see also*

postmodern); literary tradition of Calibanic discourse in novels of, 129. *See also* Calibanic discourse

black novels: the difference gender makes in achieving voice, 2

Boccia, Michael: "An Interview with Charles Johnson," 172n. 6

Bradley, David. See *The Chaneysville Incident*

Brown, Rap (Rap Brown's poem), 6–7, 8

Brown, Wesley. See *Tragic Magic*

Byrd, James, Jr., 157n. 5, 173n. 10

Byrd, Rudolph: "*Oxherding Tale* and *Siddhartha*," 84, 85, 172–73n. 7

Caliban: as defined by Caliban trope, 2–3; his enslavement through language by patriarchy, 2–3; scholarly tradition of his oppressive portrayal, 3, 157n. 3

Calibanic discourse: and the Caliban trope, 2–3; and Calibanic phallicism 6, 11, 61, 64; changing the reality of, 155; defined as the negative story of black men, 3; illustration of hegemony, 13; its centrality in the English language, 3; its effect in postmodernist and non-postmod-ernist novels compared, 4, 15, 100–102; its saturation and ironic effect on male writers, 154–55; as linguistic obstacle to liberation, 15–16; manifestation in linguistic signs and male bodies, 3; and quality of black male novels, 16–17; an unconscious discourse in male novels and culture, 3–6, 9, 11–16, 157–59n. 7, 160–61n. 5. *See also* black male counter-signifying

Calibanic discourse and *Invisible Man*: relationship and influence on black male novels, 1

Calibanic discourse and story of liberation: as central features of black male novels, 1; inseparable relationship of, 3–4

Calibanic discourse, general pattern of: in black male novels, 154. *See also* Calibanic discourse

Calibanic discourse, (re)inscription of: role of ambiguity and paradox in, 4; through characterization and narrative structure and theme, 4

Calibanic legacy: the reality beneath its revelation in male novels, 155. *See also* Calibanic discourse

Cattle Killing, The (Wideman): Calibanic discourse's (re)inscription through paradox and irony, 58; compared to *Reuben*, 43–44; complexity represented through conscious and unconscious of, 149; emphasis on male voice, 43–44; importance of on-going quest for voice, 149–50; liberating spiritual and supernatural vision and synchronous stories, 45–50; liberating stories' process and content, 46, 48, 52, 164–65n. 2; liberating storytelling and sustaining love, 51, 52–53; liberating storytelling as response to white fictions, 43–44; liberating storytelling process described, 38, 41–42, 44–45, 49, 50, 56, 164–65n. 2; liberating storytelling process inculcated by telling stories, 45, 47–48, 49–50; liberating storytelling process' movement toward ambiguity, 49, 52, 53, 57–58; liberating storytelling, the cattle myth, and oppression, 49–52, 56–57; liberation through intersubjective storytelling process, 44–58; male writers'/characters' intersubjective bonding and storytelling, 44–45, 48–52, 55–58; narrator's intersubjective bonding with and storytelling to women, 45, 47–48, 52–55; overall potential for

liberating voice, 57–58; potential silencing of liberating storytelling by great oppression, 51–53 (*see also* story of liberation); spiritual and supernatural vision, image of, 45–46; story of liberation, postmodernist potential, and novel's greatness, 58 (*see also* story of liberation; postmodern); thematized narratives and liberation, 53–58; utter despair about oppression, images of, 48–49, 51–52, 54; (white) postmodernism's highlight of Calibanic discourse, 44 (*see also* (white) postmodernism); Xhosa cattle killing myth explained, 50–52. *See also* Calibanic discourse

challenge and compromise (of story of liberation): defined, 4

Chaneysville Incident, The (Bradley): achieving human imagination, 114, 118–20; attempt to construct liberating male history, 116–21; Calibanic discourse and story of liberation, 102, 121 (*see also* story of liberation); Calibanic discourse's (re)inscription through ambiguity and paradox, 115, 117, 119–21; male community and failure of stories, 115–16; misogyny in, 114; relevance of *Philadelphia Fire*'s critique to, 121; superficially "good" ending of, 114–15, 119–21, 176n. 9. *See also* Calibanic discourse

Chesnutt, Charles W., 178n. 6

continuum of influences: Ellison, Wideman, Major, and Johnson as part of, 130, 140

The Dark and Feeling (Major), 67–68, 140–42, 144, 170n. 12

Davis, Miles, 176n. 11

Defoe, Daniel, 178n. 5

A Different Drummer (Kelley):

ambiguous male voice and liberation in, 109–13, 175–76n. 8; and Caliban trope, 110; Calibanic discourse's (re)inscription through paradox and ambiguity, 109, 110, 113–14; compared generally to other male novels, 101; failure to revise Caliban's linguistic legacy, 114; importance of and similarity to *Philadelphia Fire*, 15, 101; *Tempest*'s legacy and conscious and unconscious story, 101, 109; white voice and black liberation, 111–13; white voice and revision of *Tempest*, 112. *See also* Calibanic discourse

Dirty Bird Blues (Major): discussed in context of Major's earlier novels, 78–80; most realistic novel by Major, 79; overall implications of its negative male portrayals, 79–80. *See also* Calibanic discourse

Dostoyevski, Fyodor, 133

Dufrenne, Mikel, 179n. 9

Eagleton, Terry, 159n. 8

Eliot, T.S., 133, 134, 137, 162n. 10, 178n. 5

Ellis, Trey: "The New Black Aesthetic," 104, 174n. 1. See also *Platitudes*

Ellison, Ralph: broad influence on black male fiction and criticism, 129–30; counter-signifying in critical writing of, 133, 134–35, 177n. 3 (*see also* black male counter-signifying); opposition to Richard Wright, 129; unconscious analogy in critical writing of, 133–36, 177n. 3 (*see also* unconscious analogy, defined); white writers and tradition in critical writing, 133–35. *See also* Calibanic discourse; *Invisible Man*; *Going to the Territory*; *Shadow and Act*

Emergency Exit (Major): Calibanic discourse's (re)inscription in story of liberation, 76 (*see also* story of liberation); comparison to *Reflex and Bone Structure*, 75; self-referential narrative as site of story of liberation, 76 (*see also* story of liberation); story of liberation's silencing, 76; textual discourse's liberating/imprisoning potential for male writer, 75–76. *See also* Calibanic discourse

Fabre, Michel: "Opening of the Symposium in Tours," 163n. 12, 166–67n. 9

Fagel, Brian: "Passages from the Middle," 98

Fanon, Frantz: *Black Skin, White Masks*, 157n. 3

Fatheralong (Wideman): race and distance between black fathers and sons, 149

Faulkner, William, 131, 133, 137, 162n. 10

Favor, J. Martin: "'Ain't Nothin' Like the Real Thing, Baby,'" 175nn. 5–6

Fielding, Henry, 178n. 5

Foucault, Michel: *The Order of Things*, 6, 12–13, 157–59n. 7, 160–61n. 5, 161n. 7

Freud, Sigmund, 158n. 7, 160n. 5

Gaines, Ernest, 1

Gates, Henry Louis, Jr.: *The Signifying Monkey*, 6, 7, 177n3

Gleason, William: "The Liberation of Perception," 171nn. 2–3, 172n. 6

Going to the Territory (Ellison), 133–36

Grandjeat, Yves-Charles: "Brother Figures," 166n. 7; "'These Strange Dizzy Pauses,'" 166n. 7

Greene, Graham, 175n. 3

Gysin, Fritz: "'Do Not Fall Asleep in Your Enemy's Dreams,'" 58, 166n. 8, 167n. 14

Heidegger, Martin, 179n. 9

Hemingway, Ernest, 133, 134, 137, 162n. 10
Henderson, Stephen, 6, 7
Hesse, Herman: *Siddhartha*, 172n. 7
Hiding Place (Wideman): black male counter-signifying, and Calibanic discourse's hegemony, 9–13; —, and implied and explicit expression, 10–11; —, and sexual virtuosity and power, 10–12; —, and the white world, 12; Calibanic discourse and black male proscription, 11; —, and creation of reality, 12; —, as unconscious discourse, 11–12. *See also* Calibanic discourse
Hobbes, Thomas: *Leviathan*, 173n. 8
Hogue, W. Lawrence: "Disrupting the White/Black Binary," 175–76n. 8
Holloway, Karla F.C.: *Moorings and Metaphors*, 2, 157–58n. 7, 161n. 6, 165n. 6
Howe, Irving, 133
Hurston, Zora Neale, 178n. 6
Husserl, Edmund, 179n. 9
Hutcheon, Linda: *A Poetics of Postmodernism*, 5; *The Politics of Postmodernism*, 5

Ingarden, Roman, 179n. 9
Invisible Man (Ellison): black male counter-signifying in, 132–33 (*see also* black male counter-signifying); Calibanic legacy and restricted story of liberation, 130, 131–33 (*see also* story of liberation); implications about texts of white masters, 131–32; as precursor to black male postmodernist novel, 130, 143–44, 153, 176–77n. 13 (*see also* postmodern). *See also* Calabanic discourse

James, Henry, 137
Jameson, Frederick, 159n. 8
Little, Jonathan: "Charles Johnson's

Revolutionary *Oxherding Tale*," 173n. 11
Johnson, Charles: achievement of, 17, 151–53; Calibanic discourse in *Middle Passage* and *Oxherding Tale*, 15; Calibanic discourse's (re)inscription through unique dimensions of novels, 82–84, 99; "Caliban's dilemma" as opposition to whiteness in novels, 81, 83–84, 170–71n. 1; concept of "Lifeworld" in phenomenology of, 146–47, 178–79n. 9; conscious and unconscious "space" in novels, 151–53; "The Education of Mingo," 170n. 1; Ellison's central influence on, 143, 147, 173–74n. 12; formless being, unconscious analogy, and connection to Ellison, 143–45, 147 (*see also* unconscious analogy, defined); intersubjectivity and liberation of perception in novels, 81–83; intersubjectivity as answer to "Caliban's dilemma" in novels, 81–84, 170–71n. 1; intersubjectivity/ phenomenology as postmodernist form in novels, 83–84, 172n. 6 (*see also* postmodern); liberating intersubjectivity as central idea in novels, 82; phenomenology and opposition to Ellison's concept of reality, 144–45; phenomenology and radical approach in writing, 143–44; phenomenology as postmodernist paradigm of formless, destabilized subject, 144–45, 146–47 (*see also* postmodern); "Philosophy and Black Fiction," 144; "The Sorcerer's Apprentice," 170n. 1; (white) postmodernism's highlight of Calibanic discourse in novels, 84 (*see also* (white) postmodernism). See also *Being and Race*; Calibanic discourse; *Middle Passage*; *Oxherding Tale*

Jones, Gayl, 178n. 6
Jones, Stephen: *A Flann O'Brien Reader*, 175n. 3
Joyce, James, 134; *Ulysses*, 175n. 3

Kelley, William Melvin. See *A Different Drummer*
The King James Bible, 165n. 5, 175n. 4
Klinkowitz, Jerome, 76

Lacan, Jacques, 158n. 7, 160n. 5
Lott, Eric: "Responses to Trey Ellis's 'The New Black Aesthetic,'" 174n. 1
Lynch, Charles: "Wesley Brown's *Tragic Magic*," 176nn. 11–12
Lynchers, The (Wideman), 16
Lyotard, Jean-Francois, 159n. 8

Major, Clarence: achievement of, 17, 150–51; ambiguity, paradox, and Calibanic discourse's (re)inscription in novels, 14, 60; apparent difference from other black male writers, 150; Calibanic discourse's general influence in novels described, 60; conscious and unconscious "space" in novels, 150–51; Ellison as aesthetic standard in nonfiction of, 141; importance of yearning for liberating voice in novels, 150–51; male writers' liberation quest through writing in novels, 59–60; nonfiction's concept of self compared to Ellison's, 141–43; novels' collective and individual response to Calibanic discourse, 60; overall similarity of novels, 59–60, 174–75n. 2; self- referential narrative and story of liberation in novels, 14, 59–60; story of liberation in novels defined, 59 (*see also* story of liberation); summary of liberating quest in novels, 77–78; textual discourse's liberating/imprisoning potential in novels, 59;

(white) postmodernism's highlight of Calibanic discourse in novels, 60 (*see also* (white) postmodernism); writers' attempts to define the self in novels, 14. See also *All-Night Visitors*; Calibanic discourse; *The Dark and Feeling*; *Dirty Bird Blues*; *Emergency Exit*; *My Amputations*; *No*; *Painted Turtle*; *Reflex and Bone Structure*; *Such Was the Season*
Malraux, Andre, 133, 145
McMillan, Terry, 174n. 1; *Breaking Ice*, 138, 139
Merleau-Ponty, Maurice, 146, 179n. 9
Middle Passage (Johnson): black self as fiction, 98; Calibanic discourse's more subtle (re)inscription, 95, 99; "Caliban's dilemma" in, 96; intersubjectivity, hybridization, and changed perception, 95–99; male portrayal and Calibanic discourse's (re)inscription, 96–97; similarity of structure and theme to *Oxherding Tale*'s, 95–97, 99. See also Calibanic discourse
Morrison, Toni, *Beloved*, 159n. 9, 161n. 6
My Amputations (Major): Calibanic discourse's (re)inscription in story of liberation, 77 (*see also* story of liberation); references to *Cane* and *Invisible Man*, 77, 170n. 14; self- referential narrative as site of story of liberation, 76–77 (*see also* story of liberation); story of liberation's silencing, 77, 151 (*see also* story of liberation); textual discourse's liberating/imprisoning potential for male writer, 76–77. See also Calibanic discourse

No (Major): ambiguity and paradox of story of liberation, 66, 71 (*see also* story of liberation); ambiguity of self and sexual identity, 71;

Calibanic discourse's (re)inscription in story of liberation, 71–72 (*see also* story of liberation); comparison to *All-Night Visitors*, 66; Freudian influence in, 67–68, 170n. 12; general comparison to other postmodernist novels, 68 (*see also* postmodern); liberation quest through narrative discourse, 66; liberation quest through postmodernist form of, 67–71 (*see also* postmodern); male writer's implied role and liberation quest, 67; mergence of textual discourse and self-referential narrative, 66; self-referential narrative as site of story of liberation, 66, 67, 68–71 (*see also* story of liberation); superficially "good" ending compared to *All-Night Visitors*, 71–72; (white) postmodernism's failed potential, 68 (*see also* (white) postmodernism). *See also* Calibanic discourse

O'Brien, Flann: *At-Swim-Two Birds*, 103, 175n. 3
O'Brien, John: *Interviews with Black Writers*, 177–78nn. 4–5
Oxherding Tale (Johnson): Calibanic discourse and construction of black masculinity, 84–88, 90, 92–95; Calibanic discourse's (re)inscription through unique dimensions of, 85, 88, 90–95; "Caliban's dilemma" in, 84, 90, 93–94; contrasting power of black women, 86, 94, 152–53, 161n. 6, 172n. 4; intersubjective paradigm's liberation of perception, 84, 88, 91–93; main character's separation from other men, 88; paradox and Calibanic discourse's (re)inscription, 95; relevance of Caliban trope to male characters,

93, 173n. 10; women's role in main character's liberation, 88–90. *See also* Calibanic discourse

Painted Turtle (Major), 170n. 16
Petry, Ann: *The Street*, 129
Philadelphia Fire (Wideman): ambiguity and paradox in liberating story's ending, 34–36; Caliban as character, 34, 163n. 13; Calibanic discourse and male writers' lost sons, 19–22, 27–31; Calibanic discourse's conscious/unconscious effects on male writers, 4, 11, 13, 18–31; Calibanic discourse's hegemony over (white) postmodernism, 5–6, 13, 18, 30, 36, 162–63nn. 9–10; (*see also* (white) postmodernism); Calibanic discourse's overall effect on society, 31–36; Calibanic discourse's (re)inscription by ambiguity and paradox, 13; imaginative fictions and liberation, 28–29, 31, 165–66n. 7; intersubjectively linked characters in, 13, 37; language as source of oppression and liberation, 5–6; the male gaze, 20–21, 160n. 3; male writers' attempt to de-center Calibanic discourse, 5–6; male writer's attempted revolutionary portrayal of Caliban, 26–27; male writer's internalization and replication of Caliban's legacy, 19–22; male writer's interpretation of Caliban trope, 26; male writer's (re)inscription of Calibanic discourse, 18–27; male writer's thematizing of Calibanic discourse, 18–19, 22–28, 31, 35–36, 161nn. 7–8; males' general lack of voice and power, 24–25, 161n. 6; nightmare of male murder, 25–26; overall (re)inscription of Calibanic discourse, 35–36; potential failure of liberating story,

31–36; restriction of voice in overall discourse of, 18; role of readers in constructing liberating story, 35–36, 163n. 15; *Tempest*'s role in black oppression, 19, 22–27, 32–35; text's/writers' thematization of *Tempest* as master narrative, 4, 13, 19, 22–27, 31; Wideman's critique of language and subjectivity, 29–30, 162n. 9; Wideman's (re)inscription of Calibanic discourse as character, 30; Wideman's response to Calibanic discourse as character, 19, 27–31; Wideman's rewriting of *Tempest* as character, 19, 27–28; Wideman's story's relationship to surrogate male writer's, 19, 31; Wideman's use of language to liberate his son, 28–31. *See also* Calibanic discourse

Platitudes (Ellis): ambiguous form of, 100–101, 108, 175n. 5; black male story versus female, 104–8; Calibanic discourse's (re)inscription in, 108; disruption of narrative mimesis, 103–4; liberation of men and writers through writing, 100, 104, 107–8; male writer's empowerment by female writer, 106–8; name of female writer and her story, 105, 175n. 4; seriousness versus play, parody, and freedom, 102–5; thematized writer's attempt to use (white) postmodernism, 101, 108 (*see also* (white) postmodernism); underlying affirmation of female story, 105–6. *See also* Calibanic discourse

postmodern: concept of and its relationship to fictions, 4–5

Pound, Ezra, 134

race and racism (*see also* Calibanic discourse): impact on contemporary black men, 153–55

(re)inscription in story of liberation (*see also* Calibanic discourse): as direct evidence of Calibanic discourse, 4, 102

Reed, Ishmael, 1

Reflex and Bone Structure (Major): ambiguity of self and sexual identity, 72, 75; Calabanic discourse's (re)inscription in story of liberation, 73, 74–75 (*see also* story of liberation); self-referential narrative as site of story of liberation, 72–75 (*see also* story of liberation); story of liberation's silencing, 72, 75 (*see also* story of liberation); textual discourse's liberating/imprisoning potential for male writer, 72–75; (white) postmodernism's failed potential, 72–73 (*see also* (white) postmodernism). *See also* Calibanic discourse

Retamar, Fernandez: "Caliban," 157n. 3

Reuben (Wideman): ambiguous results of male storytelling, 37, 43; bonding storytelling and female interaction, 41–43, 165n. 5; bonding storytelling and male intersubjectivity, 38–41; bonding storytelling and white fictions, 38, 39, 40; Calibanic discourse's (re)inscription through ambiguity and paradox, 43; male "abstract hate," 39–40; male and female storytelling contrasted, 38, 41–43, 165nn. 5–6; male imagination, 38–41, 42–43, 165–66n. 7; male sexual portrayal, 14, 164n. 1; men and love, 40; story of liberation's (re)inscription of basic Calibanic theme, 43 (*see also* story of liberation); thematic and structural disruption of male story, 37–41, 42–43; (white) postmodernism's highlight of Calibanic discourse, 38 (*see also* (white) postmodernism). *See also* Calibanic discourse

Richard, Jean-Pierre: "*Philadelphia Fire*, or The Shape of a City," 163n. 15
Rogers, Alva, 174n. 1
Roney, Lisa C.: "The Double Vision of Clarence Major, Painter and Writer," 170nn. 13, 15
Rowell, Charles H.: "An Interview with John Edgar Wideman," 137, 162n. 10
Rush, Benjamin, 167n. 14
Rushdy, Ashraf H.A.: "The Phenomenology of the Allmuseri," 81, 170–71n. 1; "Properties of Desire," 174n. 14

Samuels, Wilfred: "Going Home," 178n. 4
Sartre, Jean-Paul, 179n. 9
Saussure, Ferdinand de: *Course in General Linguistics*, 29–30
Scheler, Max, 179n. 9
Scott, Daniel: "Interrogating Identity," 174n. 14
Shadow and Act (Ellison), 133–36
Shakespeare, William: *The Tempest*, 2, 4, 13, 19, 22, 23, 24, 26, 27, 31, 32, 34, 61, 93, 101, 110, 112, 157, 161n. 8, 173n. 10
shift, concept of: 157–58n. 7, 160–61n. 5, 168n. 2, 178n. 7
Silverman, Kaja: *The Subject of Semiotics*, 28, 30, 158–59n. 7, 159n. 10, 160n. 5, 162n. 9
Simpson, Lorna, 174n. 1
Sterne, Laurence: *Tristam Shandy*, 172n. 5, 175n. 3, 178n. 5
story of liberation: defined as unconscious response to Calibanic discourse, 3–4
Stubbs, George, 49, 50, 167n. 12
Such Was the Season (Major): Calibanic discourse's (re)inscription, 79; discussed in context of Major's earlier novels, 78–79; escaping self-referential narrative through woman's voice, 78–79; Major's

comments on stability of woman's voice, 78–79. *See also* Calibanic discourse

Tate, Claudia: *Psychoanalysis and Black Novels*, 158n. 7, 161n. 5
Tempest, The: as symbolic and iconic text, 2
Toomer, Jean, 178n. 5; *Cane*, 77, 170n. 14
Tragic Magic (Brown): Calibanic discourse, male voice, community, sexuality, and humanity, 102; Calibanic discourse's (re)inscription through ambiguity and paradox, 121, 125–26, 128; essentialized differences between men and women, 121, 124, 128, 161n. 6; *Invisible Man* as literary influence, 102, 126–27, 176n. 2; jazz as liberating voice in, 121–23, 125, 128, 176n. 11; main character's connection to general male portrayal, 124–26, 128; main character's rejection of male fraternity, 125–26; male general lack of voice and empowerment, 121, 122–24, 128; male lack of substantive character and sexuality, 122, 126, 128; male sexual empowerment by female, 125–26; women's voice and empowerment, 123–24, 126, 128. *See also* Calibanic discourse
Turner, Victor: *The Forest of Symbols*, 168n. 2, 169n. 8, 178n. 7

unconscious analogy (*see also* Calibanic discourse): defined, 131; the similar voices of Ellison and Wideman, 136–37, 139; in writing of Ellison, Johnson, Major, and Wideman, 131–47

white male subjects: Calibanic signification and phallocentric power, 6 white patriarchy: and control of symbols, 2–3, 157n. 4, 159–60n. 10

(white) postmodernism: explained as concept applied to black male writers, 5, 159n. 9, 174n. 1

Wideman, Daniel, 55, 56, 57

Wideman, John Edgar: achievement of, 16–17, 149–50; Calibanic discourse's (re)inscription in *Cattle Killing* and *Reuben*, 37; comments about black people's resistance to "foreign" language, 2; essentialized gender in *Philadelphia Fire* and *Reuben*, 41–42, 161n. 6, 165n. 6; "Fever," 137, 162–63n. 10; The Homewood Trilogy (*Damballah*, *Hiding Place*, and *Sent for you Yesterday*), 16; influence of Ellison and Calibanic discourse on writing, 136, 177–78n. 4; "In Praise of Silence," 2; intersubjectively linked characters in *Cattle Killing* and *Reuben*, 14, 37; novels'

contradiction of statements about liberating (white) postmodernism, 137–39, 162–63n. 10 (*see also* (white) postmodernism); "The Silence of Thelonious Monk," 165–66n. 7; statements linking Ellison to liberating (white) postmodernism, 137 (*see also* (white) postmodernism); story of liberation in *Cattle Killing* and *Reuben*, 14, 37 (*see also* story of liberation). *See also* Calibanic discourse; *The Cattle Killing*; *Fatheralong*; *Hiding Place*; *The Lynchers*; *Philadelphia Fire*; *Reuben*

Williams, Sherley Anne: *Dessa Rose*, 159n. 9

Wilson, Matthew: "The African American Historian," 176n. 9

Wolfe, George, 174n. 1

Wright, Richard, 133, 178n. 4; *Native Son*, 16, 129–30, 176n. 13